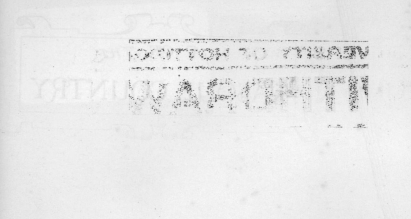

A BOOK OF THE BASQUES

MACMILLAN AND CO., Limited
LONDON · BOMBAY · CALCUTTA · MADRAS
MELBOURNE

THE MACMILLAN COMPANY
NEW YORK · BOSTON · CHICAGO
DALLAS · ATLANTA · SAN FRANCISCO

THE MACMILLAN COMPANY
OF CANADA, LIMITED
TORONTO

An Old Ploughman (Labourd).

A
BOOK OF THE BASQUES

BY

RODNEY GALLOP

Illustrated with photographs by
the Author and drawings and
a map by Marjorie Gallop

MACMILLAN AND CO., LIMITED
ST. MARTIN'S STREET, LONDON
1930

COPYRIGHT

TO MY MOTHER
WHO FIRST BROUGHT ME TO THE BASQUE
COUNTRY,

TO MY WIFE
WHOM I MET THERE,

AND

TO MY SON NIGEL
WHO WAS BORN THERE,
I DEDICATE THIS BOOK

INTRODUCTION

Dans une époque où le Pays Basque est à la mode et où n'importe qui se croît autorisé d'en parler, l'ayant vu seulement à travers les vitraux d'une limousine. . . .—J. A. DE DONOSTIA.

THERE can be few parts of the world about which so many wild and inaccurate statements have been made and so much irresponsible and unauthoritative literature has been written, as that region of South-west France and North-west Spain which is inhabited by the Basques. The mystery surrounding the origins and history of the Basque race, the difficulty of their uncouth tongue and the great reserve which they display in all their contacts with the outside world, a reserve to which is due, in all probability their survival as a race, have invested them with an air of remoteness and woven around them an atmosphere of romance.

Their lovely land of valley, mountain and sea-coast, discovered before the war by the English and Spanish, during the war by the French, and after it by pleasure-seekers of all nations, threw them into the limelight. The Basques and their country became fashionable. Henceforward it was inevitable that a horde of journalists, travel-writers and lady novelists in search of local colour should descend upon the land like a swarm of locusts, speeding through the country in car and charabanc. Some have missed it altogether and, finding themselves in Béarn or Andorra, have nevertheless seen a " noble Basque " under every béret. Others have discovered Biarritz (where, no one quite knows how, they contrive to stay at a " Basque inn ") and have ventured into the valleys of Labourd, while a few adventurous spirits have actually reached San Sebastian, Loyola and Pampeluna. It matters little that they are unable to distinguish the Breton fishermen of Saint-Jean-de-Luz from their Basque brethren, or that they do not know the difference between *cagots* and *cascarots*, between *pastorales* and *mascarades*. Each adds half a dozen new errors to those gleaned from his (or her) predecessors. Nevertheless their writings find ready publication. It would be invidious to mention names. They will be sufficiently conspicuous by their absence from the Bibliography at the end of this book.

To the best of my knowledge one Englishman, and one alone, has lived long enough among the Basques to write with authority upon their character, customs and language. This was the Reverend Wentworth Webster, English Chaplain at Saint-Jean-de-Luz for many years, who passed the remainder of his life in studious retirement at Sare. I must also mention a most useful little book, "The Basques and Their Country," by P. J. Ormond, published privately in 1924, the materials of which have been carefully sifted by one who knows how to distinguish the grain from the chaff.

In the following chapters I have attempted to paint a picture of the Basque race, their character, traditions and achievement. In order that it may be as complete and as accurate as possible, I have not hesitated to draw on all the available material. I have made full use of the works, both general and specialised, of Vinson, Michel, Colas, Donostia, Hérelle, Lhande, Nogaret, Blazy, Ormond and Webster, and of the wealth of new material by these and other writers which has appeared in the *Revista Internacional de los Estudios Vascos*, *Gure Herria*, *Anuario de Eusko-Folklore*, *Bulletin du Musée Basque* and *Bulletin de la Société des Sciences*, *Lettres*, *Arts et Études Régionales de Bayonne*.

I owe an especial debt of gratitude to the personal advice and assistance of my friends Philippe Veyrin, Miss Violet Alford and Commandant Boissel.

R. A. G.

CONTENTS

LIST OF PLATES

ILLUSTRATIONS IN TEXT

BISCAI

BISCAIÆ
FÆMINÆ

A BOOK
OF THE
BASQUES

CHAPTER I

ORIGINS AND HISTORY OF THE BASQUES

Orai bi mila urte, hainitz Erromano
Gerlan ethorri ziren Eskual Herriraino,
Kantabre hazkar heiek zioten oraino :
Nahiago dugu hil sumetitu baino !
Hitz hori ez da galdu orai arteraino.

PIARRES DIBARRART.

Two thousand years ago a swarm of Romans
Came to make war on the Basque Country.
The sturdy Cantabrians made answer to them :
We would rather die than submit !
Even to-day their words are not forgotten.

ON the shores of the Bay of Biscay, where the Pyrenees
slope down to the sea, there lies a smiling land whose
varied charm is made up of indented sea-coast, rugged
mountain and green valley, rolling hills covered with
golden gorse and forests of oak or chestnut, trout-
streams and maize-fields, shady lanes, sun-soaked vineyards and apple orchards. From time immemorial this
land has been inhabited by a mysterious race whom we
call the Basques, but who call themselves *Eskualdunak*,
and their land *Eskual Herria* or *Euzkadi*, a name which

B

may, perhaps, be derived from the Basque word for
" sun." There are few races on the face of the earth
of whose origin so little is known, and who have exercised such a fascination over ethnologists and philologists of every nationality : " The most difficult problem
presented by our history," writes Camille Jullian with
hardly a trace of exaggeration, " is that of the origin of
the Basques."

Since the publication in 1545 of the " Linguae Vascorum Primitiae," a volume of Basque verse by Bernard
Dechepare, which was followed by the historical works
of Esteban de Garibay (1571) and Andres de Poça
(1587), innumerable treatises have been written on the
subject of the Basques, their history, customs, language
and general characteristics ; and innumerable theories
have been put forward regarding their origin and their
relationship with other races, with the net result that
we are no nearer than we have ever been to the solution
of a problem which, in all probability, will never be
solved.

A young French writer, Philippe Veyrin, has pointed
out that the stages through which research into the
origins of the Basque race has passed correspond roughly
to the three ages defined by Auguste Comte, to wit, the
theological, the metaphysical and the positive age.

If this classification is adopted it is found that the
writers of the first period, the " theological " age, were
nearly all Basques living at the end of the eighteenth
and the beginning of the nineteenth centuries. The
most famous of these is the Abbé Diharce de Bidassouet,
who proclaimed in his " Histoire des Cantabres " that
Basque was the original language spoken by the Creator.
Fantastic as this assertion may appear, it was typical
of the age, and the Abbé was by no means alone in
holding such views. He went only one stage further
than the majority of his contemporaries, among whom
there was a widespread conviction that Basque, if not
divine, was at least the first human tongue. These

theories were in the main based on such startling etymologies as Guipuzcoa . . . *Gu-iz-puzk-ko-ak* . . . " We whose language was broken." This was taken to prove conclusively that Basque was the original language spoken before the Tower of Babel. Manuel de Larramendi, who wrote the first Basque Grammar, which he modestly entitled " El Imposible Vencido " (The Impossible Vanquished), gave a further and rather more convincing proof of his modesty by claiming for Basque no more than a place among the seventy-five languages which came into being after the building of the Tower.

One of the most entertaining figures of the " theological " age is the Abbé Dominique Lahetjuzan (1766–1818), for some years Curate of Sare (Labourd). Among other instructive or polemical works which he left in print or manuscript is a scarce little volume entitled " Essai de Quelques Notes sur la Langue Basque par un Vicaire de Campagne, sauvage d'origine." (The MS. draft bears the title " Notes sur la Langue Basque par Nasujtehal Aciminod, sauvage d'origine.") It is difficult to decide which is the more redolent of the age, the anagram in the pseudonym (which was abandoned on publication) or the expression *sauvage d'origine*, conjuring up visions of the " happy savage " so dear to eighteenth-century hearts. In this amusing work the Abbé exercises all his ingenuity in support of his theory which he states as follows : " *Le basque est une langue originale : la divinité de la Genèse le démontre comme vice versa : l'originalité du Basque prouve la divinité de la Genèse . . .,*" an aspect of theology which, strangely enough, has been completely overlooked by the fundamentalists. Like most of his contemporaries the Abbé brings forward no evidence in support of his conclusions beyond a series of etymologies as wild as they are fascinating to the modern reader. For instance he derives *gorphutz* (the Basque word for " body," which comes straight from the Latin *corpus*) from three Basque roots which together would mean " *une matière exhalante pétrie par l'Être Supérieur."* In Notes 6 and 7 he proceeds to show that the names of the principal protagonists of the Book of Genesis are all Basque in origin and have appropriate meanings. Adam, for example, means " He who is full of understanding." Eve (Eva : Ez-ba) means " No-Yes " (" *Il étoit naturel qu'Adam au milieu de sa joie donnât à sa femme un nom qui perpetuât le souvenir et de sa privation et de sa jouissance* "). Abel means " he who invokes through animal sacrifices," while Cain signifies " he who has committed an odious action." His excessive zeal leads the Abbé Lahetjuzan to improve on the Book of Genesis itself. For in spite of his assertion that " the originality of Basque proves the divinity of Genesis " he demonstrates to his own entire satisfaction that the Basque word *laranja :* orange (which happens to be only a mispronunciation of the Spanish *naranja*) is derived from Basque roots meaning " the fruit which was first eaten." Hence the orange and not the apple was the cause of Adam's downfall.

It may seem incredible that little more than a century ago such extravagances were taken seriously. That this was indeed the case is proved by the lawsuit brought by the Guipuzcoan priest Erroa. Like the Abbé Lahetjuzan, Erroa maintained that Basque was the language spoken in the Earthly Paradise. His colleagues, with a display of good sense as commendable as it was rare, treated him as a harmless lunatic. Erroa, however, appealed to the Chapter of the Cathedral of Pampeluna, who took the matter up seriously and, after several months of deliberations (alas that the minutes of the proceedings should not have survived !), solemnly gave judgment in Erroa's favour and publicly subscribed to his theories.

The good old times of the " theological " age may not yet be at an end, for as recently as in 1910 there was published at Zaragoza a pamphlet bearing the following title : " En el Nombre del Padre, del Hijo y del Espíritu Santo. Amen. Gloriosísimo Descubrimiento, Reconocimiento y Demonstración de la Lengua Paradisiaca en el Vascuence. Obra dedicada por su inventor y autor el presbítero D. José Garcia Oregui y Aramburu a su Augusta discípula de la misma lengua Doña Maria Christina de Apsburgo, Reina Madre y ex-Regente de España." (In the Name of the Father, the Son and the Holy Ghost. Amen. Most glorious Discovery, Recognition and Demonstration of the Language of Paradise in the Basque tongue! A work dedicated by its inventor and author the Presbyter Don José Garcia Oregui y Aramburu to his August Pupil in the same language Doña Maria Christina Hapsburg, Queen-Mother and ex-Regent of Spain.)

If Philippe Veyrin's three periods are accepted, a place must be found between the first two for the strange figure of Augustin Chaho, the turbulent philosopher, poet, journalist and pamphleteer from Soule. It would be too great an irony to class this blatant anti-clerical, who so loudly voices his disbelief in the Scriptures, with the gentle company of prelates who preceded him. Nevertheless, for all his vaunted scepticism, Augustin Chaho was as credulous as any country vicar where the Basques were concerned, and his " Voyage en Navarre " and " Histoire des Basques " are works of pure imagination. He it was, incidentally, who originated the famous legend of the *couvade*, which no amount of denial or ridicule has been able to exterminate.[1]

---

[1] The *couvade* requires a word or two of explanation. Strabo states that the Cantabrians observed a curious custom by which the father of a new-born child took the mother's place in bed beside the infant. A similar custom is recorded by Marco Polo in the province of Kardandan :—
" As soon as a woman has been delivered of a child, and, rising from her bed, has washed and swathed the infant, her husband immediately takes the place she has left, has the child laid beside him, and nurses it for forty days. In the meantime, the friends and relations of the family pay to him their visits of congratulation; whilst the woman attends to the business of the house, carries victuals and drink to the husband in his bed and suckles the infant at his side." (" Travels of Marco Polo," Ch. XLI.)
In his " Voyage en Navarre " Chaho quotes Strabo and, without mentioning any concrete instances, asserts that the *couvade* is still practised

The " metaphysical " age was inaugurated by the great German savant Humboldt, who first placed Basque studies on a scientific basis in his famous work : " Prüfung der Untersuchungen über die Urbewohner Hispaniens vermittelst der Vaskischen Sprache " (Berlin 1821). Humboldt was the first of a long line of scientists who examined the Basque problem objectively from every possible angle and put forward every conceivable theory for its solution. Camille Jullian quotes some twenty odd races which have been proposed by various writers as the ancestors of the Basques. It has been suggested, to quote a few instances, that they are related to the Turanian family, to the Uralo-Altaic group (of which the Finns and Hungarians form part), to the Ancient Egyptians and the Berber tribes, to the North and South American Indians and the fabulous inhabitants of Atlantis, to the Celts and the Caucasians, the Phœnicians, the Esquimaux and the Hittites, the Iberians, the Ligurians and the Pelasgians.

Most of these theories have by now been consigned to the scrap-heap. Modern opinion is more or less evenly divided over the question whether the Basques are descended from, or at least closely related to, the Iberians, that mysterious race which once inhabited the whole Spanish Peninsula, and which has left many traces of its existence in the shape of cave-drawings, inscriptions and tombstones. The pro-Iberians, if they may so be called, were headed by Humboldt, whose theories were adopted and developed in the main by German scientists such as Hübner, Linschmann, Phillips and

---

among the Basques. His statement was accepted at face value by no less a writer than Herbert Spencer, and in spite of all that has been done to exterminate the legend it still crops up from time to time. It has now been triumphantly resuscitated in the latest edition of Larousse. Strangely enough the idea of the *couvade* still survives where one would least expect to find it, namely in the British Isles. Mrs. Leather ("Folklore of Herefordshire," pp. 111–112) gives instances of its existence among the Herefordshire cottagers, the husband becoming proportionately worse as his wife's sufferings decreased.

Schuchardt. The principal opponents of the Iberian theory were the French professors Bladé and Philipon, the Dutchman Van Eys and above all the veteran Julien Vinson, who, until his recent death, was the doyen of Basque studies.

Vinson regards it as "infinitely probable that from earliest times the Basques have never been more than a small tribe dwelling in a few valleys of the Western Pyrenees." Moreover, even if it were proved that the Basques were descended from the Iberians, one unknown quantity would only have been substituted for another. If the Basques are Iberians, who were the Iberians? Opinion is again divided. Some ethnologists hold that they came from Africa by way of Andalusia : others contend that they originated in the Caucasus and migrated to the Peninsula through Central Europe. It is therefore difficult to agree with Camille Jullian that " Iberian and Ligurian will suffice to explain all that is mysterious in the past history and origin of the Basques."

The problem of " the oldest people in Europe " has attracted not only philologists but anthropologists who have been no more fortunate in their attempts to solve it. For a long time it was thought that the Basques were an exclusively brachycephalic race. This was disproved as a result of the researches undertaken in the middle of last century by Doctors Broca and Velasco, who found that there existed two types of skull among the Basques, the one brachycephalic and the other dolichocephalic. To quote Vinson, " there are great analogies between these two types, despite their radical dissimilarity. The first appears to resemble an African type, and the second a very ancient European type. But it is not yet possible to say : which of these two forms of skull is characteristic of and peculiar to the true Basque race : which of them is chronologically anterior to the other : and what relationships or affinities with the Basques can be found in Europe or in Asia."

Dr. Collignon, who based his conclusions on practical

experience in examining recruits for the French army, found " the purest Basque type to have brown hair and to be long-headed, with the following points : head broad at temples, narrowing to very pointed chin, tall broad shoulders of square Egyptian statue type." He considered the purest Basques to be North of the Pyrenees, where they had settled in sparsely-populated country in the sixth century, whereas the Basques South of the Pyrenees had been much adulterated by Gothic fugitives from the Moors. He judged that they undoubtedly formed part of the great Hamitic branch of the white races, that is to say, to the ancient Egyptians and to various of the races known to the general public under the generic term of Berbers. " The race is North African or European, certainly, not Asiatic." Unfortunately the definite conclusions advanced by Collignon have not been wholly confirmed by the further researches conducted by Aranzadi and Bosch Gimpera.

The latter has put forward what is not only the most modern but also perhaps the most acceptable solution of the problem. The Basques, in his opinion, are the descendants of the paleolithic inhabitants of the Pyrenean region, whose physical type is identical with that of from 25 to 40 per cent. of the modern Basques, while being practically non-existent in the neighbouring districts. This prehistoric Pyrenean race was powerfully influenced by the Iberians and either adopted their language or borrowed largely from it. This would account for the points which modern Basque has in common with the Hamitic group of languages, for the Iberians, in his view, were related to the Hamitic peoples and came to Spain from Africa, landing first at Almeria. This theory has the merit of reconciling the various results of modern research, and although it remains no more than a plausible hypothesis, it may be accepted for the present in the absence of anything more conclusive.

Thus the " metaphysical " age, after a century of active research, yielded no positive results, and the

German professor Schuchardt, for one, expressed the opinion that the origin of the Basques would never be definitely and incontestably established. The Iberian controversy has died down, and scientists have at last begun to doubt the wisdom of cultivating such an unfruitful field of research and to turn their attention to the Basques as they are to-day with all the interesting customs and peculiarities which they have brought with them out of the mists of the past. The end of the nineteenth century heralded the dawn of the " positive " age.

Let it be regarded as axiomatic, or at least accepted as a working hypothesis, that the Basques are the oldest race surviving in Europe, and that at the foot of the Pyrenees they witnessed the arrival in Europe of our Aryan ancestors. This hypothesis must cover the whole period from the Creation to the twelfth century, from which date the first well-authenticated references to the Basques. Till then, " like an honest woman they had no history." The first would-be historian of the Basques, Arnauld Oihénart, bewails the complete lack of material on the subject. " It is difficult to write the internal and external history of this race," he complains, " for there exists no single ancient document concerning them."

Roman historians make frequent references to a tribe living in or near what is now the Basque country, and speaking a peculiar language which their neighbours did not understand. This tribe they variously call Iberi, Dragani, Turdetani, Cantabri, Calagurritani, Asturi, Vascones and a host of other names. The Vascones are first mentioned by Livy in his description of the Sertorian War (77–74 B.C.), and are placed by him between the modern towns of Calahorra and Logroño. They must also have extended to the North, for Pompey established his winter quarters among them at Pampeluna, the ancient name of which, Pompaelo, is derived from his. The Vascones must therefore have already been subject to Rome, and Adolf Schulten believes their subjection

to have been effected by Cato in the second century B.C.
According to Ptolemy the Vascones extended from the
banks of the Ebro to the " *Summus Pyrenaeus*," and later
writers depict them as spreading gradually westwards
until, in the sixth century A.D., they appear to have
overflowed to the North of the Pyrenees.

Although the Latin root *vasc-* is probably a corruption
of the Basque *eusk-*, it is impossible with any certainty
to identify the Vascones with the Basques of to-day,
for from this Latin form are derived the two modern
appellations of Basques and Gascons. Only in the
twelfth century do we find a reference to the *Bascli*,
coupled with a vocabulary of some of the commonest
words in their language, which make it clear beyond a
doubt that these *Bascli* are none other than the Basques.

A comparison between the original and borrowed
words in modern Basque indicates that when they first
came into contact with the Romans some two thousand
years ago they were a pastoral people who had recently
begun to devote themselves to agriculture. It can be
assumed that after the coming of the Romans they must
have watched the successive passages of the Goths,
Franks, Normans and Moors, and it may be suspected
that they were more than spectators of Roland's defeat
at Roncevaux. In this their prehistorical period little is
known of them beyond the fact that they had established
a reputation for violence and ferocity remarkable even in
the Dark Ages. As early as the fourth century A.D.
Prudence writes of the " pagan brutality of the Vascones." Indeed they appear to have acquired the grim
merit of having made more than their fair share of
Christian martyrs. Such was their reputation in this
respect that in the seventh century Saint Amand, a
Bishop who had been driven from the Court of *le bon
Roi Dagobert*, whose " incontinence " (which may perhaps have given rise to the immortal nursery rhyme) he
had dared to censure, fled to " these tribes among whom
he hoped to win the palms of martyrdom on account of

their ferocity." Three hundred years later public
security does not seem to have improved to any great
extent, for Saint Léon, the first Bishop of Bayonne,
while trying to cross into Spain, met some " pillaging
Basques," whose language he could not understand,
and was obliged to return to Bayonne, where he met
his death at the hands of " very cruel pirates and satellites
of the Devil." The same fate overtook Saint Eusebia,
a native of the country, who is said to have been " devoted
to God among people given over to diabolical practices."
Giraldo, Canon of Compostella, must have retained bitter
memories of his experiences among the Basques, for in
1120 he described them as " a race speaking a strange
language; real savages as bloodthirsty and ferocious as
the wild beasts with whom they live."

Yet another indication of their unsavoury reputation
is to be found in the eleventh-century Provençal " Chanson de Sainte-Foi d'Agen " in which they are accused of
the decapitation of that Saint in the third century :—

> All the land of the Basques and Aragon
> On the borders of the Gascons
> Know what this song is
> And whether its burthen be true. . . .
>
> The Basques, who are from Aran, whistle :
> They say : " On no account let her depart alive."
> They lift her up and pull her from the fire,
> One of them raises the flaming sword.
> So great a blow he struck with the sword
> He severed her head completely
> As Herod caused to be done to St. John.[1]

---

[1] *Tota Basconn' et Aragons*
A l'encontrada delz Gascons
Sabon quals est aqist canezons
E ss'es ben vera 'sta razons. . . .

Cisclani Bascon que son d'Aran :
Dizon " Por ren viva nonn an "
Levan la'n pes del fog tiran.
Eros l'uns la spada flameian
Tal li doned el cab del bran
Tota la testa'n mog taillan
Con fez Heros far saint Johan.

H. D'Argain, whose critical study of this episode appears in *Gure Herria* (1926), considers the guilt of the Basques to be not only possible but probable.

If any further proof be needed that the Basques were looked upon with fear and trembling as late as the twelfth century, it is to be found in their association with the inhabitants of various other districts in a sentence of excommunication pronounced in 1179 by the Third Council of Latran : " As regards the Brabançons, Aragonese, Navarrese, Basques (Bascoli),[1] Cotereaux and Triaverdins, who inflict such cruelty on the Christians, sparing neither churches nor monasteries, widows nor young girls, old men nor children, age nor sex, but destroying and laying waste everything like pagans, the Synod condemns them . . . to the same anathema as heretics ; and orders that sentence of excommunication be published in the Churches on Sundays and other special days."

It is not proposed to give any account in this book of the historical events of which the Basque Country has been the scene. For in the main the Basques took no part in them and held coldly aloof from these innumerable wars and princely passages. Basque history, considered in its broadest aspect, is the history of the inde-

---

[1] The Basques would almost certainly seem to be indicated by this term *Bascoli*. J. Saint Pierre, who relates the history of this excommunication in *Gure Herria* (1922), remarks that it was just about this time that the word *Vascones*, which had previously been used to denote both Basques and Gascons, split up into the two words *Gascones* and *Bascoli*, *Basculi* or *Bascli*, e.g. *la Gascogne et la Basclonie* in Vezelai's "Chronicles" *circa* 1610. I am inclined to place the division a century earlier on the evidence of the Provençal poem quoted above, which refers both to the *Basconn* and to the *Gascons*.

Saint Pierre further maintains that this excommunication was directed, not against the whole Basque race, but against the hordes of Basque freebooters (*routiers*) who ravaged other parts of France at this epoch. In support of this assertion he quotes the contemporary Limousin chronicler Geoffroi de Vigeois, who complains that " God flung on Aquitaine cruel hordes such as our fathers had not seen since the time of the Normans: the Basques (*Basculi*) at their head."

pendence of the Basque provinces, and of their gradual submission, not so much to the countries to which they offered allegiance, as to the irresistible forces of time and progress. It resolves itself into the history of the *fueros* (charters), the traditional inheritance of the Basques from the Dark Ages and the warrant of their national independence, to which they clung for nearly a thousand years, and the final loss of which, when they had become a glaring anachronism, spelt the end of their independent existence and may eventually mean their extinction as a separate race.

These *fueros* or *fors* came into being at a period of which history has little to relate. The Moorish wave, which, after the great victory of Val de Funquera (to the South-east of Pampeluna) swept northward as far as Tours, came to a standstill. A reaction set in, and, little by little, the work of reconquest began until in 1212 at Las Navas de Tolosa the stain of Funquera was wiped out, and the North of Spain was finally cleansed of the infidel. Then began the infinitely more difficult work of consolidation and of the creation in the reconquered lands of a new social organisation to replace the doomed civilisation of the Arabs.

In the words of Vinson, " the exemptions and privileges resulting from the *fueros* originated in the first territorial associations formed by Christians with the object of waging war to the death against the Moors. When these crusaders, if the expression is not too bold, united under the authority of a common chief elected by themselves, were he King, Count or simple Overlord, they imposed upon him certain conditions relative above all to the possession of the reconquered lands." These conditions were incorporated in the principal *fueros*, which differed only slightly in the various provinces, and the like of which existed also in Castille, Aragon and Catalonia until their suppression in 1521. They were supplemented at a later date by a large number of local *fueros*, each peculiar to a province, a valley or even a village, which came into existence when the new territories had been wrested from the Moors, and the conquerors found it necessary to make concessions in order to attract immigrants. With this object they issued *cartas de población* (letters of colonisation) giving the colonists in free tenure the land on which they settled, granting them certain privileges and regulating the general conditions of their settlement. The *fueros*, provincial and local, grew into a legislative code consisting of " the sum total of laws and regulations dealing with all subjects from the political constitution and principal legislative measures to the smallest details of everyday life."

The *fuero* of Vizcaya, for instance, included prescriptions concerning the manner of mourning the dead : " No person . . . may make moan, tearing his hair or scratching his head (*sic*) nor lament in song . . . under penalty of 1000 maravedis . . ." Some of the *fueros* were pure folklore and consecrated pagan customs. There is a series of prescriptions in which animals are treated as reasoning beings ; others defining the obligation of a citizen to furnish his neighbour with fire ; and others providing for judicial ordeals by duel, by candle (the party whose candle first burnt out lost his case), by fire and by water.

At first the *fueros* were handed down by oral tradition, but later they were codified and committed to writing (as late as the sixteenth century in the French provinces). They were jealously guarded, and every attempt to interfere with them met with firm resistance, supported if necessary by armed revolt. As the centuries passed and the foral régime conflicted more and more with the centralising tendencies of the French and Spanish monarchs, these attempts grew more frequent, and, on the French side, the *fors* had already been seriously undermined by the *intendants* of the seventeenth and eighteenth centuries before they were finally abolished by the Revolution. In Spain they survived until the end of the

First Carlist War (1839) in Navarre, and of the Second
Carlist War (1876) in the other three provinces, when,
with a few minor exceptions, they were at length sacrificed
on the altar of national unity.

The foral régime gave the Basques full local autonomy.
The French provinces and Navarre passed under the
suzerainty of the thrones of France and Spain in the
manner described in Chapter II, while the other three
Spanish provinces voluntarily took the King of Castille
as Suzerain in the fourteenth century. Thenceforward,
however, the person of the King was the only link between
the Basque provinces and his other possessions. The
former retained their old status and titles of " *le pays de
Labourd, la Vicomté de la Soule, le royaume de Navarre,
la señoria de Vizcaya, las provincias de Álava y de Guipuzcoa.*" The King was not, as elsewhere, the owner
of the land, nor had he the right to tax his Basque subjects, who were liable only to pay a fixed annual tribute,
the burden of which they could distribute as they wished.
They had, however, the " right," which they were frequently called upon to exercise, of making so-called
" voluntary contributions " to the royal coffers. As a
corollary to their freedom from taxation the Spanish
Basque provinces enjoyed freedom of trade, and the
Castillian customs were placed inland. To such an
extent were they regarded as foreign territory that they
were included in the general embargo placed on foreign
trade with the Indies, and on occasions concluded separate treaties with foreign Powers. In 1482, for instance,
a treaty was concluded between England and Guipuzcoa.

The vexed question of Basque nobility arises directly
out of the *fueros*. It is a common error to assert that
every Basque is noble by birth. Nobility was indeed
granted to all the inhabitants of Guipuzcoa and Vizcaya
for the reason that these two provinces were never
conquered by the Moors. In Vizcaya the only proof
required for the grant of patent of nobility was that of
birth of Bizcayan parents, but since Bizcayan and Gui-

puzcoan nobility was based on land tenure the inhabitants of these two provinces were obliged to give precedence to those noble by blood. In Álava there existed the nearest approach to a feudal system recorded in the Basque Country, but in Navarre and the French provinces all the inhabitants were free men, and independent small-holders held their own side by side with the proprietors of big estates. In Navarre, however, certain lands carried with them the patent of nobility while others did not. This is explained by Nogaret as follows: "During their numerous wars in the Middle Ages, the Kings of Navarre ennobled a large number of estates in order to reward their proprietors for their services . . . one can mention villages and even whole valleys all of whose inhabitants were ennobled at once." This nobility founded in the land was only regarded as nobility of blood when the land had remained for a hundred years in the possession of one family. When Basse-Navarre was transferred to France it was found that one-sixth of the inhabitants were noble. Labourd, on the other hand, was the most democratic of all the provinces, only about one-twentieth of the land belonging to the nobles.

One of the most cherished privileges bestowed on the Basques by the *fueros* was their almost complete exemption from military service. They were, of course, called upon to fulfil the duty, incumbent on all nobles, of serving in time of war, but even then their service was subject to certain restrictions. The inhabitants of Vizcaya, for instance, were not bound to serve outside the boundaries of their province, save of their own free will. The men of Álava, like the Biscayans, had to be paid for their service and could not be made to serve in garrisons. Furthermore, access to the Basque provinces was forbidden to the regular Spanish troops.

The administrative system provided by the *fueros* was a model of simplicity. Each province elected an assembly, known on the Spanish side as the *Junta*, in Soule and Basse-Navarre as the *États* and in Labourd

THE FISHING-PORT OF ONDARROA (VIZCAYA).

A GROUP AT PASAJES.

as the *Biltzar*. The constitution of these assemblies varied, the *Juntas* being elected by universal suffrage or some such representative system, while the *Etats* were composed of representatives of the Church, nobility and *francs* or commoners, and the *Biltzar* consisted of the Mayors of the different communes. The *Junta* of Vizcaya used to meet under the celebrated Tree of Guernica, which still survives enshrined spiritually in Yparraguirre's famous song " Gernikako Arbola," and materially in a pseudo-Greek temple, as the outward and visible sign of the lost liberties. The *Biltzar* of Labourd held its deliberations in the scarcely less famous wood of Capito-Harri near Uztaritz.

The representative of the King in the Basque provinces was, in Spain, the *Corregidor* and, in France, the *Bailli* or Governor, who could, when he thought necessary, summon a meeting of the assembly without whose consent no order of the King was valid. The executive authority of the assembly was vested, in France, in the *Syndic*, whose post, though honorary, was no sinecure, and in Spain in the Deputy-General. The assemblies themselves were the great mainstay and defence of the system to which they owed their existence. They displayed an almost patriarchal rectitude in their internal administration and a great sense of dignity and independence in their relations with their Suzerain and with the outside world. It is interesting to note, in this connection, that the *États* of Basse-Navarre refused to send representatives to the *États Généraux* of France in 1649, and that when they did so in 1789 these representatives were given strict injunctions to uphold the independence of their own *États*, instructions which they carried out by retiring when the National Assembly decreed the unification of France and its division into departments.

It is hardly surprising that the French Revolution met with a cold reception in the Basque Country, although the Basques were far from content under the old régime. The eighteenth century had witnessed a steep decline

c

in their fortunes. The loss of Canada, for instance, struck a severe blow at the coastal towns, and the decline of the whaling industry, which had been a great source of revenue in the seventeenth century, was scarcely compensated by the prize money brought in by the corsairs. Overt attacks on old-established privileges grew daily more frequent and more difficult to combat. The King's agents found ways of imposing heavy taxation in spite of the *fors*, which, seen from Versailles, must have seemed an anachronism that might be allowed to subsist in theory but must be ignored in practice. Not long before the end of the century the *intendant* de Néville reported to Louis XVI that the country was " *complètement déchu*," but the King's attempts to improve matters came too late.

In comparison with the rest of France, however, the Basques were well off. They were freemen in the midst of a nation of serfs, and their financial burdens, if unfamiliar and therefore irksome, were as nothing compared with the load that crushed the life out of the French peasant. For a moment, in 1789, they seemed to welcome the new ideas. The three provinces sent their delegates to the States General. There was a feeling abroad that the National Assembly might erect an independent Basque State astride the frontier. But these hopes, if they were ever more than idle dreams, were soon dashed to the ground. The Basque provinces were deprived, not only of their privileges, but even of their identity, for a Basco-Béarnais department was created, christened Basses Pyrénées and cut up into six districts with administrative centres at Pau, Uztaritz, Saint-Palais, Mauléon, Oloron and Orthez. This was sufficient to antagonise the Basques, but there was worse to follow. The suppression of Christianity came as a stunning blow to so profoundly religious a people. Less immediately devastating but far more permanent in its effects was the Law of the 17th Ventose of the Second Year of the Republic, which abolished testamentary freedom and prescribed the equal division of a father's property among all his children, thus striking at the roots of the patriarchal system of the Basques, among whom every sacrifice is made to the head of the family.

The French Basques did not rise and fight for their King as did the dour inhabitants of La Vendée, nor for their Faith and privileges as did their Spanish brothers in the following century. It was impossible that they should do so. They had few great nobles and no military caste. Their country was no more than an infinitesimal part of France, and so mountainous that it would have been difficult to secure cohesion in a general rising. Moreover, it was swarming with troops, owing, at first, to the danger apprehended from beyond the frontier and later to the campaign of 1793–4 which was fought in Labourd and Basse-Navarre.

Instead of rebelling the Basques had recourse to their usual method of defence when threatened from outside. In the words of Pierre Lhande " *ils laissent passer* "; they let things pass over their heads and withdrew into that impenetrable reserve which is so prominent a trait of their racial character. Thus it was that the Revolution, meeting a passive rather than an active resistance, did not make the Basque provinces the scene of its worst excesses. True, the guillotine raised its gaunt spectre at Bayonne and at Chauvin-Dragon, as Saint-Jean-de-Luz was renamed, and many Basques, including Dominique Lahetjuzan, were obliged to seek refuge beyond the frontier. The leaders of the Revolution had little confidence in the whole race, and in 1793, for instance, during the war with Spain, citizens Ichon and Dartigoyte reported to the Committee of Public Safety in the following terms : " Do not rely too much on the Basques, for their fanaticism disposes them in favour of the Spaniards . . . and the camp commanders tell us that they cannot count on a single Basque, that they are in enemy country and that in the case of a reverse they would have the Basques at their throats." This impression was probably the cause of the most brutal act of the Convention in these parts, the wholesale deportation of Labourd villagers on a charge of intelligence with the enemy. These unfortunate people were interned in churches in a most unhealthy part of the Landes, where many of them died before the survivors were repatriated at the end of the campaign.

Meanwhile the Basques witnessed some of the more entertaining phenomena inseparable from revolutions. Their sonorous place-names went by the board. Uztaritz became Marat-sur-Nive ; Cambo : Montagne-sur-Nive ; Saint-Palais : Coquins-Ville ; and Itxassou was re-christened Union in the absence of most of its inhabitants. The republican calendar was translated into a sort of dog-Basque. Verses like the following were interpolated into the *pastorales* :—

Viba, Viba Francia
Viba, Viba Naçionia
Viba Republika
Eta Assamblada Guçia ! [1]

The Revolution passed and the Restoration followed. But it brought no return to the foral system.

Meanwhile Spain was in turmoil, and twice the Basques took up arms to fight with grim fanaticism for their privileges, their Faith and, both last and least, the Carlist dynasty. That this was the order of their allegiance is clear from the manifesto issued by the notorious *Cura* Santa Cruz, whose sanguinary exploits sent a thrill of horror even through the Carlist ranks. With the object of detaching the Guipuzcoans from Lizarraga, the official Commander-in-Chief of the Carlist forces, Santa Cruz accused his compatriots of " serving the caprices of one man rather than the holy interests of God, Country and King, which alone can save your *fueros*, the cause of your taking up arms."

[1] When the reader is told that *guçia* means " the whole " he should have little difficulty in understanding this verse. Like M. Jourdain, he will doubtless be delighted to discover that he can read Basque.

But nothing could save the *fueros*. To-day they are a dead letter. Only their spirit survives in the incessant smuggling which goes on all along the frontier. To the Basque smuggling is no sin : even their Bishops subscribe to this view, except when it is accompanied by falsehood or acts of violence. Assisted by their mountainous country and by the secret of their language, which makes detective work almost an impossibility, they have defeated the attempts of either Government to prevent the passage of contraband. Throughout the nineteenth and early twentieth centuries smuggling continued unabated both by land and sea, and the exploits of such men as Gambocha, Arkaitza, Emparan and Artola passed into legend. The disparity between the French and Spanish exchanges gave an added impetus to smuggling for the first few years after the war, but nowadays there is no more than the normal illicit traffic in cattle, spirits and silk.

It is not easy to obtain information on so delicate a matter, and for fear of indiscretion one hesitates to publish abroad what little one may hear. But there are always stories going round of houses built astride the frontier with one door in France and the other in Spain ; of owls hooting where no owls are ; of dogs found wandering in the mountains with Spanish shawls packed tightly under their bellies ; of firms whose bi-weekly convoys are insured against seizure by the revenue officers, and of men caught at dead of night on a Côte d'Argent golf-course, detained in prison for a year, fed by their friends on champagne and *foie gras* and finally released for lack of evidence.

The relations between smugglers and excisemen vary greatly in different parts of the country. Spanish *carabineros* are allowed to shoot at sight, but French *douaniers* are not. Smugglers, however, are not always so squeamish. A retired douanier whom I have met jumps nearly out of his skin when a neighbouring dog is summoned by its name " Guarda." For *guarda* is the warning call of the smugglers when a *douanier* is sighted, and may easily be followed by a shot in the darkness.   Yet one market day at Espelette a friend of mine saw two *douaniers* chaffing a well-known smuggler.   "*On t'aura un de ces jours*," they called; and the smuggler raised his glass to them in return.

But it will be more than *un de ces jours* before the Basque gives up smuggling or the revenue officers learn to prevent it.

CHAPTER II

PAYS BASQUE AND PAÍS VASCO

Haritz eder bat bada gure mendietan,
Zazpi adarrez dena zabaltzen airetan,
Frantzian, Espainian, bi alderdietan ;
Hemen hiru'ta han lau, bat da zazpietan.

ZALDUBY.

A mighty oak-tree in our mountains
Spreads aloft its seven branches
In France and in Spain, on the two sides,
Here three and there four ; seven in one.

THE foreign visitor has always shown a disposition to
concentrate on the French Basque Country at the expense
of the Spanish provinces. The characteristics of the
latter are more elusive, less picturesque and " romantic,"
perhaps, less " typically Basque." For this reason the
seekers after copy have fought shy of it, and have conveyed the impression that the Spanish side of the frontier
differs but little from the French, their happy hunting-
ground. This is by no means the case. Between the
Pays Basque and the *País Vasco* there is not only a political
frontier. There is also a spiritual gulf nearly as wide as
that which exists between the Old World and the New
and, curiously enough, not dissimilar to it. It is true,
no doubt, that a Basque prides himself above all things
on being Basque and that there is a strong feeling of
kinship between all *Eskualdunak.* The Basque mottoes
Denak Bat (Those that are One) and *Zazpiak Bat* (The
Seven are One) testify to this sentiment, although it is
not uncommon to hear *Irurak Bat* (The Three are One)

23

and *Laurrak Bat* (The Four are One) on the different sides of the frontier.

The feeling of unity between the two halves of the race was stronger in the Middle Ages than it is now. In those days, when war was declared between France and Spain, the two sections of the Basque Country used to bind themselves to neutrality by treaties known as *Traités de Bonne Correspondence*. These treaties, of which numerous examples are known from 1294 till 1694, were actually authorised by France and Spain, both countries realising that, owing to the poverty of their soil, the Basques could not afford the luxury of war. Until quite recently the French and Spanish frontier villages were in the habit of concluding with each other private agreements called *facéries* dealing with forests and pasture land.

Nowadays the feeling of solidarity has rather dwindled. Those sentimentalists who maintained that a good Basque must necessarily be a lukewarm Frenchman or Spaniard were made aware of their mistake during the Great War, when the Basques not only showed themselves to be among the best soldiers in the French army, but quarrelled bitterly with their Spanish brethren, whom they accused of assisting French deserters to escape into Spain and of replenishing German submarines.

In order to understand the radical differences between the French provinces and the Spanish it must be realised that on the French side the Basques form a group of some 100,000 peasants and fishermen, living in a fashion which appears primitive and backward compared with most parts of France, while the 450,000 Basques of Northern Spain constitute one of the most energetic and advanced sections of the Spanish nation. Scarcely a single Basque name of any importance is to be found in the annals of French history, with the one notable exception of Marshal Harispe. In Spain, on the other hand, from the earliest days of the struggle against the Moors the Basques have played a great part in history.

While their brothers on French soil remained a handful
of small farmers and fishermen tilling the earth and
fishing the seas from Saint-Jean-de-Luz to Greenland in
glorious anonymity, such men as Blas de Lezo (who
beat Vernon at Cartagena),
Churruca, Echaide, Oquendo and
Elcano of Guetaria, who was
Magellan's lieutenant, conde-
scendingly added new lands to
the domains and fresh lustre to
the laurels of His Most Catholic
Majesty. For long years Vasconia
remained almost a kingdom within
a kingdom. Then, in the nineteenth century, the Spanish
Basques were betrayed by their
conservative instincts, and after
the two Carlist wars it seemed
as though they had been reduced
to impotence and provincialism.  The dawn of the industrial age miraculously revived the four provinces by
providing them with new scope for their restless energy
and initiative. Meanwhile the crowded pages of South
American history had never ceased to show that Basque
explorers, revolutionaries or dictators (it depended only
upon the period) could more than hold their own with
those from the rest of the Peninsula.

The industrialisation and modernisation of the Spanish
Basque Country have led superficial observers to consider it less Basque than the French provinces. Undoubtedly, as far as externals are concerned, the more
conservative element living to the north of the frontier,
the world forgetting and of the world forgot, has a more
obvious and picturesque Basque *cachet*. On the other
hand, it is relatively speaking only in the Spanish provinces
that there has been any attempt to create a neo-Basque
culture. It must be admitted that such attempts are
not always very happy in their results. Where, for

instance, the language is concerned, the neologisms
coined by Don Resurrección de Azkue and his friends
are æsthetically unpleasing and would certainly not be
understood by the average peasant. Indeed it has been
said of Don Resurrección's famous dictionary that " *no
es Vascuence sino Azkuence* " (It is not Basque but Azkuen-
ese). But the existence of such tendencies is sympto-
matic. There is a more strongly developed racial sense
in Guipuzcoa and Vizcaya than there is in Labourd or
Soule. A more conscious pride of race has grown up
among those whom circumstances have compelled to
face the disintegrating and denationalising influences of
modern civilisation than among those who have hitherto
succeeded in avoiding them. It is possible to foresee
a time when industrialisation and mass production will
have supplanted the naïve products of Basque peasant
culture in France and when another Basque culture,
transformed to suit modern conditions, yet rooted in
the traditions of the past, may flourish in the trans-
Pyrenean provinces.

May this be a warning rather than a prophecy in so
far as the decay of the French provinces is concerned.
It is nevertheless a fair appraisal of the present tendencies
of the two regions. These divergent tendencies result
from a difference of environment rather than of temperament. The Basque inhabitants of Southern France are
méridionaux with all the accepted implications of the
word. The slothful spell of the South is upon them.
Yet one has but to cross the Bidassoa to find that the
Basques are in every sense the Northerners of Spain.
At first sight it might seem as though this contrast were
only relative; as though a Basque who seemed slothful
in comparison with a Norman or a Picard would take on
an appearance of energy when compared with a drowsy
Andalusian. But there is more in it than that. The
difference between the two halves of the race is not
relative but absolute.

The French Basques seem to lack all ambition so

long as they remain in France. They are content to live simply and humbly, and do not care to do more than the minimum of work necessary to provide them with the bare necessities of life. Imbued with no social aspirations they seldom try to " better themselves," to become doctors, lawyers and business men or to rise to administrative posts of importance. They remain and are content to remain a handful of peasants, and the Northerner will find, in his contacts with them, the unreliability and dilatoriness characteristic of Southern races. These characteristics disappear when they emi- grate to South America or Mexico. The New World awakens the essential energy and initiative which have lain dormant in the Old, and in their train come ambition and frequent success.

In the Spanish provinces a different spirit is abroad, a spirit of competence and progress. The upkeep of the roads, the harnessing of water-power for industrial purposes and the higher standard of cultivation bear eloquent testimony to a greater degree of initiative and ambition. In San Sebastian, Bilbao, Tolosa and other towns of importance the greater part of the business and administrative activity is in Basque hands. One finds not merely a Basque *bourgeoisie* such as can hardly be said to exist on the French side, but a Basque profes- sional class and commercial aristocracy. Such families as the Urquijos, the de la Sotas, the Olazabals and the Aznars find their counterpart in only two or three French Basque families. Although in many cases these Spanish Basques no longer speak the language, they are none the less intensely Basque in feeling, and it is significant that in these conditions they still remain a recognised and indeed a prominent section of the Basque race.

One is thus faced with a series of radical differences between the two sections of a race by nature homo- geneous. The root of these differences is primarily a matter of physical geography. On the northern slopes of the Pyrenees the Basques are the possessors of a soil which is not only poor and unyielding from an agricultural point of view, but lacking in the mineral wealth to be found on the southern side.   It is their natural resources which have determined the divergent line of development followed by the Spanish provinces.   Since the dawn of civilisation Vasconia would seem to have been destined to become an industrial centre.   The iron ore of North-western Spain is mentioned by Martial, Strabo and Pliny, and no sooner has the traveller crossed the frontier at Irún than he sees on the slopes of the *Trois Couronnes* (Mt. Haya) the scars of Roman mines.

There is a quaint tradition that the Basques are descended from Tubalcain, the son of Japhet, son of Noah, who, according to Genesis iv. 22, was the first man to hammer iron.   It would, however, be rash to accept the assertions of the historian Juan Iniguez de Ybargüen, who places in the year 1758 B.C. the war declared on the Basques by Laminius, son of Geron, to whom they had refused to surrender the weapons of iron with which they eventually killed him.

It is hardly surprising that, finding themselves in a land with immense mineral deposits and industrial possibilities, the Basques of Spain, endowed naturally with the same latent energy and initiative as their brothers, should have developed these qualities to a greater degree and should in turn have been transformed by their environment.   Quick to profit by the favourable combination which provided them not only with ore-producing mines but with a coast-line offering from Bilbao to Fuenterrabía a series of natural harbours for the export of their products, the Basques were not long in developing a vigorous and flourishing iron trade.   By the seventeenth century, according to Gabriel de Henao, three hundred foundries, each turning out a thousand quintals of metal a year, supplied countless clients in both the Old World and the New.

In the Low Countries the Spanish Basques maintained vast depots where they exchanged their wares for horses,

Spanish Basques.

cows, woven stuffs and works of art and craftsmanship of every kind. Bruges still has its *Biscayers Plaatz* where stood from 1497 till the last century the *Praetorium Cantabricum*, a magnificent building which served as a sort of glorified Basque Consulate. The esteem in which the Basque merchants were held by the citizens of Bruges is shown by a document dated December 1st, 1493, in which the magistrates of the city grant the " *consuls et suppôts de la Très noble nation de Biscaye* " the right of almost complete immunity from judicial interference. They could not be imprisoned for any " *dette ou cas de crisme* " except when they caused death or loss of limb, in which case their own consuls took part in the proceedings. In a word the Basque merchants in Bruges enjoyed capitulatory rights . . . and this in the fifteenth century.[1]

In spite of the semi-independence to which these circumstances testify (and it is even related that the Spanish King was once moved to complain of the substitution of the arms of Vizcaya for those of Castille), the decay of Spain brought with it a corresponding decline in the fortunes of " *la nación de Vizcaya,*" and the two disastrous Carlist wars reduced them to their lowest ebb. But the future of the Spanish Basque Country, much as one may be impelled to regret it on sentimental grounds, is bound to lie along the lines of industrial development. For, just as the stagnation of the French provinces is the logical continuation of centuries of immobility, so the industrial renaissance and development of the Spanish provinces is the inevitable sequel to their previous history.

[1] This is not the only example of precocity in the international relations of the Basque provinces. There are also records of conventions regulating the extent of territorial waters, and establishing the right of a neutral port to retain a belligerent warship for 24 hours after the departure of an enemy merchant vessel.

CHAPTER III

THE SEVEN PROVINCES

Agur eta ohore Eskual-Herriari,
Lapurdi, Bachenabar, Zibero gainari,
Bizkai, Nabar, Gipuzko eta Alabari!
Zazpiak bat, besarka, loth beitetz elgarri.
ZALDUBY.

Hail and honour to Eskual-Herria,
To Labourd, Basse-Navarre and high Soule,
To Vizcaya, Navarre, Guipuzcoa and Álava!
Seven in one, intertwined, they are bound to one another.

IN the preceding chapters the Basque Country has been frequently mentioned but nowhere clearly defined. Although this book is about the Basques themselves rather than about their country the reader can hardly be expected to have in his mind's eye a sufficiently clear picture of the latter to form the necessary background. It may therefore be useful at this stage to attempt something in the nature of a personally conducted tour of the seven provinces, coupling with it those fragments of information of the Guide Book variety which are usually offered on such occasions.

The Basque Country is very much smaller than most people realise. It comprises, in France, the three provinces of Labourd, Basse-Navarre and Soule, which together form only one-third of the modern department of the Basses-Pyrénées, and, in Spain, the four provinces of

Guipuzcoa, Vizcaya, Álava and Navarre. When Oihénart wrote his book in the seventeenth century the *eskuara* or Basque tongue was spoken throughout this area except in the southernmost part of Navarre. From place-names and other circumstantial evidence it is thought that the Basque or a similar language was once spoken far beyond these limits. Basque place-names are to be found throughout Gascony and in all parts of Spain. It is impossible, however, to state from what epoch these names date. Nowadays the language is no longer spoken even throughout the seven provinces, for a process of contraction has set in. To-day to all intents and purposes the Basque Country embraces barely a hundred miles of coast-line, and at no point is distant more than eighty miles from the sea.

In France the Basque-speaking population is still a compact mass, and if a line be drawn from Bayonne eastwards through Labastide-Clairance to a point just South of Sauveterre and then southwards through Mauléon to the Pic d'Anie on the Spanish frontier the area thus enclosed is inhabited by a solid wedge of Baskophones. Bayonne and Biarritz alone are predominantly French towns.

In Spain, however, things are different. Of the four Spanish Basque provinces only Guipuzcoa can be regarded as Basque throughout. Bilbao is a Spanish-speaking town, and the western part of Vizcaya is Asturian rather than Basque in character. Álava, considered as a Basque province, is now little more than a tradition, supported by an abundance of place-names and a handful of villages where the language is still spoken. The north-western part of Navarre, bounded by the French frontier and the border of Guipuzcoa and stretching to within a few miles of Pampeluna, is essentially Basque, but the latter city, in spite of its Basque name of Iruña, is Spanish-speaking, as is the remainder of the province lying to the East and South. There is, too, in North-eastern Navarre a forgotten stronghold of the Basque language consisting of the twin valleys of the Salazar and the Roncal, this last famous for its peculiar dialect, which was brought to light in the 'sixties by the studies of Prince Louis Napoleon Bonaparte. Much nearer the sea, however, when one climbs the wall of mountains which severs the French valley of Les Aldudes from the high plateau of Roncesvalles, one ceases with amazing suddenness to hear a word of that sonorous ancient tongue.

Labourd, the westernmost of the three French provinces, is called after Lapurdum, the Latin name of its principal city Bayonne, which was also its capital until Richard Cœur de Lion transferred that honour to Uztaritz, a decision which caused much jealousy and trouble. Bayonne still remained the capital in the eyes of many, and the English chronicler Walsingham wrote in 1440: " *Terram Basclorum cui caput est civitas Bajonae* . . ." (the land of the Basques of which Bayonne is the capital). By this time Bayonne had been granted its own separate administrative autonomy, which it retained until the Revolution made it the capital of the newly-formed department of the Basses-Pyrenées. To-day there is nothing Basque about the old cathedral city, and its atmosphere is wholly that of a French provincial town. It remains, however, the administrative and cultural centre of the French Basque Country.

Up to the first half of the eleventh century Labourd formed part of the Duchy of Gascony, which, with Aquitaine, passed into the possession of the House of Poitiers on the death of the last hereditary Duke. The whole region was divided up into small, more or less independent " *comtés, vicomtés, baronies et seigneuries,*" and Labourd became a *vicomté* in 1028. In 1152, by the marriage of Henry II and Eleanor of Aquitaine, it passed with the rest of Gascony into the hands of the Plantagenets, and after some resistance on the part of the nobles it was pacified by Richard Cœur de Lion, to whom, in 1193, Guillaume Raymond de Sault, the eighth Viscount, sold his rights. After the first few troubled years Labourd accommodated itself to English rule, which does not seem to have been at all severe. Joseph Nogaret writes: " The liberal administration of the English seneschals and the privileges enjoyed by Labourd attached it strongly to England." Patrick Ormond explains this attachment as follows: " The principal effect of the occupation was to strengthen the ports. England had to secure her means of retreat. To this end she forced the ports to provide enough ships to guard the coast: she propitiated them with free trade with England which brought in its train the need for shipbuilding. . . . She upheld them against the nobles of the interior in the tariffs which they established against the latter." [1] It is therefore no discourtesy to France to say that Labourd did not immediately stand to gain by its amalgamation with that country, which was consecrated by a treaty signed in 1450 at the castle of Belzunce (the ruins of which can still be seen not far from Saint-Jean-Pied-de-Port).

The arms of Labourd are: *D'or à un lion de gueules tenant de la dextre un dard posé en barre, la pointe en haut du même ; parti d'azur à une fleur de lys d'or.*[2] These are thought to have been originally the arms of Uztaritz and to have been adopted by the province when that town became its capital. The lion probably commemorates the early Viscounts and the fleur-de-lys the union with France under Charles VII.

Labourd is the least mountainous of the Basque provinces, and also the most tourist-ridden owing to the misfortune which has placed the villas and hotels of Biarritz, Guéthary, Saint-Jean-de-Luz and Hendaye

---

[1] P. J. Ormond: " The Basques and their Country," p. 19. Mr. Ormond has made a special study of the English occupation of Gascony, and it is to be hoped that he will soon publish the results of his researches.

[2] Cf. Louis Colas: " Contribution à l'Étude des Armoiries du Pays Basque." *Gure Herria.* 1926. Basque heraldry often deviates so widely from the accepted rules of that science that it has been found impossible to give an accurate translation into English heraldic terms.

D

on its storm-swept coast. The traveller who leaves
Paris overnight will see, after he has passed the twin
spires of Bayonne, a gently undulating succession of
downs covered with bracken, broom and gorse, stretching
away to the mountains. The charming Labourd farmhouses, turned towards the rising sun, with their long
sloping roofs and their whitewashed façades ribbed with
dark wooden beams, are scattered far and wide. These
open horizons are seen at their best in the clear luminous
light of early morning, when no deeper hues break the
softness of their vivid green, blue and white.

From Bayonne a branch line of the railway leads up
the River Nive towards the mountains of Basse-Navarre,
the second of the French Basque provinces. Entering
the narrow gorge of the Pas de Roland the train leaves
Itsassou and the *landes* of Labourd; and by the time it
emerges at Ossès the landscape and architecture have
altered. This is Basse-Navarre. At Ossès the line
forks, and the traveller must choose between changing
for Saint Étienne de Baigorri near the Spanish frontier
or going on to Saint-Jean-Pied-de-Port, the capital of
the province.

Basse-Navarre originally formed part of the Duchy
of Gascony, but in the eleventh century it was handed
over to Sancho of Navarre. This was but the first of
many occasions on which the province changed hands
before the year 1191, when it was definitely restored to
Navarre by Richard Cœur de Lion. The recalcitrant
barons were forced to submit, and the province became
one of the six *merindades* (districts) into which Navarre
was divided. For two hundred years the united province
was ruled successively by the houses of Navarre, Champagne, France, Evreux and Béarn. Its history during
this troubled period is full of violence and intrigue,
treachery, sedition and murder. Through his marriage
with Catherine of Foix, Jean d'Albret added it to his
domains. But he was not strong enough to retain it
for long. The kingdom was overrun by the Duke of

Alba, generalissimo of Ferdinand and Isabella, and Louis XII found it more convenient to sacrifice his ally Jean d'Albret to other and more pressing interests in Italy. Accordingly by an agreement signed on January 1st, 1513, at the castle of Urtubie, which is still a familiar landmark between Saint-Jean-de-Luz and Urrugne, Spain acquired the whole of Haute-Navarre and the district of Saint-Jean-Pied-de-Port, which last remained Spanish for a hundred and fifty years.

The sixteenth century brought no peace to that part of Basse-Navarre which remained under the house of Albret. The unfortunate attempts of Jeanne d'Albret to convert the Basques to Protestantism plunged the country into a sanguinary civil war in which the inhabitants suffered at the hands of Catholics and Protestants alike. These tribulations were followed hot-foot by the Wars of the League, and Basse-Navarre only entered on a period of comparative peace when, under Henry IV, it was at length united with France.

Basse-Navarre is not so much a land of mountains as a land of mountain-valleys : wide valleys of Ossès and Saint-Jean-Pied-de-Port : and narrow valleys of Mendive, Bidarray and Les Aldudes.[1] This last, a cul-de-sac cut off from Spain by Mount Auza and the Roncevaux massif and from France by the long bottle-neck gorge of Banca, shows something of the old Basque spirit of independence by steadfastly refusing to alter its clocks when summer time is adopted in France. So attractive are the mountain valleys of Basse-Navarre that one is inclined to neglect the flatter districts round Saint-Palais and Iholdy, which none the less constitute one of the most unspoilt parts of the Basque Country.

Basse-Navarre has a more southern atmosphere than the other two French provinces. The purple grapes ripening on the sun-baked hillsides of Irouléguy, the jingling bells and stripped saddle-bags of the mules, the carved lintel inscriptions which are more frequent here

[1] Said to derive its name from La Belle Aude.

than in any other province, all indicate that Basse-Navarre has retained something of the flavour of Spain in a part of the world which in reality has more northern charm than southern glamour.

A wall of mountains separates Basse-Navarre from Soule, the third and smallest of the French provinces. There are winding hill-roads that climb over from Larceveau and Saint-Palais to Mauléon, the capital of the province. Save for bridle-paths there is no other way of reaching the magnificent country which lies south of Tardets as far as Sainte-Engrâce and the gorge of Kakueta on the one side and Larrau at the foot of the Pic d'Orhy on the other. The traveller by train must return to Bayonne and make a wide *détour*, changing at Puyoo to the branch line which serves Mauléon.

From the ninth century Soule was ruled by viscounts, of whom the first rejoiced in the name of Aznar Azinarius. The dynasty founded by this almost legendary figure was not extinguished till the middle of the thirteenth century. In 1152, however, Soule passed under English domination, having previously been under the suzerainty first of the Kings of Navarre and later of the Dukes of Gascony. Its history during this period consisted principally of quarrels and disputes with the neighbouring province of Béarn, with which it has better natural communications than with the other Basque provinces.

Under Plantagenet rule Soule was restive at first, and a series of risings culminated in a big revolt in about 1255. The English were stirred to vigorous action, the rebellion was stamped out with a strong hand, and the viscounty was ceded to the Black Prince in 1261. From this date the liberal rule of the English seems to have reconciled the turbulent inhabitants of Soule and to have been maintained without serious difficulty until 1449, when the province was reconquered by the Comte de Foix aided by the Comte de Comminges and other nobles. It was then united to its ancient rival Béarn and ceased to have an independent history. In common with Basse-Navarre it suffered severely from the Wars of Religion and of the League before its final union with France.

Zuberoa, the Basque name for Soule, is explained by Julien Vinson as meaning " hot, wooded country." The arms of the province are: *De gueules au lion d'or*. The lion is *vilené*, *mantelé*, *à queue nouée*. These are the arms of the Lords of Mauléon and were adopted successively by the town and the province.

Soule has been described as the " highlands " of the *Pays Basque*. In some ways its comparative isolation from the rest of the Basque Country and its constant contacts with Béarn have made it lose something of its Basque character. Both its architecture and its dialect have been affected by outside influences. On the other hand, much of the Basque tradition has been preserved more purely in its mountain fastnesses than elsewhere. For Soule is above all the land of the *Pastorales* and the *Mascarades*, the land of ritual dancing. The shepherds who live with their flocks on its high pastures have preserved the loveliest of the ancient folk-songs, and many of the most curious and interesting tales and legends of *Basa Jaun* and *Lamiñak*.

Nevertheless in the Souletin villages it is hard to realise that one has not turned one's back on the Basque Country. The influence of Béarn is predominant in the squat little houses crouching under their tall pointed roofs of grey slate, and the graceful three-pointed belfries of the churches are quite unlike anything to be seen in the other Basque provinces.

From Sainte-Engrâce a long and arduous mule-ride takes one by rough and stony paths into Navarre to Uztarroz, the last village of the Roncal valley, in the neighbourhood of which a curious ceremony takes place each year in June. In virtue of a *facérie* dating from 1375 representatives of the Roncal proceed to the frontier and pay to those of the Béarnais valley of Bedous a tribute consisting of three cows and a certain sum in gold. Basque is spoken at Uztarroz, but once away from the

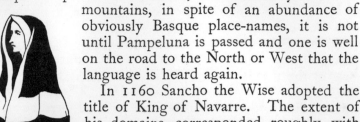

mountains, in spite of an abundance of obviously Basque place-names, it is not until Pampeluna is passed and one is well on the road to the North or West that the language is heard again.

In 1160 Sancho the Wise adopted the title of King of Navarre. The extent of his domains corresponded roughly with the present limits of the province, including, of course, Basse-Navarre. Shorn of the latter, Navarre became part of Spain under the Catholic Kings while the royal title passed to the Kings of France with Henry IV. In Spanish Navarre the King was represented by a Viceroy, and not until 1812 did the province send representatives to the *Cortes* of Spain, the famous *Cortes* held in that year at Cadíz.

The arms of the province are : *De gueules aux chaînes d'or posées en pal, en fasce, en sautoir et en orle, chargées en abîme d'une émeraude au naturel.* These are the famous chains which surrounded the tent of the Moorish Caliph and were captured at the battle of Las Navas de Tolosa (1212) by Sancho the Strong, King of Navarre, and distributed by him to the churches of Pampeluna, Irache, Tudela and Roncevaux. The emerald, unusual as a heraldic device, is said to symbolise the rich spoils taken at the battle.

No satisfactory etymology for the name *Navarra* has been found. The suggestion that it is just the Basque word *nabar* (striped—an allusion perhaps to the variety of the scenery) can hardly be accepted, any more than Vinson's ingenious theory that the *Basse* of Basse-Navarre is a corruption of the Basque word *basa* (wild).

The Basque part of Navarre is one of the most attractive regions in the whole country. In the western part of the province Basque is spoken in the valleys that flank Mounts Naparraz and Aitzola, which are traversed by the road leading from Pampeluna to Tolosa. Soon after Lecumberri a branch-road, winding over the pass of Huici, leads through Leiza to Ernani, running parallel to the border of Guipuzcoa through thick forests of oak, chestnut and beech. A wall of mountains stretching from the Trois Couronnes to the pass of Velate separates this road from another chain of valleys which escort the River Bidassoa to the sea. In among the mountains of Mendicoiz, Arinacoarreta and Izalbil one stumbles upon sombre decayed villages of crumbling unwashed stone. Vast escutcheons graven on grim and blackened mansions only serve to enhance the contrast between past and present. In Navarre almost every house has a stone coat of arms over the door, which is draped with black cloth when the household is in mourning. The arms are usually those of the whole commune or valley, which all those born within it are entitled to bear. Even the hideous stucco villas of emigrants returned from South America to end their days in the comparatively sophisticated town of Elizondo are adorned with a draughts board, the heraldic device of the Baztan valley. These arms were given to the "republic" of the Baztan in recognition of services rendered at Las Navas de Tolosa by its soldiers who, like Drake, left their game to join in the battle. In the village of Maya, birthplace of Amaiur, the first legendary King of the Basques, the chequers are quartered with a bell. At Espinal near Roncevaux every steep red roof casts its midday shadow over a graven boar; and in the valley of Bertiz Arana, where the farms are like great birds hovering with wings outstretched, the arms, a mermaid with mirror and comb, are often masterpieces of stone carving.

The waters of the Bidassoa, Navarrese at their source, are Guipuzcoan by the time they reach the sea, for the border crosses the river in the wild gorge below Vera. Vinson prefers to derive the name *Guipuzcoa* from Basque roots meaning "land of low waters" rather than to accept the more fanciful etymologies devised by some of his predecessors, such as "well of truth" or "we whose language was broken" (*i.e.* at the Tower of Babel).

In the earliest days of its history this province called itself a republic and was ruled by an oligarchy. In the fourteenth century it voluntarily took the King of Castille as its nominal overlord, as did Vizcaya and Álava, but, in common with both these provinces, with which it always maintained a close understanding, Guipuzcoa continued to hold aloof from the historical events which took place around it. Indeed it might with justice be said that the history of the province is summed up in its armorial bearings : *Coupé au premier parti de gueules à un roi vêtu et couronné d'or, tenant en sa dextre une épée d'or et de gueules à douze canons d'or posés en trois pals ; au second d'or à trois arbres de sinople placés sur une seule ligne audessus d'ondes d'argent et d'azur.* The water and the trees can only represent the sea-coast and forests of Guipuzcoa in which for so long the Basques led their own independent existence. The King is probably Alfonso VIII of Castille. The cannon are thought to commemorate the victory gained by the Guipuzcoans over the army of Jean d'Albret in the passes of Ochondo and Velate on December 12th, 1512.

While Guipuzcoa is the only province on the Spanish side which is purely Basque through its whole length and breadth, it is in a way the most elusive and least individual of all. Neither in its architecture nor in its scenery, neither in its dialect nor in its customs, has it any strongly-defined characteristics. The country is hilly although, except in the Goierri, the mountainous region of the South, there are few high peaks. The valleys are fertile, and the serried ranks of golden maize-stalks lend a touch of distinction to the autumn landscape. The farms lack the glistening coat of whitewash of the French provinces and have neither the dark external beams of Labourd nor the balconies of Basse-Navarre.

It is relatively difficult to get away from civilisation in Guipuzcoa. Even in the more remote villages one

OLD HOUSES AT ORIO.

finds electric light and telegraph wires; and, what is
more disturbing, the spirit of the twentieth century.
The tourist is likely to be disappointed in the towns,
for there is little to attract him in Tolosa or Azpeitia,
and, from the Basque point of view, still less in San
Sebastian, except, of course, during the "Basque Week"
held each July. The chief beauty of the province lies
in the sea-coast, a broken, indented line of cliffs with
every few miles a port, a little town of tall white houses
crowded round a massive brown church that looks more
like a fortress. First of these is Fuenterrabía or Fonta-
rabie,[1] familiar to every tourist. Then comes Pasajes,
the bottle-necked harbour from which Magellan set
forth, with gaunt cliffs towering over the twin villages
of San Pedro and San Juan whose vaulted streets pass
beneath their houses. After San Sebastian comes the
lovely *corniche* leading to Orio, Guetaria, Zumaya (Zulo-
aga's home) and Motrico, the one more picturesque than
the other.

Beyond Motrico the road enters Vizcaya. First
comes Ondarroa, beloved of artists, and then Lequeitio,
the present home of the exiled Hapsburgs. Vizcaya is
not unlike Guipuzcoa in its general appearance. The
countryside is a little more barren, and in places long
scars of grey rock show through the shallow soil. There
are in consequence fewer scattered farmhouses, a fact
which, coupled with excellent communications, has contributed to the
more rapid disappearance of old traditions in this province. A hill country
of gentle contours extends from the
coast to the industrial towns of Bilbao,
Durango and Eibar. To the south of
the railway the mountains rise in a
series of jagged limestone peaks.
Among them lies the valley of Arratia,

[1] Derived, neither from *fons rapidus* nor from *fontaine d'Arabie*, but
from its Basque name Ondarrabia, meaning "sandy way."

the wildest part of the province, where the *alboka* is still played, and where, within living memory, the men wore their hair long, knotted in a pig-tail during the week and flowing over their shoulders on Sundays.

The earliest reference to Vizcaya describes it as being in the eighth century a *señoria* under a certain Ozmin. In 880 Alfonso of Leon attempted to conquer the province but was defeated by Lope Zuria (the " White ") at Arrigorriaga. For a long period Vizcaya was ruled by the family of Haro, one member of which, Diego de Haro, was present at the battle of Las Navas. The union with Castille was consecrated by a treaty dated June 21st, 1356. But Vizcaya broke away again, and it was not until 1480 that the union was finally effected.

The arms of the province are very curious : *D'argent au chêne terrassé de sinople brochant sur une croix latine de gueules, accompagnée de deux loups passants de sable posés l'un devant, l'autre derrière le fût et ravissant chacun un agneau ensanglanté de gueules.* The oak is the famous Tree of Guernica, under which the *Juntas* of Vizcaya met to issue laws and the Sovereign received the oath of fidelity, himself swearing to maintain the privileges of the province. This ceremony was observed for the last time by the ill-fated Don Carlos during the second Carlist War (1873–76). The Cross symbolises the Christianity of Vizcaya. The two wolves are those which, according to an old tradition, crossed the front of Lope Zuri's army immediately before the battle of Arrigorriaga and were taken, after the event no doubt, to be an omen of victory. Whatever the origin of the name Vizcaya it was not that attributed to it by a Castillian who, in a petulant moment, derived it from *bis Cains* (Cain twice over) !

Nor is Álava, the fourth of the Spanish Basque provinces, derived from the Basque word *alaba* (daughter), as some would have it, on the assumption presumably that the least Basque of the four provinces is the daughter of the others. The origin of the name remains unknown.

The province has adopted arms which were originally those of the town of Portilla: *De gueules au château crénélé d'or, sommé de trois tours du même, et un dextrochère armé d'argent, issant de la porte dudit château vers senestre, tenant une épée d'or posée en bande, dont il menace un lion rampant du même, le tout posé sur une montagne d'argent; l'écu entouré d'une orle d'argent portant en lettres de sable l'inscription: En Aumento de la Justicia contra Malhechores.* In 1332, when Álava accepted the suzerainty of Castille, the *fuero* or charter of Portilla was extended to the whole province, which adopted the town arms at the same time.

In some ways Álava is the exact opposite of Soule, for the latter is more Basque in reality than in appearance while Álava looks intensely Basque in both its scenery and its architecture, although only four or five villages in the North-eastern corner of the province have retained the language. I am hardly competent to write of Álava, for my impressions have been formed exclusively from a railway carriage. I remember only that, as the train left Vitoria, the capital of the province, and wound between the mountains towards the Guipuzcoan border, all the Basque ingredients seemed to be there: little villages clustered round grim brown churches; black bérets amid the maize fields, oxen ploughing or dragging rude carts with solid wheels, scattered farms crouching under the weight of their broad sloping roofs, seen as flecks of white against green hillside or blue mountain slope. It was hard to believe that the spirit of Eskual Herria had fled for ever from these lovely valleys. And I asked myself how soon the ancient language and traditions would die out in the other provinces, and the Basques and all that they stand for be no more than a vanished memory.

CHAPTER IV

CHARACTER

Bethi aintzina   Ever forward
Chuchen chuchena   Straight and upright
Dabil Eskualduna.   Goes the Basque.

ANON.

Eskualdun fededun.   The Basque is faithful.

BASQUE PROVERB.

OF the prehistoric Basques—and one does not have to go very far back to reach their pre-history—it is possible by collating the sparse references of antiquity to conjure up a picture which, for all its lack of detail, is probably not too inaccurate in its main outlines. The Vascones, assuming them for the moment to have been the ancestors of the Basques, were rude and uncivilised folk who lived on acorn bread, clothed themselves in strips of woollen cloth and were shod with boots of twisted hair. Their usual pursuit was war, varied with a little relaxation in the form of hunting and fishing. They fought without helmet or armour and, if worsted, took to their mountains expressing their defiance of the enemy in " wild mocking cries," which no doubt resembled the *irrintzina* of to-day, a long, wavering yell, something between a laugh, a shriek and a horse's neigh, to which the Basques give

44

vent on festive occasions. They preferred death to captivity, it is said, and, if taken prisoner, either killed each other or insulted their captors with the object of inciting the latter to put them to death. Of their religious observances Strabo relates that at the full moon they danced and feasted in front of their dwelling places in honour of a nameless god. He adds that they used to plant on a dead warrior's tomb as many lances as he had slaughtered enemies. Little more is known of the ancient Vascones; yet, although there is no certainty that they were the ancestors of the Basques, theirs is just such a past as one would imagine the latter to have had.

As the theories put forward concerning the origins of the Basques can be divided into three distinct periods, so also may the views held, or at the least publicly expressed, concerning their character. With sinister unanimity the writers of antiquity depicted them as fierce and turbulent barbarians. Their conversion to Christianity, which may probably be placed in the neighbourhood of the sixth century,[1] modified their reputation to no appreciable extent. They remained the " *inquieti Vascones*." In the twelfth century Aimeric Picaud, a Norman pilgrim, passed through the Basque Country on his way to Santiago de Compostela. In the fourth folio of the " Codex Compostellanus " he has left an account of his journey in which he records the joy with which he saw the peasants trooping into church on Sundays. In one village a group of young men joined with the pilgrim band in prayers for their safe arrival. The next day, finding himself on the brink of an unfordable river, Aimeric Picaud was overjoyed to be met by a boat manned by these same young men. He was sadly disillusioned, therefore, when his new friends stopped in mid-stream to relieve him of his few valuables before dropping him on the other bank, where they completed

---

[1] Some authorities, including Nogaret, place it as early as the second century, while Louis Colas ("*La Tombe Basque*") thinks that it cannot have been complete till the tenth century.

his discomfiture, with a truly mediæval touch, by accompanying him on his way "*en le chevauchant comme un âne.*" One feels, therefore, that he was not quite free from a grain of un-Christian resentment when he described the whole race as "black, perfidious, faithless, corrupt, violent, savage, given over to drunkenness and evil-living. . . ."

As the centuries rolled on and the lawless exploits of the Basques came to be viewed with growing displeasure by their neighbours and consequently to be more difficult of accomplishment, they seem to have turned their energies into another channel and to have acquired a reputation for boisterous high spirits, which is the keynote of the second period. The first evidences of a certain love of horseplay are already to be seen in the humiliating experience of Aimeric Picaud. More general testimony is forthcoming from the pen of the Venetian historian Andrea Navagero, who travelled through the Basque Country in 1528 on his way to Blois (where he died in 1529), from Granada, where he had made literary history by introducing the poet Boscán to the metres of contemporary Italian verse, thus paving the way to the lovely "Eclogas" of Garcilaso and the lyricism of the Spanish Renaissance. After a detailed account of the whaling industry at Saint-Jean-de-Luz he writes:—"The people of this country are very gay and are quite the opposite of the Spaniards, who can do nothing save gravely. These people are always laughing, joking and dancing, both men and women. . . ." Le Pays, writing about a hundred and thirty years later, remarks that "joy begins there with life and ends only with death." He also comments on the unusual agility of the Basques which caused them to be in great demand as servants.

Quite in the spirit of the time is the book written by Pierre de Lancre, Counsellor of the Parliament of Bordeaux, who was sent in 1609 to extirpate sorcery in Labourd. His account of this mission does not indicate that it was conducted with the impartiality and enlightened freedom from superstition for which one might have looked in so eminent a person.   He is easily convinced of the wickedness of the Basques, which he ascribes to the fact that, in the form of cider, a drink which must have been peculiarly abhorrent to a Bordelais, they partake largely of apple-juice, " which is the cause of their biting so willingly at that apple of transgression, which made our first father offend against the commandment of God."   In other passages de Lancre describes the Basques as being " light and quick in body and spirit, liking late evenings and dancing . . . and not restful and grave dancing " (one thinks of the ponderous Counsellor snatched from the polished delights of Bordeaux), " but loose and turbulent."   Similar accounts, inspired with a more friendly spirit, are to be found in the works of Sebastian Moreau, Abel Jouan, Aarssens Sommerdick and other travellers of the sixteenth and seventeenth centuries.

One is impelled to wonder to what extent this tendency to depict the Basques as a gay and lively people was more than a concession to a prevailing fashion.   Although they are far from being a doleful race, their natural liveliness tends to be concealed by their dignified demeanour, and it is not the side of their nature which they are most prone to exhibit before strangers.   Although the legend of the imaginative and poetical Basque, imbued with *Weltschmerz* of a somewhat Celtic hue, which grew up a couple of centuries later, is in reality equally false, one is less astonished that it should spring from the first impressions of superficial travellers.   Or did the Basque character indeed undergo some sort of metamorphosis during the nineteenth century, and the whim of an Empress, concentrating the limelight on a little-known corner of France, change the character of a whole race, causing it to withdraw into the reserve which is its most patent characteristic to-day ?

On the whole it seems more probable that when the

eighteenth century went out and Romance with a big R came in, there was a change of fashion. With chameleon-like adaptability writers accepted the new theory that the Basques, whom they had previously united in regarding as the gayest section of a convivial nation, were the successors of Rousseau's "noble savage," the romantic scions of a doomed and dying race. The third or "romantic" period appears to have been introduced by that monster of inaccuracy Augustin Chaho, himself a Basque from Soule. In 1835 (the date is significant) we find him referring to the "dignity of a free man" and the "sentiments of his original nobility." The seed was sown which some sixty or seventy years later was to bear such meretricious fruit. The novelists stepped in and consecrated the legend; tourist agencies, compilers of guide-books and managers of *Syndicats d'Initiative* propagated and exploited it; generations of tourists swallowed (and continue to swallow) it whole.

The completely successful Basque novel has not yet been written. Many writers have tried their hand at it, including one lady from over the water, who, after a visit of forty-eight hours to the *Côte d'Argent*, wrote a book which has found reputable publishers in both continents. The most distinguished attempt, partly because it was the earliest and partly because, whatever its faults, it is at least extremely well written, is Pierre Loti's "Ramuntcho." This immensely popular novel, which has run into nearly two hundred and fifty editions in France alone, contains the best descriptions of the Basque countryside that have ever been penned. With an amazing combination of intuition and perception, Loti, from his house at Hendaye, succeeded in steeping himself in the intimate spirit of the landscape. In "Ramuntcho" not only does he exercise that unrivalled mastery of the literary palette which made him equally at home with the colour of Britanny, the Levant and the Far East, but he shows that he has felt the formal beauty of the Basque Country, has loved the quiet and delicate contours of its mountains and valleys. The work abounds in those vital touches which, apparently insignificant in themselves, have the power of conjuring up an entire scene, and the intuitive choice of which seems to be almost a monopoly of French writers. This gift for the sober and economical use of the essential detail is all the more appreciable since it is above all the detail which lends individuality and distinction to the Basque landscape. Those blue mountains and green valleys, those golden maize-fields and poplar-bordered streams are to be found elsewhere. But one could never mistake the aspect of the villages, clusters of white-washed houses with chocolate beams and shutters and the scarlet gash of red peppers drying on the balconies, the *pelote* court never more than a stone's throw from the church, which seems to collect the other buildings round it as a hen her chickens. Nor could one fail to recognise the disposition of the outlying farms, innumerable specks of white, each set on a hillock and turned towards the rising sun, the threshold hidden by the gently swelling curve of the land and reached by white paths that wind through green apple-orchards or skirt a field of maize stubble. More vital even, more disproportionate in their incidence, are the living things which stand out in the clear light a valley's breadth away. Fawn-coloured oxen, quiet and gentle, drag a creaking cart with solid wheels, goaded from before by a peasant whose shoulders are curved like the contours of his native hills, and whose black béret tilted up at the back is pulled low over his eyes. Along the dusty winding of the road go men and donkeys, little black-smocked boys on their way to school, old women bound for market, a postman, a priest, a *douanier*, in haphazard but decorative procession. All these things Loti saw; and he understood their æsthetic value and their underlying pattern. It is all the more strange, therefore, that he should have failed to bring those same qualities of intuition and perception to bear on the

E

human psychology of this land which exercised so great a fascination over him.

Apart from his mistakes in describing the habits and customs of the race, Pierre Loti failed utterly to understand the Basque character. Neither Ramuntcho nor Gachucha nor even the minor characters talk, think or act like Basques. Perhaps Loti realised some of his shortcomings, for he gave Ramuntcho a foreign father, as though to explain by the obscure forces of heredity all that is improbable in his nature. Without attaining quite the mystic dream-quality of the Northern Celts, Loti endowed his protagonist with a prodigious imagination and a taste for philosophical speculation, which have a certain Celtic flavour and may well have been imported from Brittany. At all events they are far removed from the clear-thinking, practical mentality of the Basques. To one who has moved with some degree of intimacy among them there is nothing more ridiculous than the idea of a Basque smuggler, with one eye fixed on the radiant heavens while the other wanders over the face of the waters in anxious expectation of a cargo of contraband, indulging in lengthy meditations on the possibility of a hereafter and the vanity of human religions. It is not among the Basques that you must look for " honest doubt." The fact is that Loti, with an unpardonable lack of scruple, has made Ramuntcho the vehicle of his own sophisticated self-questionings.

Still further removed from reality are the imaginings of Francis Jammes. In " Le Mariage Basque," the second of two tales which together make up " Cloches pour Deux Mariages," he portrays a young Basque with as priggish an incapacity for any lapse from the paths of smug virtue as the heroes of the stories which were poured treacle-like down the unprotesting throats of our own Victorian young.

More honest attempts to depict the Basques as they really are have been made by Pierre Lhande (himself a Basque) in " Mirentchu," and André Geiger in " Maï la

Basquaise." Yet both, perhaps unconsciously, make certain concessions to the public craving for the unusual and the exotic, and these two novels are to some extent marred by a tendency to overemphasise the isolation of the Basques and those traits in their character which are least universal. Romance dies hard, and the public clings tenaciously to its legends, with the result that the best-intentioned novelists have not yet succeeded in shaking themselves free of this pernicious influence and in penetrating into the rarer air of Comtian positivism.

One would like to be able to announce the advent of a fourth and "positivist" period in the delineation of Basque character, but fair and accurate appraisals of the race are as rare now as they have ever been, and, seeking for an analysis of Basque character combining balance and brevity I have been able to find only two passages which satisfy these conditions. Canon Dibildos, writing in *Gure Herria*, resumes his impressions of his own people as follows :—" Sober thought, courageous action and cheerfulness, these are the three characteristics which mark our race." The second passage represents the considered verdict of the late Julien Vinson, who lived for more than half a century among the Basques :— " They are full of prejudices," he writes, " and retain ancient superstitions which Catholicism has not been able to eradicate. They are firmly attached to even the least important of their customs, but they have a solid foundation of uprightness, although their ignorance, their obstinacy and the extreme liveliness of their imagination [1] lead them frequently into false judgments. They are gentle and agreeable, but irascible and dangerous in the heat of their temper. I do not think that they are spiteful and vindictive as they have been said to be. They are keen and enthusiastic, carried away by a trifle and as easily disillusioned. Though habitually serious, they are prone to let themselves go over games and the pleasures of the table. Their gaiety then becomes noisy

---

[1] The only point on which Vinson seems to me to be radically wrong.

and interminable. They make a habit and a cult of hospitality in the widest sense of the word."

It is now time to discard scissors and paste and to broach the more delicate task of recording, condensing and classifying the thronging crowd of personal impressions. There are few tasks, at first sight simple, which prove more difficult than the analysis of a nation's psychology. Let the reader try to condense into a few lines his impressions of, say, the French or the Germans. In place of the neatly-docketed generalisations consecrated by tradition, there will spring to his mind an inextricable tangle of personal experience, fraught with self-questioning and contradiction, in which the particular will dwarf the general and the exception will loom larger than the rule. This is more than ever the case when one thinks of the Basques. Their reserve and uncommunicativeness towards the foreigner produce a discouraging impression of elusiveness. One knows that one will never quite reach the back of their mind or fathom the full depth of their nature, and one is reduced to studying them at second-hand, as it were, through their actions and their achievement. It is even doubtful if they understand themselves, for, not being naturally introspective, they hesitate to embark upon the hazardous sea of self-analysis. "The Basque spirit," writes Laurent Apeztéguy, himself a Basque, "is indefinable. We persist in thinking that it exists, that it is one of those realities which one feels and realises without being able to discern its outlines or even its most essential substance."

Some temerity is required to embark on a task at which so many have failed, and my personal observations will therefore be offered with the greatest diffidence. Here, as a framework on which to embroider, are some impressions of Basque character: loyalty and rectitude; dignity and reserve; independence and a strong sense of race and racial superiority; a serious outlook tempered by a marked sense of humour and capacity for enjoyment; deep religious feeling; and a cult of tradition amounting almost to ancestor-worship: all these correlated and directed by a deep-rooted simplicity and a courageous, objective view of life.

To my mind this last point is the key to the whole problem of Basque character. So many writers have been led by the deliberate elusiveness of the Basque to think that his reserve hides more than is really there. Puzzled by their own inability to probe beneath the surface, they have complicated the problem unnecessarily and have created a legend, the legend of " Ramuntcho." To maintain that imagination is not one of the primary qualities of the Basque, that the lack of it is indeed the key to his racial character, is not to say that his thoughts are occupied exclusively with material things, but rather that he unquestioningly accepts his ancestors' views of the essential problems of life and death and wastes no more time in idle speculation.

On the belfry of the old church at Sare, which stands out white against the purple bulwark of La Rhune, are painted the following lines :—

> *Oren guziek dute gizona kolpatzen*
> *Azkenekoak du hobira igortzen.*
>
> (All the hours shower blows on man,
> The last sends him to the tomb.)

Even more final in its brevity is the oft-quoted " *Vulnerant omnes, ultima necat* " of the weather-beaten church at Urrugne, where on a wet day in 1813 Wellington stabled his horses. Less resigned and therefore rather less true to Basque character is this other inscription graven on a house near Cambo : " *Le temps passé m'a trompé, le présent me tourmente et l'advenir m'espouvante.* " A farm at Saint Martin d'Arossa (Basse-Navarre) bears over the door the two words " *Orhoit hilceaz* " (Remember death), and variations on this sombre theme appear in inscriptions in other parts of the country. I would mention also the sentence carved above a door of the Institut Sainte-Marie in the Rue Saint-Jacques at Saint-Jean-de-Luz : " *Ici fait l home ce qui peut et fortune ce que. elle veut. Jean Decasa bielhe. me fit faire* 1632." These maxims all breathe the same spirit of fatalism, tempered, except in one case, with Christian courage and resignation. They testify also to an essentially serious outlook on life, and their directness and brevity seem to exclude all doubt and imaginative speculation.

A marked lack of imagination and poetical sense is discernible throughout Basque literature, both written and oral. The religious works, of which the former is almost exclusively composed, are characterised by the entire absence of mysticism. These solid and musty tomes exhale a spirit of sound, precise and healthy doctrine, harnessing the practical to the ideal in such a way as to obtain the best positive results. More than any written literature the legends handed down by oral tradition reveal the true spirit of the race. They are mediæval in atmosphere, redolent of the Gothic, with all its wealth of fantastic invention, its freshness and its *naïveté*. But they are entirely materialistic and devoid of allegory or indeed of any abstract thought. Even the words of Basque folk-song, sung to airs of the greatest beauty, are usually lacking in the lyrical qualities that are so often found in folk-poetry. When they are not humorous or satirical, only their evident sincerity and lack of self-consciousness save them from appearing trite and commonplace.

It is difficult to decide whether this serene, unimaginative outlook explains or is itself explained by the deeply devout nature of the Basques. In few parts of the world does any faith or creed exercise on its devotees a hold so firm and yet so free from fanaticism. " *Qui dit Basque dit Catholique* " runs an old proverb, and in the sixteenth century, when Protestantism made so much headway in the Kingdom of Béarn, it failed to secure any footing in the neighbouring Basque provinces.   Jeanne d'Albret is said to have made eleven converts, neither more nor less.

Basque faith is as free from Northern mysticism as it is from Latin superstition.   Although the Basques, like all primitive races, are by nature superstitious, they do not let superstition encroach upon their religion.   There is in their worship relatively little of that cult of images, so idolatrous in its essence, which one finds further south, where the comparative virtues of the Virgin of This, That or the Other have often been the cause of bitter dissension and strife.   Nor have the Basques exaggerated the habit of making vows or presenting votive offerings to their favourite saints.[1]   Yet they do not neglect the externals of worship.   One has only to watch them in church, or in one of the frequent religious processions, to see how reverent is their demeanour, how grave and dignified their expression, as free from cant as from shamefaced self-consciousness.   Their faith is simple, natural and unquestioning; lacking in any display of emotion or sentiment.   It has a patriarchal quality which recalls the Old rather than the New Testament, the Psalms rather than the Gospel.   For the Basques have not lost the conception of a Righteous God, who will reward the virtuous and show no mercy to the wicked. Even Pierre Lhande, himself a Basque and a priest, admits that his people fear their God more than they love Him.   A mother, he remarks, will not say to her child " Don't do that, for you will make Jesus unhappy," but " Don't do that or God will punish you."

In the Middle Ages so close was the connection between the religious and the secular life of the Basques, that in

---

[1] Nevertheless on the inside of my bedroom door at the inn at Loyola I found a little card with a portrait of Saint Ignatius.   Above the Saint's head was written in large letters : AL DIABLO.   No ENTRES !   (To the Devil.   No admittance !)   Below was a quotation from one of the Jesuit fathers to the effect that the Saint's picture was " most efficacious in all assaults and infestations of the Enemy . . .," a sort of moral Keating's Powder in fact !

some places the church served not only as a place of worship but also as a centre for assembly. In Saint-Jean-de-Luz, for instance, all important public meetings were held in the church until well on in the seventeenth century.

The priest still plays a very intimate rôle in the life of his flock, for he is their real friend and counsellor. Being usually of Basque peasant stock himself, and having acquired the wider outlook which comes with education, he is full of sympathy and understanding for all their troubles and difficulties, and can yet give them wiser and more experienced counsel than they could find in their own hearts. Above all he takes care that there shall be no wide gulf fixed between them and him. Though quiet and unostentatious in his ways, he is ready at any moment to go out shooting or, with his cassock girt up, to join in a game of *pelote*. A hundred years ago it was not unusual to see the village priest lead the *Saut Basque* on a Sunday evening He does not expect his flock to conform to an unattainable standard of virtue, but aims at the highest ideals compatible with practical results. Not for nothing was Saint Ignatius of Loyola a Basque. Were the clergy men of a lower moral standard the Basques would be in danger of becoming " priest-ridden." As things are their influence seems to be greatly for good.

It would be presumptuous to pass judgment on the Basques from a moral point of view, for it is far harder to decide whether a race is virtuous than whether it is pious. The two qualities do not always go hand in hand, and there are more different standards of virtue than there are of piety. Suffice it to say that the Basques give the impression of being clean-minded, clean-living people, with an almost patriarchal standard of public morals, founded less on any religious or ethical code than on the material interests of the family and community. As a matter of course they speak out with the utmost frankness everything that is in their minds, and it never occurs to them to mince their words even before their womenfolk, who nevertheless see therein no cause for blushing. In their songs and legends there is seldom any deliberate obscenity. Adultery is most severely condemned. Should the slightest breath of suspicion link the names of two persons who are not free to marry one another, these may awake one morning to find a tell-tale trail of freshly-cut grass or rushes linking the doors of their houses, as a mark of public disapproval. Even the remarriage of a widow is looked upon askance. Should she brave public opinion she will as likely as not be kept awake on her wedding night by " rough music," and the beating of tin cans, the ringing of bells and the blowing of horns will continue till dawn. This custom, called the *galarrotza* (night-noise), which is by no means peculiar to the Basques, is still kept up even in the towns, and was revived not long ago in Saint-Jean-de-Luz for the remarriage of an old *cascarot* fish-wife to a man thirty years her junior. Although the Basques show such strong disapproval of conjugal in-fidelity, they are singularly lenient towards the mis-conduct of unmarried persons. Should a girl find herself in trouble she will be held up to ridicule in improvised songs, but she will not be expected to marry her lover, nor will she have any difficulty in finding a husband. The latter indeed will not merely overlook the existence of an illegitimate child, but will welcome it into his home just as primitive man must have welcomed every prospective pair of able hands.

As strong as the religious feeling of the Basques is their sense of race. If asked whether they are French or Spanish they will invariably reply : Basque. One of the most frequently quoted examples of pride of race is the repartee made by a Basque to a Montmorency who had been bragging of his family, which, he said, dated back a thousand years. " And we," replied the Basque, " we cannot be dated at all." In some respects their strong sense of their own superiority resembles that peculiarly British quality which has made our ancestors, and, it must be admitted, not a few of our contemporaries, disparagingly divide the races of Europe into the two classes of " Dutchmen " and " Dagoes." Basque pride is satirised by Cervantes in that chapter of " Don Quixote " where the Biscayan coachman leaves his mistresses unprotected in their carriage in order to defend, by force of arms, his honour as a nobleman. Aubrey Bell quotes an amusing modern parallel to this episode :—" A chauffeur while driving his mistress considered that he had been insulted by a passer in the street, and leaving mistress and motor proceeded to punish the offender till the police intervened."

In the past these intransigent folk have not always been over kind to the " stranger within their gates," and the *fueros* included the most severe regulations against *cagots* and gypsies.

The *cagots* or *chrestias* were a mysterious race living not only in the Basque provinces but in Brittany and other parts of France. In appearance they were fair and physically under-developed and had narrow and curiously pointed heads. De Rochas (" Les Parias de l'Europe ") states that they had, by way of hair, a kind of very blond down and that their shrivelled nails curled over the quick at the end of their fingers. Their ears lacked the lower lobe and, if one is to believe popular tradition, were unequal in size. The folk-song " *Agotak* " has a verse which runs :—

> This is how you may recognise the *cagot* :
> You must look first at his ears :
> One is bigger, and the other
> Is round and covered with
> Long hair on every side.

Opinion has long been divided as to their origin, and at one time they were thought to be isolated colonies of Goths, a theory to which their Basque name *agotak* seemed to lend colour. It appears now to be generally admitted that these unfortunate people were the descendants of leper colonies. This at least would explain, and to a certain extent excuse, the severity of the *fueros*, which provided the most severe penalties, including that of death, for marriage with a Basque or for any other breach of the regulations affecting them. Curiously enough they were exempted from taxes and were granted the monopoly of certain occupations, especially of carpentering, since wood was regarded as being a non-conductor of infection. On the other hand, they were obliged to live in isolated villages and forbidden to mix with Basques in crowded places. In the churches they used a separate door and a gallery divided off by a grille which can still be seen in a number of places. *Cagots* were even forbidden to walk barefoot lest they should defile the earth, and in some localities they were obliged to wear a distinguishing mark. In theory their disabilities were abolished by Louis XIV, but in practice they lasted much longer, especially on the Spanish side, where the *agotak* only ceased to be ostracised and began to intermarry with Basques in the latter half of last century. An interesting description of the atmosphere in which they lived is to be found in the opening chapters of a Spanish novel, " El Barrio Maldito," by Felix Urabayen. The " accursed quarter " therein described is the Barrio de Lozate, a mile or so from Arizcun in the Baztan Valley. I visited it one day in the hope of seeing a *cagot*, but I must admit that, if I seemed to detect a hint of degeneracy in the features of the inhabitants, it may have been nothing more than auto-suggestion.

More spasmodic but sometimes even more relentless was the treatment meted out to the gypsies who arrived in the Basque Country at the end of the sixteenth century, having been expelled from Spain, where, as in the Balkans, they professed the Moslem faith. Despite the persecution to which they were subjected and the frequent orders for their expulsion, they have survived till the present day and can still be identified at Ispoure, at Saint-Palais and perhaps in the *cascarots* of Ciboure.

Although there has been intermarriage of late years they have not yet lost those characteristics which distinguish them throughout Europe, and it is not surprising that the ancient prejudice against them still subsists.

To his consciousness of the individuality and superiority of his race the Basque adds a deep-rooted sense of its continuity, a sense which is instinctive rather than conscious, and is manifested particularly in his deep respect for the traditions of his ancestors and in the serenity of his attitude towards death. There is no more conservative race on the face of the earth. The *aintzinekoak*, " those who have gone before," are held in the deepest reverence, and their ideas and mode of life are regarded as a sacred model from which later generations will not deviate an inch. It is no use trying to instil ideas of modern progress into these peasants, for they are always ready with the one irrefutable answer:— " What was good enough for my father is good enough for me." This intense devotion to tradition explains much which might otherwise be puzzling in the race, and not least its survival relatively untainted by the universal fustian of the twentieth century. When the Basque emigrates to South America or Mexico, and is no longer under the influence of his own racial environment, he becomes a different man. He throws off this clogging conservatism, responds to the call of progress and develops unsuspected qualities of energy and initiative. But there is a risk that he may cease, to all intents and purposes, to be a Basque.

Respect for racial traditions and the sense of racial continuity are the principal factors which have determined the Basque attitude towards family life. Most striking is the lack of importance attached to the individual in comparison with the family, or with its tangible symbol, the house. Almost any sacrifice may be demanded of him for the benefit of the house, and it is only fair to say that it will usually be voluntarily and indeed gladly offered. The essential identity of the conceptions of house and family is revealed by the fact that patronymics are never formed as in other countries from a Christian name or from an occupation. With hardly a single exception they are names of houses. Thus Etcheberri means " new house "; Jaurreguy, " manor house "; Elissamburu, at the head of the church; Zubilibia, the two bridges; Dargaineratz, rocks rising one above the other. The " new house " may have fallen into ruin, the two bridges may have disappeared, but the house will retain its ancient name, and the family, so long as they live there, will be known by no other. Sometimes, owing to ill-fortune, a house has to be sold; or it may pass through the female line to the descendants of a son-in-law. There will then be a difference between the name of the house and that of the occupants (although the latter name will originally have been derived from that of some other house). This distinct family name, however, will be used almost exclusively for legal purposes and the neighbours will take no notice of it. (Pierre Lhande states that many young men learn their legal surname for the first time when they receive their calling-up papers for military service.) The family will find that the house is of more account than they are. " Ceci tuera cela." They will be assimilated to it and perforce named after it. Speak to a Basque of Pierre Topet and he will not know whom you mean : but speak to him of Etchahoun [1] and he will raise his béret to the memory of the greatest of all bertsolaris.

Basque family life, based originally on the patriarchal system, is essentially autocratic. The etcheko jauna, or head of the house, retains his despotic power till the hour of his death. He does not abuse it, for in all matters of importance affecting the welfare of the house, such as the purchase of a cow or the rotation of crops, he takes counsel not only with all the members of the family but even with the servants. Once his decision is made,

[1] Literally " good house." For Etchahoun and bertsolaris, see Chapters V and VII.

however, it is respected by all. When he dies his
possessions and authority pass by an unwritten law
into the hands of that one of his children who has long
since been chosen to be *etcheko primu*, or heir of the house.
This may be the eldest child or the youngest : it may
be a boy or it may be a girl Whichever child has been
chosen, the decision will not have been made without
long and careful deliberation, and there will be none to
challenge it. " *Le Roi est mort : vive le Roi.*" The
etcheko primu succeeds his or her father as *etcheko jaun*
or *etcheko andre*. In the latter event the authority will
be vested in the *etcheko andre* herself, and her husband
will be of no more importance than any other member
of the household. There is a moral obligation on the
etcheko jaun to support all the members of the family and
to provide adequate dowries for the daughters of the
house.

These domestic customs appear to be of ancient
origin. The *fueros* made special provision for full
testamentary freedom, and this was one of the few
privileges which the Spanish Basques were able to rescue
from the wreck of their liberties after the Carlist wars.
In France their traditions have not been similarly
respected. A law passed on the 17th Ventose in the
2nd Year of the Republic abolished testamentary freedom
and prescribed the equal division of a man's property
among his children. It was not to be imagined that this
law, based on ideas of equality and the rights of the
individual, ideas which are both foreign and repugnant
to the Basque mind, would be welcomed by a race the
lodestar of whose domestic tradition is parental authority
and filial respect. The Law of the 17th Ventose has
never been modified in its essentials, and for over a
century the Basques have waged warfare against its
provisions, circumventing them by every means in their
power, in order to save their lands, small enough already,
from being further split up, and their houses, indivisible,
from being sold. Where the younger children have

shown sufficient devotion to surrender their rights in favour of the *etcheko primu*, this has proved no difficult matter. But when, encouraged by the law, with their respect for tradition undermined by modern ideas, they insist on their rights, it becomes a hard task for the heir of the house to raise the money required to buy them out and so to preserve the house and lands intact. In many cases, thanks partly to lax administration of the law, this has been successfully accomplished. On the other hand, many homes have been broken up and have come under the hammer, victims of this conflict between the new ideas and the old.

The innate consciousness of the Basques that they are a people apart probably accounts to a large extent for two of their most noticeable traits, to wit independence and reserve. Independence is reflected as much in the individual as in the mass : more so indeed, for History can offer hardly a single example of collective action on the part of the Basques. Authorities set up by themselves have often met with difficulty in carrying out their decisions. When, for instance, the hamlet of Accotz was incorporated in the municipality of Saint-Jean-de-Luz, a change which conferred considerable benefits on the inhabitants, the latter resisted all attempts to make them pay taxes or bear their share of other communal burdens. Those who come into contact with the Basques to-day have to put up with a good deal from their independence and obstinacy. When a Basque has made up his mind about a matter threats will avail nothing and persuasion extremely little.

The impenetrable reserve of these people is akin to their spirit of independence, of which it is to a certain extent the expression. The peasantry remain unaffected by any tactics which the foreigner may pursue to pierce their reticence. The Basque cannot be called a xenophobe in the accepted sense of the word, for he does not hate foreigners. His attitude is more detached. If xenophobia still bore its literal meaning of " fear of strangers," then its use might be more apt. For the attitude of the Basque towards the stranger is founded less on dislike than on distrust and suspicion. It is both the conscious armour of the individual whose experience and outlook are too circumscribed to afford him protection from the dangers which beset the guileless, and the unconscious weapon of a race whose language and geographical isolation suffice no longer to protect it against the perils which threaten its survival. This attitude is plainly evident in two Basque proverbs :—" A foreign land is a land of wolves " ; and " Heavy is the hand of foreigners."

Even Frenchmen and Spaniards who have lived in the country since childhood admit that, while they have no enmity to contend with, they are never treated as aught but foreigners. I, too, can speak from experience. When I first started collecting folk-songs I did not hesitate to approach a peasant at home or in the fields and ask him to sing. Invariably I was greeted with silence or with an evasive answer, while the suspicious mind was wondering what was my real object. It was not long before I learnt to expect songs only from those with whom I had come into contact in some other way, and in whose eyes my presence was already explained.

Few foreigners see through this dour mask to the light-heartedness and sly, whimsical humour which lie beneath. Mayi Elissague, authoress of a charming little volume of " Silhouettes Basques," tells a story which serves admirably to illustrate the peculiar quality of this humour. One day while she was watching a *pelote* match she fell into conversation with an old man beside her who was following the game with intense interest and appreciation of all its finer points. Having told her his name, which she recognised as that of a famous player of bygone years, he proceeded to recount to her all the victories of his youth. " Did you never have any defeats then ? " she asked him slyly. " Defeats ? " he said ; " ah, it is my opponents who tell the story of those ! "

There is one word which covers all the qualities that go to make up Basque character; a word which unites the conceptions of independence and " superiority complex," of high spirits and deep reserve. That word is " insularity." In spite of the apparent paradox the Basques are insular, as insular as we are ourselves. If the British traveller bears this in mind he will no longer be surprised to find himself stared at in the villages, to hear a facetious remark or laugh which he guesses rightly to be at his expense, to find that his friendly advances break down before a polite but solid wall of reserve. Is not that exactly how he himself will probably treat a foreigner at home ? Let him watch the young men, and appreciate their natural ease of manner, their cheerful good humour, the geniality of their intimate jokes and their air of conscious superiority, and he will end by likening them in his mind to a group of English public-school boys. They have, like ourselves, a natural simplicity in personal relations which is utterly foreign to the Latin temperament. When they are not busy laughing at the idiosyncrasies of the tourist, it would seem as if they realised that there is an affinity between the Briton and themselves.

There is no need to emphasise how intensely they dislike " *le snobisme basque*," as they call the present vogue for their race and their country, how they despise the hordes of inquisitive sight-seers, armed with béret, *makhila* and *espadrilles*, who invade their privacy; the ridiculous novels and films which distort their life and customs ; and all the pseudo-Basque festivities, organised for the benefit of an " Internationale " of profiteers by the *Syndicats d'Initiative* of the fashionable seaside resorts. At Biarritz one day at a so-called *Fête Basque* a procession wound through the town, in which there figured an ox-cart complete with a " Basque peasant couple." Unfortunately for the organisers the whole effect was spoilt by a voice from the crowd shouting :— " There's nothing Basque there but the oxen ! " That voice interpreted the feelings of the race.

F

Much has been written about the place occupied by women among the Basques. Strabo was shocked at the important rôle which the Cantabrian women were allowed to play. Modern writers seem to be unable to avoid one or other of two extremes. They depict the Basque either as treating his womenfolk like menials or as putting them on a sort of semi-divine pedestal, which would be unusual, to say the least, in a nation of peasants. The fact is that he places women on his own level (or very nearly), but in a completely different sphere. The difference is one of kind rather than of degree. The women of the house will serve their men-folk first, and will not start their meal till the latter have finished. While the men ride they will often walk behind. Yet they seldom do men's work, they are universally respected, their supremacy in their own sphere is unchallenged and, as has been shown, there is no Salic Law in Basque successorial custom.

At various times in history, moreover, the women have asserted their rights and independence with no uncertain voice. M. Pierre Dop of Saint-Jean-de-Luz has in his possession a curious document headed " Doléances du Sexe de Saint-Jean-de-Luz et Cibour au Roi." This is a petition addressed by the " *très humbles et très soumises sujettes citoïnnes* " of the two towns to Louis XVI, who had just convened the States General of 1789. The petition is nothing less than an appeal for female suffrage, expressed with an eloquence and a discursiveness thoroughly redolent of the eighteenth century. Although these rather premature suffragettes admit that they have not " at present the knowledge necessary to set right a bad Government," they argue that the best public adminis-trators must necessarily be those who have the fullest experience of domestic economy, *i.e.* themselves. Once in power they would first of all devote themselves to the reform of female education. No longer would they learn to " *composer notre maintien, symmétriser nos gestes, cadencer nos pas, danser avec grâce et chanter avec mélodie,*" but they

A Street in Ciboure.

would devote themselves to more serious pursuits. Then they would slay the hydra of " monstrous celibacy." All confirmed bachelors would be declared unfit to occupy any responsible position, and their possessions would be confiscated to provide dowries for such spinsters as were less favoured by nature. Perhaps on the whole it is just as well that Louis did not grant this petition.

      *   *   *   *   *   *

It may be thought that this account of the Basques, like so many others, has idealised them. It is therefore only fair to touch, however lightly, on the other side of the picture. For the Basques, like every other race, have their faults. There is in their character a streak of hardness which is primitive in its neglect of the more cultivated virtues of compassion and altruism. This hardness is not so much of a positive as of a negative order, and springs rather from the natural outlook of a race which has never apprehended modern ethical conceptions than from any definite defect in their moral composition. It suffices, however, to explain certain somewhat unlovable traits in their character, such as their lack of consideration for others, their unconcealed contempt for every form of weakness and deformity and their indifference to suffering both human and animal. They have little or no affection for their beasts, and their cruelty is principally the result of thoughtlessness rather than wanton brutality. At the same time one does not like to see the pointed steel goad used on the oxen. Nor can there be any excuse for the revolting " *Antzara Jokoa* " or Goose Game, now happily obsolescent.[1]

Their lack of the sporting spirit is really astonishing in a race endowed with such a remarkable taste and aptitude for all outdoor sports. The Basque, usually so reserved, displays his feelings on the *pelote* court with all the expansiveness of a pettish *prima donna*. If he is losing he will scowl at his opponent, gesticulate at the crowd and make no further attempt to win the game. He has

[1] Cf. p. 248.

no hesitation in dynamiting his rivers for fish or in shooting a sitting bird. He will even take pleasure in a Sunday morning massacre of song-birds like any " *chasseur de casquettes* " from Daudet's Tarascon.

There is very little that can be called sporting in the methods used for slaughtering the pigeons which cross the Pyrenees in migratory flight. A big tree (known as a " *palombière* "), lying on the route invariably followed by the birds is the traditional scene of the annual massacre. A watcher is set ; nets and decoy birds are placed in the tree. As soon as the flock is sighted crowds of children lining the hills start shouting and gesticulating to prevent the birds from deviating from their course. Then, just as they reach the tree, a flat piece of wood, shaped rather like a heart and so cunningly contrived that it imitates the flight of a hawk, is thrown into the air. The birds dive, the nets are drawn tight and the hapless victims die an ignoble death.

Nevertheless the abiding impression left by the Basques is that of a fine stalwart people, healthy and robust in mind and body, a race of hardy mountain folk with mountain virtues, who know their own minds and can defend their traditions and convictions with a courage and a spirit of independence amounting almost to fanaticism, and whose hearts are set on one thing, namely, to endure.

CHAPTER V

LANGUAGE AND LITERATURE

Quand nous fûmes à Bayonne
Loing du Pays
Changer nous fallut nos couronnes
Et Fleur de Lys
C'était pour passer le pays
De la Biscaye
C'est un pays rude à passer
Qui n'entend de langage.
COMPOSTELLA PILGRIMS' SONG.

When we came to Bayonne
Far from our homes
We had to change our crowns
And fleur-de-lys,
For to pass through the land
Of Biscay
A hard land to pass
Which understands no tongue.

FROM time immemorial the Basque language has enjoyed a fame amounting almost to notoriety. Most of the classical writers who refer to the Vascones make special mention of the uncouth tongue which distinguished them from their neighbours, describing it as " barbaric and not to be borne." Since all the dialects of the Peninsula must have seemed uncouth and barbaric in comparison with the *lingua Romana*, it is significant that they should have singled out for special mention what one would like to regard as the Basque language. But do these quotations refer to either Basque or its ancestor ? Therein lies a problem which has already been discussed in connection with the origin of the race and which may never be solved.

Unfortunately, the Romans were not interested in philology, and have left on record no details of the language which so inspired their aversion. Moreover, they showed a singular lack of scruple in their transcription of native geographical names, when they did not ignore them altogether. One need not therefore be disturbed at finding little or no Basque savour in most of the place-names which they mention. It is none the less possible, with a little good will, to find such resemblances, and Professor Achille Luchaire makes use of them in support of his contention that in Aquitania and Northern Spain there existed in classical times a language or group of languages resembling Basque, with the aid of which it is possible to interpret many names of places, men and gods mentioned in Roman writings and covering an area much more extensive than that of the present Basque Country.

Similarly, Iberian inscriptions, as deciphered by Hübner and Boudart, yield such manifestly Basque words as *Ilibaricoen*, *Hilibeturicoen*, etc. The resemblances between Iberian and Basque have been fiercely challenged and as fiercely defended by specialists. Nogaret, after weighing the evidence on both sides, concludes : " At all events, this much can be held to be scientifically established :—

" 1. Although little is known of the Iberian language, it seems that its system of declension is approximately the same as that of Basque.

" 2. The names of places and even the names of people in ancient Aquitania and in the North of Spain (valley of the Ebro and Pyrenean region) have often a completely Basque appearance and can easily be interpreted in that language. One may therefore conclude that Basque is most probably the language spoken by the Aquitanians, or the survival of an idiom very closely related to the Aquitanian language ; and that both of these in turn must have been more or less closely related to Iberian."

The first generally accepted evidence of the existence of Basque is to be found in a Latin document dated 980 delimiting the diocese of Bayonne, in which local place-names are reproduced in a more or less recognisable form. The science of transliteration seems to have made some slight advance since Roman times. But it is necessary to skip another couple of centuries in order to reach anything more satisfactory than place-names.

The " Codex Compostellanus " already quoted contains the first known vocabulary of the Basque language (the *Bascli*, it is amusing to find, are therein described as being "*ex genere Scothorum*"), consisting of a list of eighteen common words with their meanings, of which the following are examples :—*Urcia* (God),[1] *orgui* (bread), *ardum* (wine), *aragui* (flesh), *araing* (fish), *echea* (house), etc. With the exception of the word *Urcia* which has been replaced in modern Basque by *Jaungoikoa* or *Jinkoa* (literally " the Lord on high "),[2] these words are all in current use to-day.

A similar but later vocabulary is to be found in the " Journal " of the German knight, Arnold von Harff, another pilgrim to the shrine of St. James, who left Cologne in 1496 and returned there in 1499, after visiting Rome, Venice, Cairo, Mount Sinai, Jerusalem, Santiago and the Mont-Saint-Michel, a round tour which at that date must have appeared an unprecedented example of

---

[1] The word *urzi* or *ortzi* now means the " sky " according to Azkue, or " thunder " according to Van Eys. From it is derived the word *Ortzegun* or *Ostegun*, meaning " Thursday " (cf. German *Donnerstag*). In this connection it is interesting to note a resolution passed in the year 589 by the Provincial Council of Narbonne :—" We hear that many persons celebrate Thursday in the manner of the pagans. He who, except on feast days, shall solemnise that day, let him be excommunicated. . . ."

[2] This word has passed into current English use in the expression " By Jingo," which first appears in 1690 in the form " High Jingo " and is used in Motteux's translation of Rabelais (1694) to render the French " *par Dieu*."

transatlantic hustle. Von Harff made a point, in every country through which he passed, of noting in his " Journal " a few words and phrases in the local idiom, including the equivalent of " *Schoin junfrau kumpt bij mich slaeffen,*" which he renders by a Basque phrase so inaccurately transcribed that it has set all the present-day experts at loggerheads. Von Harff himself prefaces his vocabulary thus : " In *Pascayen* they have a language of their own which is very difficult to write." I reproduce part of the Basque-Platt Deutsch vocabulary with the modern Basque and English appended :—

Pascaysche spraich.

Item ogea . . . broyt   (ogia . . . bread)
Arduwa . . . wijn   (arnoa . . . wine)
Oyra . . . wasser   (ura . . . water)
Schambat . . . wat gilt   (zembat . . . how much ?)
   dat
Gangon dissila . . . got gheue dir guden morgen
(Gabon Jainkoak dizula . . . God give you good evening)
Bat . . . eyn   (bat . . . one)
Bij . . . tzwey   (bi . . . two)
Yron . . . drij   (hirur . . . three)
Lae . . . vier   (lau . . . four)
Boss . . . vunff   (bortz . . . five)
See . . . sees   (sei . . . six)
Sespe . . . seuen   (zazpi . . . seven)
Tzortzey . . . acht   (zortzi . . . eight)
Wedeatzey . . . nuyn   (bederatzi . . . nine)
Hammer . . . tzien   (hamar . . . ten).

Basque had appeared in print long before this, however. A brief vocabulary more accurately transcribed than von Harff's appears in a work by Lucio Marino Siculo, published at Alcalá in 1530 under the title " De las Cosas Memorables de España " (" Of the Memorable Things of Spain "). While this vocabulary has the distinction of being the first known example of printed Basque, the first consecutive Basque text to appear in print was Perucho's song in the third part of the " Celestina."

This was closely followed by a short Basque passage in Rabelais' " Pantagruel " (Book II, Ch. IX). It will be recalled that Pantagruel meets Panurge, who is described as " *beau de stature et élégant en tous linéaments de corps, mais pitoyablement navré en divers lieux, et tant mal en ordre, qu'il semblait être échappé es chiens.*" Panurge, questioned by Pantagruel as to the cause of his distress, answers first in German and then in Arabic, Italian, English, Basque, Dutch, Spanish, Danish, Greek, Breton, Latin and finally French. The substance of his reply in each case is that he is miserable and hungry and wants something to eat.[1] In spite of this helpful clue the Basque reply, which Rabelais probably took, phonetically as he thought, from the dictation of some Basque lackey, baffled all the earlier commentators down to Prince Lucien Bonaparte. This is the text :—

> *Jona andie guauſ-*
> *ſa gouſſietan be harda er remedio be-*
> *harde berſela yſſer lada.   Anbates otoy*
> *y es nauſu ey neſſaſſu gourray pro-*
> *poſian ordine den.   Nonyſſena bayta*
> *faſcheria egabe gen heraſſy badia ſa-*
> *daſſu noura aſſia.   Aran hodouan gual*
> *de eydaſſu naydaſſuna.   Eſtou ouſſyc*
> *eguinan ſoury hin er darſtura eguy*
> *harm.   Genicoa plaſar vadu.*

Julien Vinson was the first to make anything resembling

---

[1] In English he says : " Lord, if you be so virtuous of intelligence, as you be naturally releaved to the body, you should have pity of me. For nature hath made us equal, but fortune hath some exalted and others deprived : nevertheless is virtue often deprived and the virtuous man despised ; for before the last end none is good."

sense of this curious passage. His interpretation is as follows :—

" Great Lord, for all ills there must be a remedy. To be as one should be, that is the difficulty. I have besought you so greatly. Do so that there may be order in our conversation, which will occur, without disrespect, if you will make me eat my fill. After that ask me what you will. So, please God, it will not be difficult for you to pay for two."

Vinson's version has not been unanimously accepted, as is shown by the following alternative proposals for the first sentence alone :—

" Great Lord, in all things one must take the remedy in the proper way after having sweated " (Beignatborde).

" Great Lord, for all things there must be a remedy : there must ; otherwise how much trouble ! " (Louis Dassance and Jean Elissalde.)

" Great Lord, for all things there must be a remedy, as there must be for the field lying fallow " (Elgezabal).

" Great Lord, all things must have the proper remedy ; otherwise it is trouble wasted " (Mugarre).[1]

The first entire work to be printed in Basque was a little volume of religious and lyrical poems by Bernard Dechepare, a priest living in Basse-Navarre, which was published at Bordeaux in 1545 under the title of " Linguæ Vascorum Primitiæ." This is not only the first but one of the most striking monuments of Basque literature. It was Dechepare's hope that his work would act as an incentive to his compatriots to use their language as a literary medium, a hope which he expressed in a poem beginning :—

> *Euskera, euskera,*
> *Ialgi hadi kampora.*

(" Tongue of the Basques, come out into the open.") But it was not until some three centuries had passed that there was any general response to his call.

[1] Cf. " Le Texte Basque de Rabelais." *Gure Herria.* 1921.

Twenty-six years later Leizarraga's Basque translation of the Gospels was published at la Rochelle by order of Jeanne d'Albret at the expense of the Parlement of Navarre. This work is of the utmost importance from the point of view of the evolution of the language. In 1638, under the jejune title of " Notitia Utriusque Vasconiæ," Arnauld Oihénart published a history of the region, which he followed up in 1657 with a collection of 537 Basque proverbs and a number of poems. Books of this nature were exceptional, however, for until the end of the eighteenth century little was written in Basque beyond religious works, many of them translations. These are headed both chronologically and in interest by the " Guero " of Axular, Curé of Sare, which, published in 1643 at Bordeaux, remains the acknowledged masterpiece of the Labourd dialect. Bernard de Gazteluzar, d'Argaineratz, Harizmendi and Etcheberri followed in Axular's footsteps, and were succeeded in the eighteenth century by Augustín de Cardaveraz, Manuel de Larramendi (of dictionary and grammar fame), Sebastian de Mendiburu, Haraneder and another Etcheberri, whose complete works were reprinted in Paris in 1907.

The nineteenth century witnessed the first serious attempts to solve the mystery of the Basque language and to place Basque studies on a scientific footing. Many of those who took a leading part in this renaissance of learning were themselves Basques, and the result was a marked increase of literary output in the vernacular. Among the poets mention must be made of Hiribarren, whose long poem " Eskualdunak " is a description of the principal towns and villages in the French provinces. Others are Elissamburu, Larralde, Dibarart, Sabino Arana, Yparraguirre, who wrote " Gernikako Arbola " (" The Tree of Guernica "), which has come to be regarded almost as a Basque national anthem, and that strange and tragic figure Etchahoun of Barcus.

Thanks to the researches of Pierre Lhande, who has not only explored the civil and ecclesiastical archives of

Barcus, but investigated and collated the oral traditions surviving in that neighbourhood, we know something of the stormy life of Etchahoun, so characteristic of the romantic age in which he lived. There is something so intensely Basque in his personality that it seems worth while to summarise what is now known of him.

Pierre Topet d'Etchahounia was born in 1786 at the house of Etchahounia near Barcus (Soule). He was the eldest son of peasant parents who, if not wealthy, were quite comfortably off, but he was never happy at home, for his father disliked him, principally, if the evidence of his poems is to be believed, because Pierre bore him no physical resemblance. As a young man he fell in love with the daughter of poor folk, but his parents would not hear of the marriage. They went so far as to threaten that, if he persisted in it he would be deprived of his birthright as *etcheko primu* (heir of the house). When Etchahoun saw that this threat, one of the most drastic that a Basque father could devise, was intended seriously, he gave way. The bad grace with which he did so is expressed in the curse which he is said to have pronounced against his father and which has become proverbial :—

> " May God curse Gaztelondo Topet
> And all those who give their hearts to penniless maidens ! "

He complied with his parents' wishes, however, and, in his own words, " On my twenty-second birthday, to my misfortune, I took a wife." This wife, one Engrâce Pelento, a year his senior, was almost as unwilling a bride as her husband was a reluctant groom. Tradition says that she loved another man, and certainly the marriage was not a success. Engrâce had influential relations who on more than one occasion caused Etchahoun to be imprisoned for ill-treating her. During one such term of imprisonment, however, the faithlessness of Engrâce became manifest. On his return Etchahoun tried to shoot the betrayer of his honour, but had the misfortune in the darkness to kill the wrong man. For this crime he was sentenced to a further term of imprisonment. Escaping from his prison at Agen he returned to Barcus and publicly announced his intention of setting fire to the house of his enemy. Nevertheless when the house eventually caught fire he was able to prove an alibi and was acquitted, although the peasants believe to this day that the fire was his handiwork. He made repeated efforts to return to his home, but his brother and his son as well as his father and his wife were against him and turned him away from the door. All his middle age was spent in poverty and exile. Although in his verse he never ceased to make mock of the priests and was generally held to be an agnostic, he claimed to have made pilgrimages to Santiago and Rome and to have heard Mass regularly every fortnight. He spent long periods in the mountains with shepherds and charcoal-burners, and acquired a great reputation as a bard whose improvisations made him a welcome guest everywhere save in his own home. Towards the end of his life Etchahoun " repented " and was reconciled with the Church. He died in 1862 in his own house, although nothing is known of the circumstances of his return. It is unlikely that he effected a reconciliation with his family, for after his death the latter made a public bonfire of all his manuscripts, fearing that these would bring a curse upon the house. In consequence the majority of his poems survive only through oral tradition. Some of them figure, not always under his name, in Sallaberry's " Chants Populaires du Pays Basque," and I have taken down others, hitherto unrecorded, from peasants in Soule.

Etchahoun has been described as the combined Villon and Verlaine of Basque literature. His work is characterised by the intense bitterness and rancour born of disillusionment, by the violence of his hatred and by the implacable acerbity of his satire. He made no secret of his vindictive feelings towards his wife and his relations, who are not spared in his verse. His poems are in the form of folk-song. They display the same alternation between narration and dialogue, the same brusque gaps in the logical exposition of a narrative which lend such racy vividness to the folk-song style. Indeed Etchahoun's poems are in reality folk-songs which by a fortunate chance or by their own compelling power have escaped the deformation and the anonymity which is usually the fate of such poems. For all Basque folk-songs are born, as were the poems of Etchahoun, on the lips of a gifted improviser. The only essential difference is that the greater names are remembered while the lesser are forgotten.

At the present time, on both sides of the frontier, a number of writers are carrying on the work of moulding Basque into a literary language, although the unity of their endeavours is much hampered by differences of dialect and method. On the one hand, a consciously intellectual clique with their centre at Bilbao and their leader in the energetic, mercurial and somewhat combative figure of Azkue have evolved a style and vocabulary quite beyond the comprehension of the ordinary peasant. In France, on the other hand, an unassuming little group of priests, including Daranatz, Saint-Pierre (Anxuberro), Barbier, Moulier (Oxobi), Elizalde (Zerbitzari), the late Laurent Apezteguy and Blazy (the editor of *Gure Herria*), aim at developing and enriching the forms of folk literature by writing simple tales, plays, legends, fables and lyric and satyric verse within the easy comprehension of all their countrymen. The success of their endeavours is proved by the fact that many of their poems have passed into the realm of folk-song and can be heard in the most remote villages and farms. The antagonism between these two groups resembles that which exists in Greece between the partisans of the " *katharevousa* " and those of the " *demotikē*." The former aim at returning as far as possible to the vocabulary and syntax of Ancient Greek while the latter write in the popular speech of to-day with all its later accretions.

A considerable impetus has been given to the literary

Working in the Maize-fields at Berroeta (Navarre).

A Basque Farmyard (Labourd).

use of Basque by societies such as the Academy of the Basque Language, the "*Eusko Ikaskuntza*" of San Sebastian and the "*Euskalzaleen Biltzarra*" of Bayonne, aided by various periodicals written wholly or partially in Basque. First among these is the *Revista Internacional de los Estudios Vascos*, and others worthy of mention are *Gure Herria* (Bayonne), *Argia* (San Sebastian), *Eskualduna* (Bayonne) and *Euzkadi* (Bilbao). On various occasions when these societies or reviews have organised literary competitions there has been no lack of entries, some of them of a high standard.

Finally, as a sign of the growing attention paid to the language one may adduce the existence of Basque chairs at the Universities of Toulouse, Bordeaux and Paris. In 1922–3 I found at the University of Hamburg a flourishing little Basque class under the direction of the late Professor Urtell. During the war, with characteristic thoroughness, the Germans utilised the presence of numerous prisoners-of-war of different nationalities for the systematic study of some three hundred different languages and dialects with the aid of gramophone records and phonetic texts. For lack of any better classification Basque was placed among the Romance languages, and Hermann Urtell acquired a good theoretical knowledge of it at a prison camp in the Harz Mountains. There were seven of us, if I remember right, who sat at his feet, translating alternately from Leizarraga's "Gospel" and from a supernatural tale which Urtell had phonographically recorded from a Basque prisoner (quoted in Chapter IX). Six of the little class (for I was the merest *dilettante*) were bent on finding resemblances between Basque and the most improbable languages in which they happened to have specialised. I remember that Gaelic, Georgian and Malay were among them. I never heard, however, that any of my co-disciples were strikingly successful.

Basque printed literature is neither extensive nor varied. Nor does it equal in interest the unwritten literature handed down by oral tradition. An intriguing hint that there may once have been an interesting literature in Basque or some kindred language is furnished by Strabo, who states that one particular Iberian tribe were " the most literate of the Iberians and that they conserved historical writings and poems of great antiquity." If Basque was ever the language of some highly-developed civilisation (and from internal evidence there is every reason to doubt it), that civilisation has irremediably disappeared.

The Basque language has always been famed for its difficulty. The Basques say that the Devil came to their country to learn it, but that, after seven years, having got no further than *Bai* (Yes) and *Ez* (No) he gave it up in disgust. They add that he forgot even these two words as soon as he had passed through Bayonne on his way out of the country. In the Middle Ages Scaliger, who described Basque as " one of the fourteen languages that Latin did not destroy," exclaimed : " They say that they understand one another, but I don't believe it ! " He admitted, however, that " this language has nothing barbaric, strident nor aspirated."

To the would-be student the difficulties presented by the language are fourfold. First there is the intrinsic difficulty of the excessively complicated syntax and morphology which are utterly unlike those of any Indo-European language. To think in Basque requires an entirely different attitude of mind from that inherent in other more familiar languages. The verb, in particular, constitutes a positively mountainous obstacle.

The next difficulty lies in the lack of facilities for study such as good simple grammars and dictionaries. Azkue's dictionary is a monumental work which has gone far to improve the situation in this direction. Unfortunately it is both expensive and unwieldy. In 1922 *Gure Herria* began the publication of a " Grammaire Pratique de la Langue Basque," by Henri Gavel, which has been continued in almost monthly instalments ever since and

is still far from complete.   Unfortunately, it is not quite
as practical as the title suggests.   Similarly, in 1926,
Pierre Lhande commenced the publication of an excellent
dictionary of the French dialects.   This was to come out
in bi-annual instalments, but only two of these have
appeared in four years and the dictionary has got no
further than the letter D.   Correspondence courses in
Basque can, however, be taken with the Abbé Eyheramendy
of Saint-Jean-le-Vieux who has pupils all over Europe.

On the whole this second difficulty is not so great as
the third, the extensive differences between the written
and spoken languages.   The Basques clip their words
even more than the English, and it is not unusual to hear
whole phrases which seem to lack a single consonant.   A
peasant from Basse-Navarre is as likely as not to turn the
phrase *dudarik gabe* (without doubt) into something that
sounds like *du'aika*.

The greatest difficulty of all, constituting even more
of an obstacle in the path of the learner than the com-
plexity of the syntax, is the amazing diversity of the
dialects and the lack of any standardised language even
for writing purposes.   There are eight
universally recognised dialects ; Biscayan,
Guipuzcoan, Navarrese and the almost
extinct Roncal on the Spanish side ;
Labourdin, Western Basse-Navarrese,
Eastern Basse-Navarrese and Souletin
in France.   The Biscayan dialect stands
by itself, and so, in a lesser degree,
does Souletin, which has a vowel sound
like the French *u* not to be found in
the other dialects.   When French and
Spanish folk-dancers have met in London, Paris, Bayonne or San Sebastian for
public performances, they have failed
to understand each other's Basque and have been reduced
to conversing in French or Spanish.

The eight main dialects can be divided into innumer-
G

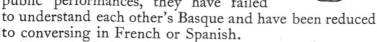

able sub-varieties. Prince Lucien Bonaparte whose linguistic map of the Basque Country was published in London in about 1870, records twenty-five distinct dialects. The truth is that the language varies from village to village, from house to house, and indeed one might almost say from one individual to another. History can offer but few examples of foreigners learning Basque. The Emperor Charles V is said to have mastered it. In 1617 an Augustine monk named Etienne Materre, who had settled at Bayonne, published in Basque a " Christian Doctrine " of which there is a copy in the Bodleian. Sylvain Pouvreau, a *protégé* of Saint Vincent de Paul and secretary of the famous Jansenist Duvergier de Hauranne, Abbé of Saint-Cyran,[1] translated a number of religious works into Basque while he was Vicar of Bidart (1642–4). He was also the author of one of the first French–Basque dictionaries. The publication of this work, which had been preceded by that of Voltoire's " Trésor des Trois Langues," and of Micoleta's " Modo Breve de Aprender la Lengua Viscaina," which appeared in Spain in 1653, testify to a certain demand for such text-books. The works of Lardizabal and Larramendi, author of the " Imposible Vencido " and of a Spanish–Latin–Basque dictionary, show that in the following century there were still people who aspired to " vanquish the impossible."

Among the men of a later age who learnt the language for the purpose of philological study two names are pre-eminent, those of the Rev. Wentworth Webster, Vicar of the English Church at Saint-Jean-de-Luz at the end of last century, and the German *savant* Schuchardt, who accomplished the amazing task of acquiring the Labourd dialect during a six months' stay at Sare.

It must not be thought that only the learned have succeeded in mastering Basque. Gavel mentions the

---

[1] The Abbé was himself a Basque (indeed he was Curé of Itxassou in 1607) and there is a close affinity between Jansenism and the Basque religious outlook.

Flemish wife of a Gascon *douanier* posted in Basse-Navarre who learnt Basque perfectly while her husband failed to acquire so much as a smattering of the language. I have also been told of a British sailor who has settled in Bilbao, where he keeps a tavern and speaks fluent Basque. The present landlord of the Hôtel Oppoka at Ainhoa, a Gascon of the name of Suhas, married the daughter of the former innkeeper and learnt his wife's language in two years.

"Basque," writes Henri Gavel, "is a very fine language. In softness and sonority its pronunciation nearly equals that of Italian or Spanish, especially in the dialects which do not exaggerate the *h*. The grammatical system is very simple and very logical, and the only fault with which it can be charged is an exaggeration of synthetic methods in conjugation. But this fault is beginning to disappear, for an evolution has set in, more advanced in some provinces than in others, but noticeable in all, by which more analytical methods are tending to replace this unnecessarily complex system. On the other hand, there is nothing rigid in the grammatical construction and in the wealth of suffixes which permit the formation of numerous derivatives. All these characteristics make Basque a very simple language and one most suitable for poetry."

With this account one may find oneself in disagreement on some points. With all respect to Gavel, Basque remains essentially a synthetic and agglutinative language. In common with other agglutinative languages, such as Hungarian and Finnish, it conveys an idea, not in the analytical manner of English, for example, but by an intensive use of suffixes through which words of an inordinate length are often formed. As an illustration of this method the phrase *arropa elizarakoak* (Sunday-go-to-meeting clothes) may be quoted. *Arropa* and *eliz* are nothing more than the French words *robe* and *église*, but the remainder of the phrase is conveyed as follows:—
Eliz : church. *Eliza :* the church. *Elizara :* to the

church. *Elizarako :* pertaining to (going) to the church. *Elizarakoak :* those pertaining to (going) to the church. Thus the adjective is formed from a noun plus a definite article plus a preposition (or rather post-position), plus another preposition plus a definite article plus a plural suffix.

Hungarian and Finnish share with Basque the use of postpositional suffixes, *e.g.*

Hungarian.	*Fejemben :* head-my-in.
Finnish.	*Paassani :* head-in-my.
Basque.	*Nere buruan :* my head-the-in, or
	Buru nerean : head my-the-in,

and other peculiarities such as the lack of any clear distinction between the verb and the noun, the absence of gender, etc. But they differ greatly in many respects and it would be unsafe to draw any conclusions from such analogies as exist, the more so since there is not the slightest resemblance in their respective vocabularies.

The vocabulary of Basque falls into three groups. The first consists of words borrowed from Latin or from the Romance languages and *patois*. " Certain infallible indications," writes Nogaret, " which Romance experts can easily recognise, show that this influence began to make itself felt in Roman times." *Bakea* (peace) must have been derived from *pacem* in the time of the Cæsars, when the *c* was pronounced hard, while *gurutzea* (cross) was clearly taken from *crucem* at a much later date, presumably that of the conversion of the Basques to Christianity. The borrowing process is still going on. Not only are all Basque words for recent inventions such as " train," " bank," etc., and also for many abstract conceptions, imported from French or Spanish, but there is a growing tendency, especially in the less isolated districts, to borrow quite unnecessary words and thus displace genuine Basque terms. Thus *pensatu* (*penser*) exists conjointly with *uste* (to think) and *kitatu* (*quitter*) is tending to replace *utzi* (to leave). Innumerable examples could be quoted of a tendency which is becoming a serious menace to the purity of the language.

The second group consists of a small number of words borrowed from languages other than Latin or its derivatives. The names of certain plants and vegetables, for instance, are said to resemble their Celtic synonyms.

The third and by far the largest group consists of words of purely Basque origin. With only one or two exceptions these bear no resemblance to any known tongue. When George Borrow, in " The Bible in Spain," tried to show that there were resemblances between the vocabularies of Basque and Hindu, he was unconsciously bearing out Arago's epigram : " *Le Basque partage avec le Celtique le privilège de faire dire à son sujet d'innombrables extravagances.*" [1]

This section of the vocabulary is of exceptional interest for the indications which it affords that Basque is the tongue of an ancient and primitive race. Certain words may date back to neolithic times, for the terms of most sharp-edged or pointed instruments are derived from the word *aitz* (stone) e.g.

Aitz-urr : lit. stone for pulling to pieces : *i.e.* pick or mattock.

Aitz-hortz : lit. stone-tooth : *i.e.* bill-hook.

Aitz-kor : lit. raised stone : *i.e.* axe.

Aitz-koltu : lit. small raised stone : *i.e.* hatchet.

Aitz-tto : lit. small stone : *i.e.* knife.

Aitz-tturr : lit. small stone for tearing : *i.e.* scissors.

Aitz-kon : lit. stone-point : dart.

[1] For that matter Borrow himself wrote :—" Much that is vague, erroneous and hypothetical has been said and written concerning this tongue." (" The Bible in Spain," Ch. XXXVII.) So he is condemned out of his own mouth.

One of the " extravagances " of which Arago may have been thinking is that perpetrated by Julian de Churruca, who sought, in his " Lauroguei ", to explain certain passages of the Apocalypse by means of the Basque tongue, and predicted the return of the Messiah in 1823. Like the exponents of the famous Pyramid Theory, he survived to realise his mistake.

There is even a verb *aitzkatu,* meaning "to attack" (*-ka* is a suffix meaning "by blows with . . .").

The names of the days of the week seem to show that the Basque week originally consisted of only three days, for the words for Monday, Tuesday and Wednesday are :—

Astelehena : the first (day) of the week.
Asteartea : the middle (day) of the week.
Asteazkena : the last (day) of the week.

The names for the four other days are clearly of later date.

The numerals are based on the decimal system, but with the exception of *sei* (six) they do not resemble those of other languages. Forty is twice twenty; sixty is thrice twenty and so on. There are pure Basque words for all numerals up to a hundred but none for a thousand or higher figures.

Three general characteristics of the vocabulary indicate if not great age, at least a very primitive mentality. These are the lack of collective terms, the lack of abstract words and the extensive use of onomatopœics.

While Basque contains words for every kind of tree and animal found in the country, the words for "tree" (*arbola*) and "animal" (*alimalia*) are of comparatively recent Latin extraction. Similarly, there are original words for most of the colours and for all parts of the body, but none save those derived from Latin for "colour" (*kolore*) and "body" (*gorphutza*). There is also no general word for "sister," but one for a man's sister (*arreba*) and another for a woman's sister (*ahizpa*).[1]

The lack of abstract words stands out in strong contrast with the wealth of the vocabulary where pastoral and, to a lesser extent, agricultural terms are concerned. The one over-worked word *gogo* has to cover almost every mental and moral attribute of the individual. It is used irrespectively for soul, mind, desire, will, mood,

---

[1] Of the two similarly distinctive words for "brother," however, only one survives except in Vizcaya.

fancy, or thought. There is no true Basque word for Heaven or Hell, nor even, sign of a true democracy, for King or Queen, Count or Marquis.

In the " Concise Oxford Dictionary " onomatopœia is defined as " the formation of names or words from sounds that resemble those associated with the object or action to be named or that seem naturally suggestive of its qualities." At an early stage of civilisation, before any conventional system was adopted whereby certain sounds were invested with quite arbitrary meanings, human speech must have consisted almost exclusively of sound mimicry. The further a language develops the less dependent it grows on onomatopœia. Yet the fact that children still talk of " bow-wows " and " puff-puffs " proves that onomatopœia is nearer to nature than such irrational (or should one say ultra-rational?) words as " dog " and " train." In addition to obvious onomato-pœics such as " cuckoo," " yap," " howl," etc., English still contains a large number of words such as " sizzle " and " rustle " clearly intended to copy the sounds which they signify.

A further group of words, which must be classed as onomatopœics since they are " naturally suggestive of the object or action named," are those which translate into terms of sound impressions received by the eye. These impressions are nearly always those of movement. Such words as " flicker " or " wobble " conjure before the eye a vision of movement and often prove comprehensible to foreigners ignorant of their meaning. The fact that the eye has at least as much influence as the ear in the formation of these words is shown by expressions like " ding-dong," which reproduces the oscillating movement of the clapper rather than the regular note of the bell.

Basque, being essentially a primitive tongue, is richer in onomatopœia than the civilised languages of Europe. As is only natural, all animal cries are represented by onomatopœics, e.g. *urruma* (lowing of cattle), *irrintzi* (neighing of horses), *karanka* (cackle of geese). Some-times the names of the beasts are based on their cries, e.g. *kokoko* (hen), *pipuak* (chicks), *ttirritta* (cicada). There is a marked difference between the way in which the Basques hear and reproduce the sounds about them and that which is more or less common to the Indo-European races. In Basque the sound of bells is represented by *bilin-balan* or *bimbi-bambaka*, and that of boiling liquids by *bur-bur* or *gar-gar*. There are numerous adverbial expressions based on onomatopœia which are not usually so formed in other languages : e.g. *darga-darga* (drinking in gulps), *mauka-mauka* (eating greedily), *hitipiti-hatapata* (walking on all fours), *tarrapatakan* (clattering downstairs) and *gili-gili* (tickling).

This last example brings us to the verge of the second group of onomatopœics, those in which the word renders acoustically an impression received through the eyes. Of such expressions there are innumerable examples in Basque : e.g. *birristi-barrasta* (carelessly), *inki-manka* (undecided), *kili-kolo* (ill-balanced), *dirdira* (trembling), *nyir-nyir* (seeing double), *armiermua* (spider), *tchintchitola* or *pimpirina* (butterfly), *dilindan* (hanging). Perhaps the best example of Basque onomatopœia which I have met is a little bit of dialogue from one of the folk-tales :—

" How fast you are spinning to-night ! "

" Yes, yesterday I was spinning *frin-frin* and *firun-firun* : to-day I am spinning *fran-fran* and *furdulu-furdulu*."

It will be noticed that nearly all these onomatopœics are formed by the repetition, either simple or in a slightly modified form, of the first half of the word (cf. English "hurdy-gurdy"). The initial consonant may be modified (*keko-meko :* undecided) or one may be added (*inki-minki :* toppling over); there may be a vowel change (*glizka-glazka :* hair-cutting), or the two pheno-mena may appear together (*kirri-marra :* scribbling). The frequent addition or substitution of the letter *m* is curious. It may be no more than a coincidence that in

Turkish the repetition of a word, with the letter *m* substituted for the initial consonant, amounts to a kind of collective generalisation. For instance, *Pasha-Masha* means " Pashas and people like that."

So strong is the influence of onomatopœia in Basque that words of Latin origin are often treated in the same way. *Trikun-trakun* (swindling), for example, which might at first sight be taken for an onomatopœic, is really derived from the French *tricher*.

Another form of onomatopœia found only in primitive languages consists in strengthening a word by repeating it. In Basque, for instance, *bero* means " hot " and *bero-bero* means " very hot." Sometimes the meaning is modified rather than strengthened. I seem to have heard that in some African or Polynesian language with a very limited vocabulary a certain word, let us say it is *tan*, means " eye." By extension *tan-tan* has come to mean " policeman," the train of thought being that a policeman is a man with two eyes which are always fixed upon you. There is nothing quite so picturesque in Basque. A curious example, however, is the word *garagar* (barley) from *gari* (corn), presumably an allusion to the large number of ears in barley. In his dictionary Azkue gives a very good example of the furthest extension of this principle : viz. *bilo* (hair) : *bilo-biloka* (a fight between two women who grasp each other by the hair).

In addition to the ordinary diminutives formed by adding the suffix *-tto* (pronounced *-tyo*) there are a number of diminutives formed by the modification of the initial consonant or vowel, e.g.

Zakhurra : dog	*chakhurra :* little dog.
Gatu : cat	*ttattu :* little cat.
Armiermua : spider	*irmiermua :* little spider.

I have even heard a Basque say *tyout petyit* when talking French !

Without a shadow of doubt the most difficult part of speech in Basque is the verb. I shall not attempt a

technical description of its workings, but there are one or
two aspects of it which are so peculiar that they cannot
be passed over.

The original form of Basque conjugation seems to have
been a " strong " one without an auxiliary, which is still
preserved nowadays in one or two verbs of motion.
In the intransitive verb the subject is indicated by the
initial consonant: e.g. *noa :* I go; *hoa :* thou goest;
doa : he goes. In the transitive verb, however, the
initial consonant indicates the object and a suffix the
subject: e.g. **n**a*kar***zu** : you carry me; **d**a*kar***gu** : we
carry him. If the object is in the plural, the suffix *-zki*
is inserted after the verbal root: e.g. *dakar***zki***gu :* we
carry them. Furthermore, the indirect object, if there
is one, is also expressed within the verb: e.g. *dakarzki-
zugu :* we carry them to you.

The more usual form of conjugation is effected by
means of the auxiliary verbs *naiz* (I am) for intransitive
and *dut* (I have) for transitive verbs, in conjunction with
either a past participle or a form of verbal locative or
gerundive meaning something like " in the act of . . ."
These two auxiliaries are in reality but two different
aspects of the one infinitive *izan*. The principal difficulty consists in the fact that the auxiliary is more than
a verb, and embraces the conceptions of time, person of
subject, person of object and person of indirect object,
e.g. *dut* (I have it), but *diot* (I have it to him), *dautzut* (I
have it to you), *zaitut* (I have you), etc. In order to ring
the changes on all possible combinations of these four
conceptions a vast number of verbal forms are necessary,
the more so since, in addition to the usual moods (indica-
tive, subjunctive, conditional), there are others such as
the potential. Needless to say these forms vary considerably in the different dialects.

In translating into Basque the sentence " I give the
book to the boy " (my apologies for this little bit of
Ollendorf) by the phrase *Liburua mutilari ematen diot,*
one is literally saying, " Book-the boy-the-to in-the-act-of-

giving I-have-it-to-him." That, at least, is the simplest way of looking at it. According to the most modern views, however, it is not quite as straightforward as this. Nogaret writes : " One of the characteristics of Basque is the passivity of the verb : the transitive verb is conceived in a passive manner : when a Basque wants to say ' I have a house,' what he really says is ' A house is had by me.' "

Another curious way of looking at things is shown in the phrase *Iruten ari nuzu* (I am spinning) which literally means " in-the-act-of-spinning doing you-have-me."

Basque often seems quite unnecessarily to imply consciousness of the person addressed when this person is not in any way connected with what is said. A slight digression is necessary to explain this. The use of " thee " and " thou " is rare in Basque, as it implies definite disrespect of the person so addressed. The second person singular is seldom used among the members of a family, and a mother usually addresses her child as " you " even when it is still a baby in arms. In talking to persons to whom the second person singular would be used, however, the verb varies according to the sex of the person addressed, even if the verb so affected is in the first or third person. For instance, a Basque would change *du* (he has) to *dik* if he were addressing a man or *din* if he were addressing a woman, to either of whom he would use the second person singular. There is also another form *dizu*, used in addressing especially respected persons. This subtle and seemingly pointless variation is the only gender distinction in Basque. I have never heard that it appears in any other language.

CHAPTER VI

THE PASTORALES OF SOULE

Misterio admirablerik
Errepresentatu ukhen dugu
Eztakigu zien goguak
Ahal tugunez satisfatu.
EPILOGUE OF " ROLAND."

An admirable Mystery
We have acted.
We do not know
Whether we have fulfilled your desires.

Beztimenta. Anderiak ahal bezain eijerki, sustout Ratafia eta Grosilla.
J. B. HARDOY.

Costumes. The ladies dressed as finely as possible, especially Ratafia and Grosilla.

IT was a spring day at Tardets. The warm April sun shone down on the *pelote* court, and behind the wall glistened a snowy flank of the Higher Pyrenees. To the right the Pic d'Anie and Mount Gastarria were hidden by a steep hill with tall trees that cast a grateful shadow over the eager hundreds who thronged the seats of wood and stone.

Something more unusual than a *pelote* match had drawn the peasants from all the surrounding villages. It had been announced that on this Sunday the *jeunesse* of

Tardets would act the Pastorale of "François I," an example, albeit a modern one,[1] of those traditional outdoor plays, the performance of which has been peculiar to Soule for three or four centuries.

In the middle of the court, exposed to the heat and glare of the sun, stood the theatre, a primitive affair. The stage was of boards supported on trestles and barrels, about four feet above the ground. Three or four steps led up to it, and at each corner was a tall post decorated with flags and branches of fir. Between the posts hung green garlands and paper streamers. At the back of the stage was a rough backcloth of white linen sheets, at either end of which was an opening through which the players could pass. That on the left was reserved for the " Christians," the " good " characters of the play, and that on the right for the "Turks," in token of which it was surmounted by a black puppet, a sort of Dancing Jack with pointed horns. This was the *idole*, sometimes called *Mahoma*. In the centre a small square gap in the backcloth formed a window behind which sat the *pastoralier*, who, like the Greek *tragododidaskalos*, combined the functions of stage-manager, prompter and author of the piece. Above the *pastoralier's* window was the band, perched in an insecure looking bower, high above the stage, surrounded and surmounted by flags and greenery. The musicians were four or five in number, armed with brazen instruments all of different size and pitch.

When we arrived the performance had already begun. We had missed the procession (known as *montre* or *passe-rues*) when the whole troupe, the Standard-Bearer leading the motley crew of " Christians," " Turks " and " Satans," go riding or driving round the town before entering the theatre enclosure. Likewise we had missed the " assault upon the stage " by the Standard-Bearer boldly waving the tricolour, followed up the wooden steps by two " Christian " warriors ; and the recital of the Prologue (*Lehen Pheredikia*, literally " first sermon ")

---

[1] " François I " was first performed in 1901.

by a young man who welcomes the audience, gives a brief
account of the play and finally announces his intention
of summoning the actors. The Prologue is written in
verses of four short lines and intoned on an ancient
Gregorian chant :—

Ex. 1.

Jin - ko - ak   e - gun houn dei -zie - la   Jau - nak e - ta an - dre - ak

Hun - ki jin zi - rai - e - la   Tchi - pi - ak   e - ta han - di - ak.

According to strict tradition, after the first two lines
and at the end of the verse, the reciter raises his hands
to the height of his head, and then, with a semi-circular
movement, brings them down to his side: for the
beginning and end of the Prologue he stands stock still,
hat in hand, but while he is describing the plot he walks
to and fro across the front of the stage singing a verse
in turn from each corner and from the middle.

All this we had missed, and at the moment of our
arrival there was no one on the stage save, at each corner, a
guard, a lad of sixteen or seventeen, armed with a long
musket and dressed in white trousers and espadrilles,
short black smock and scarlet béret, and with a red Navarrese handkerchief knotted loosely round his throat. The
band was blaring out a slow march when suddenly from
behind the backcloth two figures appeared. They could
only be " Christians," for they had come through the
opening reserved for the " good " characters, and moreover there was a predominance of blue in their handsome
uniforms, and blue rosettes adorned their cocked hats
and the cane which each held. They were in fact two of
François' courtiers. As the band continued to play they
filed gravely, one behind the other, to the front of the
stage. At the corner they executed a three-quarter turn
outwards, and continuing their march to the other
corner, repeated their turn before retiring to the back of

the stage, where two chairs awaited them just in front of the *pastoralier's* window.

Then the music stopped and they sat down. But a moment later they rose to their feet and strode together towards the front of the stage. At the same time one of them, who was clad in a blue doublet, raised his voice and on a single high-pitched note intoned the first two lines of a quatrain. At the front of the stage each wheeled outwards and strode back to his seat as the one with the blue doublet was finishing his verse, the third line a whole tone higher and the fourth on the original note.[1] Again they sat down, again they rose and came forward while the other chanted an answering verse. So the dialogue continued, verse by verse, until the scene was at an end.[2] Then the band recommenced the same slow march and the two actors filed out, punctiliously retracing

[1] The quatrains are divided into four irregular lines each of which can be fitted into two bars of 6/8 time. The number of syllables in each line varies from 5 to 10 and the half-bar may consist of a dotted crotchet (one syllable), crotchet and quaver (two syllables) or three quavers (three syllables). In the " Performance of Music in Spain," J. B. Trend writes that in the twelfth century " Poema de Mio Cid " (in which the number of syllables to a line varies from eleven to twenty) " as in all early Spanish and Portuguese poetry that was sung by minstrels, practically every line has four down beats and four up beats, a system probably derived from folk-dancing " (Proceedings of the Musical Association, Session LV. p. 67). He adds that " good modern readers fit the line approximately into four bars of 6/8." If the quatrain is regarded as consisting of two double lines instead of four short ones, its metrical system is found to be identical with that of these early Spanish models.

[2] Wentworth Webster writes : " Metre, measure, feet, pauses in poetry or music are nothing but the cadenced steps, the march, the dance of the actor on the stage. The verse (*versus*) is only the turn described by the actor when he reaches the edge of the stage. . . . All this can be seen preserved by tradition with the most complete exactitude, in a Basque Pastorale " (Wentworth Webster : " Les Loisirs d'un Etranger au Pays Basque," p. 217).

A. Léon, on the other hand, writes :—" These marches and counter-marches seem clearly to be an imitation of the comings and goings of the celebrant at Mass. . . . Such comings and goings take place only in the truncated ritual of the countryside, where the absence of a deacon obliges the celebrant to move about during Mass " (A. Léon : " Une Pastorale Basque, Hélène de Constantinople ").

their steps and executing the same curious turns at the corners, which are thought to derive from the liturgical drama of the Middle Ages. This scene was but one of many which followed. Each was enclosed within the same formal entrance and exit. Each verse of the thousand or so which made up the play was declaimed in the same manner and to the same tune, if tune it can be called. Only the pitch of the voice varied, each individual actor choosing his own. It is difficult to convey an impression of the effect which this extraordinarily conventionalised technique produces on the spectator. There is no attempt at realism in either setting or acting. Just as there is no scenery, and as, till recently, there was no attempt at historical accuracy in the costumes, so there is no attempt to convey the sense of the dialogue, but only to make it audible to an out-door audience. The melodic and rhythmic monotony of the chanting does away with any possibility of expression in the recitation, and the stiff drill-like movements of the actors reduce the variety of gesture to a minimum. Yet upon consideration it seems best that it should be thus. The actors are only peasant lads, shepherds, farm-hands or village artisans, often illiterate. Usually they have no experience of acting, even in such plays as these, for it is only once in every twenty years or so that a particular village acts a Pastorale, and only those born in the village can take part in it. Were these peasants to attempt to act their parts as we understand acting, or to speak their lines in a natural manner, there is no doubt that the result would be lamentable. As it is, however, there is something strangely and unexpectedly impressive in their rigid stylisation of the performance and above all in the sincerity and gravity with which they play their parts ; and there is an elemental beauty in the clear manly voices, ringing out from the theatre across the valley to the green hillside and distant farms, the homes of these pastoral players.

The Pastorale of François I.

As scene followed scene events moved rapidly on the stage. It transpired that one of François' officers, a young man in a cocked hat and black uniform, was suspected of treachery. He was brought in; his hands were bound, though only with a piece of twine, and a moment later the protagonist of the play, François I of France, entered for the first time. The King was a well-built young man, dressed in a black velvet cap and doublet edged with ermine, white breeches and black top-boots. It might well have been said of him, as Cavalli the Venetian said of the real François:—" His appearance is altogether regal, so that, without ever having seen his person or his portrait, at the first sight of him, a stranger would say : ' This is the King '." Speaking his lines with intensity and power he proceeded to order the trial of the traitor. Then the band struck up, and on to the stage came three black-gowned lawyers in horn-rimmed spectacles. They were followed by a queer female figure clad in flowery silks trimmed with lace, and wearing on her head an elaborate green headdress. With her left hand she coyly held her skirt off the floor, and with the other she fluttered a fan, painted (pleasing anachronism) with bull-fighting scenes at San Sebastian. Long curls hung down either cheek, but as she turned formally at the first corner there was revealed the back of a closely-cropped head. For the part of Louise de Savoie, François' mother, like all female rôles in the Pastorales, was played by a man, strict tradition forbidding the intermingling of the sexes.[1]

The trial of the traitor was soon over, and, the prisoner having been found guilty, the sentence was executed without delay. The Hangman, a grotesque figure in a frock-coat and top-hat, appeared from the " Turks' " entrance and proceeded to improvise a gibbet out of one of the posts at the side of the stage. Meanwhile three

---

[1] There have, however, been cases (G. Hérelle quotes eighteen) of Pastorales acted by women alone. The last of these performances, that of " Hélène de Constantinople," took place at Ordiarp in 1909.

H

girls (real girls this time, known as *servantes de la scène*), who were stationed behind the scenes ready to put a stitch into any of the actors' costumes, entered and spread a white sheet and pillow on the ground. The prisoner knelt upon the pillow and, throwing wide his arms, broke into a song of prayer to God and farewell to Earth. He sang to an ancient traditional air of modal character, one which is used in every Pastorale and which is usually sung by the angels who, though unaccountably absent in " François I," figure in most of the plays. Sung with a freedom innocent of all rhythm this air is unbelievably poignant and lovely and seems to carry the hearer straight into another age and another world [1]:—

Ex. 2.

Oi Jin - ko e - gi - az - ko - a Ze - lu lur - ra - ren krea - tzai - lia

E - man i - za - da - zut Hil - tze - ko ko - ra - ge - a.

> " O God of Truth, (sang the traitor)
> Creator of Heaven and Earth,
> Grant Thou to me
> Courage to die.
>
> Before I die
> I commend my soul to Thee
> And I pray for
> The pardon of all.
>
> The Queen has compassed my death
> Through no fault of mine.
> Farewell, Earth, farewell,
> Now I must take leave of you."

Then he rose to his feet and, within sight of all, the hanging took place: that is to say, the Hangman pulled a cord on the gibbet and the traitor lay down on the sheet.

After François and his men had filed out to the strains

[1] In Chapters VI–X the musical and other examples have been collected by the author except where otherwise stated.

of the band there was seen a tall figure seated on a chair at the back of the stage. A typical old Basque, he had broad but rounded shoulders, angular features and smooth-shaven chin. On his lap he was holding what resembled an elongated wooden box which, after a moment, he lifted on to his right knee, supporting it against his left arm and now revealing it to be a *ttun-ttun* or *tambourin de Gascogne*. Simultaneously with his other hand he raised to his mouth a *tchirula*, or three-holed pipe. On this he blew out a cheerful but ordinary little tune (it was in fact the well-known French song " *Bon Voyage, Monsieur Dumoullet* "), while at the same time he kept up a rhythmic thrumming with a little stick on the strings of the *ttun-ttun*. This is the traditional instrumental music of the Basques and is almost identical with our own English pipe and tabor.[1]

To this music is done the " Dance of the Satans." As the *tchirulari* struck up, two fantastic figures sprang out on to the stage. These were no commonplace stage devils with horn and tail, but lithe and graceful youths in dancers' trappings. They wore vermilion bérets and narrow little coats of scarlet with gold froggings, covered in front with a white plastron thickly worked in gold. Their breeches, too, were of scarlet, with a wide band of

---

[1] The *tchirula* is in every respect similar to the English pipe and has two holes on top and one underneath. The six strings of the *ttun-ttun* can be tuned by means of keys, and the instrument may once have been used otherwise than as a tabor. The stringed tabor is only found on the French side of the frontier. The Spanish Basque instrument is a kind of small drum slung from the left arm like the English tabor depicted in the Betley window. In the Spanish provinces the *tchirula* is replaced by the *tchistu*, a black pipe, bigger and fuller in tone. The *tchistulari* is usually accompanied by another musician equipped with a side-drum.

gold braid, and splayed out at the knee over thick white stockings of open-work crochet. On their feet they wore dark spats, braided and spangled, over white espadrilles. This elaborate costume suited their even more elaborate dance. Bodies erect and immobile, arms held stiffly a little way from their sides, they seemingly glided to the front of the stage. Then a *pas battu* brought them back. Again they advanced, and this time they executed that most difficult ballet step the *entrechat*: the *entrechat quatre*, at first, simply crossing and uncrossing their legs in the air: then the more difficult *entrechat huit* and finally the *entrechat douze*. Nearly two feet up into the air shot the tense muscular bodies, and seemed to hang for a moment suspended while the twinkling feet crossed and recrossed two and even three times before dropping lightly back to earth. We gasped, for the *entrechat douze* is a step seldom attained by even the most renowned ballet dancers. While we were still breathless with amazement these two peasant " Satans " executed a final variation, the *entrechat en cabriolet*, and then set about their task of carrying off the very lively corpse of the traitor which, outstretched on its white sheet, had been smoking a cigarette. The entire scene was over in a minute, but whenever, throughout the performance, there was a corpse to be carried off or any moment's interval in the action, the *tchirulari* appeared and the " Satans " sprang out to repeat their thrilling dance.

In older plays the " Satans " have a more active rôle. There are usually three of them, known as Jupiter, Bulgifer and Satan, and they carry a whip or stick with an iron claw, recalling the fork carried by the devils of the mediæval Mysteries. Besides dancing and removing the dead it is their rôle to go up and down the stage, tempting the virtuous and urging on the wicked.

When the Satans had gone, François I reappeared on the scene and began a series of military marches and counter-marches with his generals and courtiers. To the strains of the band they moved up and down and finally took

up their positions in a line across the front of the stage.
Suddenly our attention was attracted by a glint of scarlet
and silver away to the left beyond the theatre, and a
moment later a splendid cavalcade appeared. These
were the " Turks," the " Reds," the Enemy, who,
curiously enough, were all considerably taller than the
" Blues." Mounted on sleek, well-fed horses, they
came riding across the grass to the open space in front
of the stage. Their costume was not unlike that of the
Satans. It consisted of a scarlet coat with a white
plastron, yellow breeches and black riding-boots. But
its principal glory was the tall headdress, the *Koha*, a
fantastic Christmas-cracker crown faced with little
mirrors to imitate the glint of brilliants, and surmounted
by a huge bouquet of feathers, ribbons and artificial
flowers.

The Turks formed a line in front of the stage, and
immediately their leader's voice rang out in a quatrain
of defiance which was taken up by " Turks " and
" Christians " in turn, each " Turk " turning his horse
round in a complete circle upon completing his verse.
Soon the music struck up the *leitmotiv* of the " Turks," a
lively air, very different from the grave march which
heralded the entrance of the " Christians." Then
François and his men moved round and took up a
position along the left-hand side of the theatre. The
" Turks " dismounted and, threateningly brandishing
their canes, climbed on to the stage and ranged themselves along the other side. It became clear that there
would be a battle; but first further parleyings and
challenges had to take place. When the music stopped
one of Francois' warriors advanced from the ranks,
flung his arm forward in a defiant gesture and strode
across to the " Turks," shouting a couple of lines of
challenge. Then in silence he marched down the enemy
lines, glaring into their faces and, finishing his verse,
returned to his place. A moment later one of the
" Turks " went through the same mimicry, brandishing

his cane in the air, his voice wilder and his movements more violent than those of the " Christian " had been, and as he finished his quatrain his fellow-warriors stamped out the last three beats. It was like some fantastic kind of " Sir Roger de Coverley."

These heroic speeches ended. The *pastoralier* sitting in his tent held the red and the blue flags above his head and crossed them. Upon this signal the two little armies marched to the centre of the stage and solemnly crossed swords. The band struck up the traditional battle tune (the French eighteenth-century " Clé du Caveau "), and the two lines danced together back and forth in a slow skipping step, striking each other's swords above their heads. A battle could hardly be more completely conventionalised. When the music stopped two of the " Christians " left the ranks and lay down as though dead on white sheets which had been spread out as before by the *servantes de la scène*. This mimicry was repeated until all the " Christians " lay dead. Then the " Turks " in wild triumph strode out through their exit, saluting *Mahoma*, who, in turn, signified his satisfaction by agitating arms and legs.

This curious opposition between " Christians " and " Turks " is the underlying idea of all the Pastorales. In Webster's words each one of these plays is " an episode in the eternal struggle between good and evil, between Satan and God." It is, however, difficult to say how far the Basque peasant is aware of this symbolical, metaphysical aspect of the Pastorales. It is even doubtful whether the *pastoraliers* themselves aim to do more than satisfy the very general and natural desire to see heroes and villains on the stage and to have them always clearly and sharply defined. In the Pastorales the heroes are always called " Christians " and the villains are always called " Turks," regardless of race or religion. In " François I " they are French and Italians respectively : in " Abraham " they are Jews and inhabitants of Sodom and Gomorrha, in " Astyage, Roi de Perse,"

they are Medes and Persians, and in " Jeanne d'Arc "
they are French and English.   As regards their distinguishing colours Georges Hérelle thinks that the blue
of the " Christians " may date from the time when blue
was the colour of the Kings of France, as opposed to the
red of the British invader in Aquitaine.   It is probable,
however, that this colour symbolism is more primitive
and elemental.   According to a fifteenth-century work
called the " Blason des Couleurs," blue signifies the sky
(and by extension Heaven), together with loyalty, courtesy,
friendship, kindness, renown and beauty, while red stands
for fire (and by extension Hell), and anger, fury and
violence.   When, therefore, the Pastorale characters
wear their costumes of red or blue these are as outward
tokens of the qualities which they may be expected to show.

I refrain from giving a full account of the many
important events in the life of François I which were
enacted before us.   The performance lasted from
eleven to four o'clock with no intermissions and
indeed with no divisions other than the brief Satan-
dances.   There were challenges and battles, negotiations
and treaties, armistices and *plébiscites*.   The Connétable
de Bourbon, one of François' principal Generals, went
over to the enemy and came and went with the " Turks."
He and the Chief Turk rode up in front of the stage and
tried to treat with Queen Claude and the Queen-Mother,
who scornfully rejected their advances.   Later we beheld
a representation of the battle of Pavia at which François
was taken prisoner and shut up in a small wooden crate,
and of the ensuing treaty (signed with a fountain pen),
followed by the surrender as hostages of two little princes,
François' sons, dressed in miniature Satan costumes.
New and unexplained characters appeared on the scene :
a Bishop, a huntsman with two dogs, a strange figure in a
battered top-hat whose comments and grotesque antics
delighted the crowd ; Charles V, whose combination
of Court dress and *koha* portrayed his rôle of alternate
ally and enemy.

At last, at about four o'clock, when tree-shadows were beginning to invade the stage, the actors gathered to form a circle, and the *pastoralier* stepped from his tent to conduct the Hymn of Thanksgiving which concludes every Pastorale.

There remained only the recital of the Epilogue and the open-air dancing. The company divided to either side of the stage, and the Epilogue was then declaimed to the same chant and with the same ritual as the Prologue, save that now the Christian and Turkish Standard-Bearers accompanied the reciter across the stage waving their flags. Beginning by thanking the audience and apologising for the shortcomings of the actors, the reciter proceeded to draw a vague moral from the play. He concluded his lines by bidding farewell to all and announcing that the dancing would begin.

The Standard-Bearers, mounted on two chairs which had been brought forward to the centre of the stage, continued to wave their flags from side to side. The band broke into an air called *Moneindarrak*, and the whole company, forming a circle, began to dance a *saut basque*. The *jautziak* or *sauts basques* occupy a curious place in Basque folk-dance, for they are neither wholly ritualistic nor yet purely recreational. Though they are danced on any Sunday or feast-day and at weddings and similar festivities, men alone take part in them, and there is something about the stiffness and gravity of the dancers which suggests archaic ceremonial rites. With light springing steps, in no way acrobatic, yet difficult by reason of their intricacy, the whole circle moves round a few paces to the right, then turns about and moves to the left again. The *Moneindarrak* is but one of the eighteen or nineteen *jautziak* or *jautzi-buztanak* (*suites de sauts*), which differ only in tune and in the order of the eighteen steps of which they are composed. To the untrained eye they all look much the same.

After their dance the actors observed a remarkable custom, traditionally associated with the Pastorales.

THE VILLAGE OF ERNANI (GUIPUZCOA).

THE MASCARADES DANCING A SAUT BASQUE.

While they all crowded forward on the stage one of their number put up to auction to the onlookers the privilege of dancing the first *saut*. Not individuals but whole villages bid, and it was extraordinary to hear tiny hamlets offering hundreds of francs for this most ephemeral and unsubstantial honour. After lively bidding the dance was finally knocked down to the villagers of Alos-Sibas for 760 francs. Amid loud applause twenty young men in black suits and bérets climbed gravely on to the stage and danced under the critical eyes of all those whom they had outbid. When they had finished the next *saut* was put up and knocked down to Gaztelondo for 460 francs. Even the third fetched between two and three hundred.

This auction provides a means by which surrounding villages can unobtrusively bear their share of the expenses of the play. Until quite lately admittance was free, and the only direct source of income was a plate handed round the audience, preceded by a man armed with an enormous bottle of wine, of which he offered a glass to everyone. Even nowadays with paid admission receipts do not always cover expenditure. Should there be a surplus, however, the actors do not divide it amongst themselves but lavish it all on a banquet.

There has been much speculation over the origin of the Pastorales, although little is known of their history. The first performance for which there is presumptive evidence is that of " Saint-Jacques " at Tardets on August 29th, 1634. The next recorded performance was not till January 3rd, 1750, when " Sainte-Elisabeth de Portugal " was played at Esquiule, and we find no detailed account by an eye-witness before 1839. In that year J. A. C. Buchon saw " Les Trois Martyrs " at Sainte-Engrâce and wrote a description of it in the Pau " Mémorial des Pyrénées." The play lasted twelve hours,[1] and it is likely that Buchon's attention wandered, for he seems

---

[1] In those days it seems that the actors did not learn their parts but repeated each verse after the prompter.

to have given free rein to his imagination. Chaho, Francisque Michel and even Webster all proved themselves unreliable observers, and it was not until the twentieth century that Albert Léon, J. Saroihandy and above all Georges Hérelle studied the Pastorales in a thorough and objective manner.

The Pastorales are acted only in Soule and exceptionally in one or two villages of Basse-Navarre. There is nothing to suggest that a similar tradition ever existed in the other Basque provinces. Every Soule village still boasts its *instituteur de pastorales*, who, however, always has some other profession; schoolmaster, farmer or the like. He is not only the stage manager of any play that is produced but also custodian and if need be copyist of the manuscripts. For in almost every case the original manuscript has been lost, and to-day the plays survive only in the uncouth hand and the rough exercise-books [1] of the *professeurs de tragérie*, as one at least has pompously called himself.

Georges Hérelle records a total of sixty-seven surviving plays, which fall into seven different groups : those taken from the Old Testament (e.g. " Moise," " Judith et Holopherne "); New Testament and early Church History [2] (" L'Enfant Prodigue," " La Destruction de Jérusalem "); lives of the Saints (" Sainte-Ursule "); classical antiquity (" Oedipe," " Astyage Roi de Perse "); *Chansons de Geste* (" Roland," " Les Quatre Fils d'Aymon "); romances of chivalry (" Warwick ou Histoire de Julie et d'Hippolyte comte de Douglas "); French History (" Jeanne d'Arc," " Napoléon I," " Guillaume II ou la Campagne de France 1914–1918 ").[3]

[1] Many of these have now found their way into the Bibliothèque Nationale and the libraries of Bayonne and Bordeaux. The oldest surviving manuscript dates from 1723.

[2] The absence of any form of Passion Play is remarkable and is usually attributed to the disinclination of the Basques to allow any human being to play the rôle of the Saviour.

[3] An unkind fate prevented me at the last moment from attending the first performance of " Guillaume II " at Barcus on April 15th, 1929.

It is clear from this range of subjects that the original authors of the plays took their plots for the most part from those cheap little books, such as the " Bibliothèque Bleue," which used to be peddled throughout the French countryside. The plays are full of anachronisms and incongruities, many of which can be traced to these sources. Jerusalem is destroyed by heavy artillery, for instance, and Saint-Eustace aims a shot-gun at the miraculous stag. The King of Persia concludes an alliance with the King of Wallachia. The inhabitants of Sodom are called Cocor, Patar, Mademoiselle Maneton and Mademoiselle Catilie. On the stage these ladies are dressed in the latest (or very nearly the latest) fashions. Roland steps over a flower-pot to represent his passage through a forest, and Napoleon, being a great man, is acted by the tallest lad in the village. Charlemagne and Nebuchadnezzar alike wear the Legion of Honour, and in at least one performance of " Abraham " the voice of Jehovah emanated from a top-hatted head looking over a wall.

Except for the dancing there is nothing profoundly original in the Soule theatrical tradition. It is only one of many regional theatres which existed in France and Italy, inheriting the repertory and technique of the mediæval Mysteries, until they died of atrophy or ecclesiastical persecution. The opposition of good and evil, the simplicity of production, the rôle of the Satans, the chanted versicles, the conventionalised stagecraft and

---

I am indebted to Miss Violet Alford for the information that the Prologue was sung by the King of the Belgians in a khaki uniform and gold crown, a costume which he shared with the British Sovereign ; that the Kaiser was played by the miller of Barcus in a white dolman with the German colours ; that the French entered Mulhouse to the traditional skipping step associated with battles ; that a black cardboard model of Rheims Cathedral was shelled by a Big Bertha a couple of feet long ; that the Kaiser and the Crown Prince finally ran away off the stage and disappeared among the crowd ; and that the Kings of England and Belgium blindfolded the German emissaries and led them to Foch to sign the Armistice.

many other points of detail derive directly from the Mysteries.

The principal interest of the Pastorales lies in the fact that they are a fragment of the Middle Ages, which has survived intact into the twentieth century. How long they will preserve their freshness and vitality it is impossible to say. Already there are not wanting signs that the old traditions will not be respected for ever. In the words of Hérelle " relics of the past can never be rejuvenated."

CHAPTER VII

FOLK-SONG : THE WORDS

Etchahun Ziberun, Otchalde Lapurdin,
Buruzagi dirade kantoren egitin.
Ez gitutzu gu beldur, nor nahi jin dadin ;
Erranen dit orotan nik gur 'Uskal-Herrin :
Jokaturen dugula hek plazer dutenin.

ETCHAHUN.

Etchahun in Soule, Otchalde in Labourd,
We are the greatest among bards.
We are afraid of no one.
I declare it everywhere in our Basque Country
That we will compete whenever they want us to.

PUBLIC interest in folk-song dates from the latter half of
the eighteenth century, when the publication of Percy's
"Reliques" and Macpherson's "Ossian" created a new
vogue which resulted throughout Europe in the rescue
from oblivion of countless anonymous masterpieces. Folk-
lore in all its aspects has now become a recognised science.
Although all poems and stories taken down from peasant
lips are not necessarily of intrinsic literary beauty, there
is a great fascination as well as sound scientific value in
their collection and study, for there are few things in
which a nation reveals its character so fully as in its
folk-literature.

It is from this point of view that one should approach
Basque folk-song. One may look in vain for anything

resembling the Border Ballads, the long epic poems of Finland or the stirring songs of the Balkans. Nor are there to be found, as in some countries, works of great lyrical beauty, or fragments rivalling in concentrated vigour some of the four-line *coplas* of Spain. Yet among the folk-songs of the Basques there are some which have the beauty of simplicity and sincerity, and many which are engaging in their humour. Collectively they throw a valuable light on the mentality and outlook of the people who sing them.

It might almost be said that the Basque is born into the world with a song on his lips, so great and so intimate a part does song play in his whole life. Among his first impressions will be the tender lullabies crooned to him by his mother as she rocks him in her arms or gently sways the wooden cradle to and fro. A little later he will learn all sorts of children's songs, many of them just nonsense rhymes, others intended to accompany games or dancing. In church he will join in the hymns of which the music so closely resembles the tunes which his family sing at home, love-songs, these last, and satyrical poems of which he will pick up the words as he grows to manhood. There is nothing pretentious in the songs of his race. They are sung without any instrumental accompaniment, in long soaring phrases in which the tune obediently follows the metrical vagaries of the words, and the words themselves are not time-hallowed poems which must be respected, but themes on which one may embroider as one goes along. These songs will be woven into the pattern of his life. He will sing them while he is watching sheep on the gorse-covered hillside; ploughing or stripping the golden maize stalks; leading the patient oxen to market and stopping every now and then to draw his goad across their necks, while the solid cart-wheels creak an obligato to his song.[1] A bar or two; then a

---

[1] An ingenious author has asserted that this shrill creaking was deliberately devised by the peasant for the entertainment of his oxen. In actual fact its cause is rather more prosaic, namely neglect to grease the axles.

few seconds pause ; another phrase ; then again a rest ;
thus he will continue half unconsciously the whole day
long. Sometimes he will just express his contentment
with life in general :—

> Early in the morning as the day dawns
> I drive my sheep out to pasture,
> Then I lie stretched out in the shade.
> Who is more content than I ?
> Mine is a happy lot,
> For in this hut none is my master.

or,

> I am young and cheerful
> And always ready to laugh,
> Content, happy and gay ;
> Nothing worries me,
> For I am friends with all
> And bound to none.[1]

In like manner does the housewife sing over her work,
and the fisherman in his boat, although it is a curious
fact that this race of hardy seamen have hardly any songs
particularly associated with the sea.

With this one exception there is no aspect or incident
of everyday life which does not inspire the Basque with a
song. Any theme, however trivial, will suffice. The
language lends itself admirably to rhyming improvisations, and every man is, more or less, his own poet. The
influence of this facility, however, is not wholly for good.
It results in an enormous output of verse, but reacts
unfavourably on the quality. When it is so easy to invent
a new song there is less incentive to memorise the old
ones, and less likelihood that a good song, once written,
will be universally adopted and preserved. Relatively
few songs are sung over a wide area or in an unvarying
form, and this fact accounts principally for the scarcity
of really memorable poems. Another consequence of
this fatal facility is that the words are almost always of
later date than the melody and are often quite out of

[1] Charles Bordes : " Douze Chansons Amoureuses du Pays Basque."

keeping with the latter. One finds the most trivial rhymes harnessed to gravely beautiful airs, and it is quite usual for one melody to be associated with several different sets of verses. Here, for example, is a love-song, simple but sincere, which I heard not far from Saint-Jean-de Luz, sung to a sad and lovely air :—

> My father and my mother have sent me
> From my home in Arbonne to Saint-Jean-de-Luz
> In order that I may see you no more.
>
> But do not let this cause you pain or sorrow,
> For love is more faithful from afar,
> And, my beloved, I will never forsake you.

At Itxassou, barely twenty miles away, I heard the same tune again with the following words :—

> Monsieur Sirrist's donkey, what a brute he is !
> The flies bite him and he kicks out with his heels.
> He has torn Mari Tyipiri's skirt at the back !

It is not always easy to date these songs, but it is safe to say that very few of them can have been written before the second half of the eighteenth century. Some can be dated by the events which they describe, and others by the mention of the year in the first line, e.g. :—

> In eighteen hundred and twenty-four
> There was a mission in the village of Bidart, etc.

It is possible that great Basque epic poems may once have existed. If so they have been irretrievably lost, or survive only in isolated fragments, such as the following lines which are still sung :—

> Up, up, men of the house, for the sun has risen ;
> From the sea rings out a trumpet of silver,
> And there is gathering on the coasts of Holland.[1]

Nogaret believes in the existence of these lost epics. " It is probable," he says, " that in olden times songs were sung to commemorate the great deeds of the heroic

[1] J. D. J. Salaberry : *op. cit.*

age, or the numerous warlike episodes which occurred on the distant expeditions of these bold and hardy seafarers." Charles Bordes, on the other hand, held that "wrapt up in themselves, coming little into contact with their neighbours and remaining great individualists, the Basques found in their own history no themes for epic poems." Whatever the cause may be, the fact remains that among the thousands of songs figuring in the collections of Iztueta, Sallaberry, Bordes, Donostia, Azkue and others, the historical legends can almost be counted on the fingers of one hand.

By far the oldest Basque poem, if it is genuine, is a curious little fragment called the "Song of Lelo," which was discovered in 1590 among some old manuscripts by Juan Ibañez de Ybargüen. Here is one of the many translations proposed for the first few lines :—

> Lelo, Lelo is dead.
> Zara has killed Lelo.
> The foreigners from Rome
> Would vanquish Biscay
> And Biscay raises the war-cry.
> Octavian is Lord of the Earth
> But Lecobidi is Lord of Biscay.[1]

There are a number of other verses, but even those who are persuaded of the authenticity of the opening are doubtful as to that of the remainder.

At about the same time Estebán de Garibay published what purported to be a number of ancient Basque songs, among which is a fragment on which doubts have been cast owing to the fact that it is composed in the metre of the Spanish *romances* :—

> A thousand years has the stream flowed in its course
> Since the Guipuzcoans entered into the house of Gaztelu
> And vanquished the Navarrese at the battle of Beotibar.

---

[1] Francisque Michel : "Le Pays Basque." In the *Revue Internationale des Etudes Basques* Don Julio de Urquijo has expressed the view that the words *Lelo Il Lelo* have no meaning and that they constitute a formula expressive of grief such as "Lackaday." They bear a certain resemblance to the Serbian exclamation *Oi lele*, meaning "Woe is me."

I

Garibay also published a number of laments for the dead, the singing of which he describes as a very widespread custom in the fifteenth century, although it was, in fact, forbidden by the *fueros*.

It is impossible to be sure that any of these early poems are not literary fakes. The " Chant d'Altabiscar," which, in the middle of last century was accepted by many as a genuine Basque epic dating from the days of Roland, proved to be a hoax. It was composed in French by one Garay de Monglave, whose friend Louis Duhalde translated it into very bad Basque.

Of the few legends which seem to be old at least half are obvious importations. One meets, in transparent disguise, such old favourites as " Malbrook s'en va-t-en Guerre," " Jean Renaud," " Le Juif Errant," and, grown prematurely grave, " Little Billee " :—

> "You, the smallest of my crew,
>   You, my favourite of all,
>   Go, climb up to the masthead
>   And see if there is land in sight."

> " My dear master, I am sad at heart,
>   For I see neither land nor sail ;
>   If you must eat somebody
>   Let me be the first to die."

The third verse is the same as the first : but this time the cabin-boy replies :—

> " My dear master, great is my joy,
>   For I see land, the towns of England
>   And your sister Marianne
>   Sewing on the balcony." [1]

Besides these foreign legends there have survived a handful of songs based on grim tragedies of the Middle Ages. So elliptical and circumstantial is their style, so rapid the alternation between past and present, between narrative and dialogue, that it is usually difficult to re-

---

[1] Charles Dufau in *Gure Herria*.

construct the events which inspired these songs.   Nevertheless the names of men and houses figuring in " The
Lady of Ruthie " and " The Song of Berterretche " have
been identified in the fifteenth-century annals of Soule.
" The Song of Berterretche " is a particularly good
example :—

The alder has not pith, nor does the reed have bark.
I did not think that noblemen spoke lies.
The valley of Andoce, oh the long valley !
Though it be weaponless thrice has it pierced my heart.
Berterretche from his bed speaks low to the maidservant :
" Go see if there are men in sight."
Straightway the maid told him what she had seen,
Three dozen men going from door to door.
From his window Berterretche greets my Lord Count
And offers him a hundred cows and their bull.
Treacherously spoke then my Lord Count :
" Come to the door Berterretche, you shall return forthwith."
" Mother give me my shirt, perchance the one that I shall never cast off.
Those who live will remember the dawn that follows Easter."
Oh the haste of Mari-Santz as she sped past Bostmendieta !
On her two knees she entered the house of Bustanoby at Lacarry.
" O young Master of Bustanoby, my beloved brother,
Without your aid my son is lost."
" Be silent my sister, I beg you do not weep ;
If your son lives he is gone to Mauleon."
Oh the haste of Mari-Santz to the door of my Lord Count !
" Alas ! my Lord Count, where have you my fine son ? "
" Have you sons other than Berterretche ?
He lies dead over by Espeldoy ; you who are alive go tend him."
Oh, the men of Espeldoy, they of little understanding,
Who having the dead so near knew nothing of it !
The daughter of Espeldoy, she whom they call Marguerite,
Gathers up the blood of Berterretche in handfulls.
Oh, what fine linen there is to be washed at the house of Espeldoy !
Of the shirts of Berterretche they say there are three dozen.[1]

The marriage of Baron Charles de Luxe et de Tardets
and Marie de Jaurgain which took place in 1584 inspired
a beautiful song which is still sung in the three French
provinces.   The first and last verses are as follows :—

[1] Salaberry : *op. cit.*

There are two golden lemons at the Manor of Jaurgain d'Ossas
The Lord of Tardets has demanded one of them.
He was told in answer that they were not yet ripe,
When they ripened, then he should have one.

" Mother, you have sold me like a mare,
And exiled me, alas ! into Spain.
Had my father been alive as you are
I should not have married into the house of Tardets." [1]

Nowadays the peasants have no recollection of the events
which this song recounts.   They usually turn the Manor
of Jaurgain into the Castle of Tardets, and the Count
into a mythical King of Hungary.

Another ballad is based on events which took place in
Soule in the seventeenth century :—

I rose early in the morning on my wedding-day
And was dressed in silk ere the sun was risen :
I was an *etcheko-andre* at mid-day
And a young widow when the sun set.

" Monsieur d'Irigaray, my Lord, raise your head,
Or do you already regret having married me ? "
" No, I do not regret having married you,
Nor shall I regret it so long as I live, my beloved.

I had a mistress, secret from all the world,
Secret from all the world, and confessed but to God :
She sent me a bouquet of rare flowers,
Or rare flowers with poison in their midst."

For seven years I kept a dead man in my room,
By day on the cold floor, and at night enfolded in my arms.
I washed him with lemon-water one day in every week.
One day in every week, and that was a Friday morning. [2]

Soule has no monopoly of legends, however.   In the
Baztan there still exists the ancient house of Ursua, now a
dilapidated ruin, which forms the scene of a fine song
collected in the neighbourhood by Father Donostia,
who retells its story as follows :—

[1] Jean de Jaurgain in " La Tradition au Pays Basque."
[2] Salaberry : *op. cit.*

" A son of the house of Ursua took to wife a girl from beyond the mountains which surround the Baztan valley. She came with a great train, for the people say that she was a princess. The marriage was celebrated with all the pomp that can be imagined. But the groom found on his wedding night that his bride had not brought to the altar that jewel which, since it is of the spirit, is more precious than wealth and beauty. He concealed his dismay. The following morning he bade his wife put on all her finery in order that he might show her the possessions of the house ; those ' seven mills and eight white palaces ' of which the song tells : and there in the open air without further explanation he killed her. Her body was found in the Hermitage of Saint-Anne. Thus far the poem. Tradition relates that the Lord of Ursua saddled his horse and escaped. According to another version of the tale he boldly sent an emissary to the house of Lantana to bid them fetch the body of their daughter." [1]

It seems probable that the older poems were finer than those composed nowadays, for many of the longer songs start well and then tail off into obscure and commonplace dialogues, in which there often appears to be little or no connection between the various verses. In these cases it is probable that of the original song the first verse alone survives, whilst the others have been borrowed or improvised to fill the gaps caused by deficient memories. There is, for example, a song which begins :

> One day I was embroidering in my room.
> From the sea I heard a sailor singing,
> A sailor singing, and this was his song. [2]

In all probability this was originally a copy or variant of the lovely Spanish " Romance del Conde Arnaldos." As sung to-day, however, it tells an involved and colour-

[1] R. P. José Antonio de Donostia : " De Música Popular Vasco," p. 38.
[2] Dufau in *Gure Herria*.

less tale of a maiden who is abducted by a sea-captain and prefers death to dishonour.

Some of the most charming and original little poems are the lullabies. These are regrettably rare on the French side of the frontier and have been collected for the most part in Navarre and Vizcaya. They are essentially brief, seldom consisting of more than a single quatrain. The mother takes the child into her arms or rocks the cradle, and sleep is often the burden of her song :—

> Lullaby, sing lullaby,
> God on high
> Grant to this babe
> Four hours of sleep.

If the child will not close its eyes she will try persuasion :—

> Lullaby, my darling.
> We will both go to sleep :
> You now and I later,
> We will both go to sleep.

or bribery :—

> Baby, have a little sleep,
> And I will give you a sweet.
> Your father will give you one,
> Your mother will give you two,
> And the Lord God will give you a dozen.[1]

Sometimes she will sing little nonsense rhymes to amuse the child :—

> Binbili, bonbolo, go to sleep.
> If we were in France
> The ass would drum,
> The ox would dance
> And the goat would play
> The tambourine.

She will warn it of the dangers that surround it :—

> Bonbolontena, my darling,
> Do not go to sleep in the wood,
> For the wicked eagle would come and take you
> As though you were a little hare. [2]

---

[1] Donostia : " Eskual Eres Sorta."   [2] Donostia : *ibid.*

She will give rein to her fancy :—

> From the famous country of France
> Come the noble professions,
> Scissor-grinders
> And pig-doctors.[1]

meditate on her own life :—

> At one o'clock I was born,
> At two I was baptized,
> At three I fell in love
> And at four I was married.[2]

or on her troubles :—

> The little child is crying ;
> You his mother must feed him.
> His father is in the tavern,
> The rascal, the gambler, the rogue.[3]

Among the lullabies there is a tendency, which re-appears throughout Basque folk-song, to divide the quatrain into two parts, the first two lines depicting a scene from Nature while the other expresses an emotion :—

> A lovely elm beside a stream,
> Three roses in May.
> She who knows not love
> Knows no sorrow in her heart.[4]

or :

> On the sea a mist is lying,
> Towards the bar of Bayonne.
> I love you more even
> Than the bird loves her young.[5]

Even when, as in these two examples, the first half of the quatrain has no direct symbolical connection with the second half, there is usually an affinity of mood ; and the contrast between the objective and the subjective welds the little poem into a wonderfully complete and satisfying whole.

[1] Azkue : *op. cit.*   [2] *Ibid.*   [3] *Ibid.*
[4] Donostia : " Eskual Eres Sorta."   [5] *Ibid,*

The children's songs are no more pretentious than the lullabies. In every country one comes across the same sort of nonsense songs consecrated by tradition. In the Basque Country the children sing :—

> Trilili and Tralala.
> That is the mother of all song.
> For me bread and ham ;
> For you the horns of an ox.

There is a little song for dancing children on the knee like " Ride a Cock Horse," and another for teaching them to count their fingers or toes like " This Little Pig went to Market." The following are the first and last verses of a song which adds a line at each repetition like " This is the House that Jack Built " :—

> The wolf has come to kill the goat,
> The goat eats the maize.
> Drive, drive, drive away the goat.
> The goat was in our maize field.

> Death has come to kill the man,
> The man kills the cat,
> The cat kills the mouse,
> The mouse gnaws the rope,
> The rope strangles the ox,
> The ox drinks the water,
> The water puts out the fire,
> The fire burns the stick,
> The stick beats the dog,
> The dog worries the wolf,
> The wolf kills the goat,
> Drive, drive, drive away the goat,
> The goat was in our maize field.[1]

Here is another nursery rhyme, a typical one, since the Basque child's nursery is usually the farmyard :—

> I had three chicks and lost four.
> Where has their mother gone ?
> The mother of the chicks was the hen ;
> The fox twisted her neck.
> " Purapura," I called to her from the door,
> " Cluck-cluck," she replied from the stew-pot.

---

[1] Charles Dufau in *Gure Herria*.

Lullabies and nursery rhymes are few in number in comparison with love-songs and satirical songs. It is strange that love, which elsewhere has inspired the greatest masterpieces of poetry, should be the theme of the most commonplace and insipid of Basque folk-songs. Few of these express the idealism of love: more often they are painfully materialistic, as in the following example—

> I went to Barcus
> To eat a kid
> In my cousin's house.
> It was a good spread;
> There were roast cutlets
> And they had brought beer,
> Fresh bread and
> Sweet wine.
> The only thing lacking
> Was yourself, my sweetheart.

Here and there one comes across a verse or two of some distinction in praise of the loved one:—

> My beloved has beautiful hair,
> Red in colour;
> The skin of her hands is white as finest silver
> And she is more full of charm than any other.

> I have a house
> As fine as any castle.
> You shall dwell there seated in a silver chair.
> And none shall say to you that which you do not wish to hear.

> In the mountains I have sheep with their shepherds
> And on the sea ten ships with their sailors;
> In Catalonia I have ten mules
> Laden with silver pieces.[1]

Another song exceptional for both its beauty and its brevity is the following:—

> White wood-pigeon whither are you flying?
> All the passes into Spain are full of snow.
> To-night you will take refuge in our house.

---

[1] Bordes; *op. cit.*

> I am not afraid of the snow nor of the darkness.
> My beloved, for you I would pass through night and day,
> Through night and day and through deserted forests.[1]

More often Basque love-songs restrict themselves to the expression of the most conventional sentiments. Quite irrelevantly the nightingale is praised for its song (though one peasant poet, striving after originality or perhaps with his tongue in his cheek, substitutes the parrot!) The object of the poet's affections is compared to a flower in a garden; the swallow is invited to convey assurances of eternal fidelity, and the moon to shed her tender radiance on the head of the loved one. It is all very hackneyed and unconvincing. Still less inspired are the all too numerous laments of unrequited love, or the endless dialogues between faithful and unfaithful lovers. They are as doleful and, when unrelieved by humour, as sordid as the dingy ballads beloved of the British private soldier. They go through the whole theatrical gamut of self-pity, regret, entreaty, reproach, indignation and despair.

In one of these dialogues a young girl shows herself too clever to be taken in by the blandishments of a specious suitor. When the swain addresses her thus :—

> Good-day, oh new-born star, sun with the lovely eyes,
> For your sake I would leave the village where I was born
> To come and live with you, oh star full of charm!

She answers :

> You talk well, yes, you talk well and honestly;
> But what I want to hear from you is this :
> When will you make me your star or your sun?

To his :

> I am sick at heart, I tell you truly,
> I am ill with fever for fear you should not be mine.
> I beseech you, cure me, that I may not die of sorrow.

---

[1] Salaberry : *op. cit,*

She retorts :—

> For every ill there is a remedy.
> If you have the fever go to the leech,
> And do not come to me for a doctor.

The Basque can never stray far from his particular vein of malicious, mocking humour. In most of his songs irony and wit take the place of emotion ; for he can seldom resist the temptation to make fun of his own (or other people's) most intimate feelings, and he seems as afraid as any English schoolboy of being suspected of lofty sentiments. It is typical of this attitude that the two stanzas quoted above, beginning " White woodpigeon," are followed by a third of which the first line is :—" The pigeon is beautiful in flight : it is still more beautiful on the dish." This sly and rather mediæval humour replaces the cult of nature in Basque verse. Indeed, observation of nature does not seem to be a strong point. One comes across songs in which partridges sing in hedges, and " the cuckoo has her young in a little hole high up in an oak tree." Rare are such songs as this :—

> Sadly sings the bird in the cage,
> Though it has plenty to eat and to drink.
> It longs to be outside,
> For liberty is so beautiful.
>
> O bird in the open, look into the cage.
> Keep away from it if you can,
> For liberty is so beautiful.

Birds figure more often in malicious gossip songs, in which they disguise an allusion to some neighbour :—

> The nightingale sings beautifully,
> It charms the whole neighbourhood.
> Last night in a hedge
> There were two of them.
> They were beautiful and charming
> In every kind of way.
> And they were very taken with each other,

> One was a male bird and the other a female.
> No wonder then that they mated.
> There is no doubt
> That the male bird
> Would not have gone to that hedge
> If he hadn't seen
> That the female was ready to meet him half way.

Sometimes, more poetically, they are used for purposes of comparison :—

> In the mountains how lovely is the red-legged partridge,
> But one cannot trust his handsome looks.
> My beloved is much the same,
> For she gave me a promise and then went back on it.[1]

or again :—

> When the broom is in flower
> The bird alights upon it.
> The bird can fly through the air
> When the fancy takes him.
> Even thus has flown away
> The love between you and me.

If one does not find much evidence of the appreciation of beauty in Basque folk-song, humour is always near at hand. Every little incident which takes place in the village provides an excuse for a song : a *pelote* match, a game of cards between tipsy women, a successful piece of smuggling, or the theft of a broomstick. The particularly revolting murder of an old woman committed by a servant girl at Espelette in 1916 is narrated at great length in a song beginning :—

> A horrible affair in the village of Espelette
> Took place in the middle of the war.
> It is not enough for men to shed blood,
> Women must now take to being butchers.

The Basque improviser is always ready to poke fun at his neighbour. There are songs satirising a would-be sportsman :—

[1] Charles Dufau in *Gure Herria.*

Pierre of Uhart, oh what a good shot he was !
By chance he found a hare in the corner of a hedge.
It had been dead for a fortnight and, oh how it smelt !
To eat it one must have a healthy appetite ! [1]

a dishonest blacksmith :—

Joachim Raymond, blacksmith of Ituren,
Now you are angry because we know
That no Saint can trust you ;
You have melted down Saint Christopher and made bells of him ! [2]

a village lady-killer :—

In the red field are the partridges
And among the beech-trees are the doves.
A gallant young man is
Little John of Mendiberri. [3]

or an immoral priest :—

The Curé of Biscaye has a little son,
Who calls him uncle as he tells him to.
The Curé celebrates Mass and his son helps him,
But he calls him uncle as he tells him to.

Another group is formed by the songs, now unfortunately growing rare, sung in honour (or dishonour) of the various trades. One such poem, not unlike the English " Farmer's Boy," sings the joys of being a charcoal burner, but with a characteristically Basque twist it concludes :—

As soon as my purse grows fat
Why should I remain a charcoal burner in the mountains ? [4]

In another song a young girl reviews the different trades with a view to choosing a husband :—

[1] This song is sung to the air given on p. 136, and has the peculiarity that each line begins in Basque and ends in French. It is said to have been improvised at a competition organised many years ago by M. D'Abbadie d'Arrast.
[2] Donostia : " Como Canta el Vasco."   [3] *Ibid.*
[4] Dufau in *Gure Herria.*

> If you marry a sailor
> You'll live on sardines and cod.
> If you marry a muleteer
> You'll eat your fish with oil.[1]

and so on.

There are a number of songs, too long to quote, about horse-dealing. Of these the best-known are " Ezkerra's Mare," " The Mule of Ikazketa," and " The Mare from Pampeluna." In this last a farmer is bamboozled by an Andalusian horse-dealer into buying a lame mare. He only reaches home with difficulty and gets into hot water with his wife :—

> Oh what a miserable little mare,
> Old, too, what's more.
> On her you have spent
> All the household money.
> For a sou I'd be glad to sell
> Both the horse and the husband.

Needless to say there is no lack of songs devoted to the ups and downs of married life. The following is more subtle than most :—

> I have a French husband
> Who is fond of the inn.
> He won't always come at once
> For he likes his freedom
> As in the days of his youth.
> His back is bent
> And his beard is of two colours.
> But may God preserve him !
>
> I have a Spanish wife
> Better than I deserve.
> Her hair is like newly-washed linen.
> To her hands I would entrust
> Silver and gold.
> She has no serious blemishes,
> Only that she is black and green in complexion
> And just a little quarrelsome.

---

[1] Salaberry : *op. cit.*

Many of the songs are delightfully carefree and irresponsible :—

> My father gave me for my dowry
> (Oh my dowry, my dowry !)
> A sow with her young,
> A hen with her chicks
> And a string of onions.
>
> The wolf ate my sow
> (Oh my sow, my sow !)
> The fox ate my hen
> And the rats ate my string of onions,
> So farewell to my dowry ! [1]

Drinking songs are less numerous than one would expect. Their themes are divided between the pleasures of the cup :—

> Oh Noah, illustrious man of the Ancient Law,
> You were the first to plant the vine.
> Who put it into your head to cultivate so precious a plant ?
> It is Man's consolation in times of trouble.

and the pain of the return home. The tune of the following song is so singularly appropriate that I cannot resist quoting it :—

GOIZIAN ON.[2]

Good in the day, good too in the night, Juice of the grape you
al - ways find good, you al - ways find good.
You start to walk home, but your
You get up a - gain, but your
feet will not work, So you fall and lie down on the
feet will not walk, So you fall down a - gain on the
ground, and lie down on the ground.
ground, and lie down on the ground.

---

[1] Dufau in *Gure Herria*.   [2] Donostia : " Eskual Eres Sorta."

In the taverns of the Baztan the old men have a quaint sobriety test. Balanced on one foot on a *fereta* (a conical wooden receptacle banded with metal), they sing a song which in the original is rather a tongue-twister :—

> On the tip of the twig of the branch
> Of the apple-tree on the hill-side
> A little bird perched singing :
> " Liralirali and liralirali."
> Who can dance well to this tune ?

Religious songs, of which there are many, fall into two groups, the first consisting of songs improvised by the peasants themselves and sung during their daily life, and the second of hymns used in the Church services. The former, like the *saetas* of Andalusia, are the spontaneous expression of Basque religious feeling. They are sincere and robust rather than mystical, and are usually short, simple and direct :

> Love bore Thee in anguish ;
> Men raised Thee on high
> And crucified Thee.[1]

In the Bertiz Arana valley it was till recently the custom at the end of the bracken-cutting season for the peasants to form nocturnal processions on the mountain side, carrying flaming torches and singing a song about the Ten Commandments. I have heard similar songs about the Seven Sacraments and the Last Judgment. In some religious songs the dialogue form reappears, as in the following fragment in which a Christian addresses a condemned soul :—

> " Oh damned soul,
>   What is your torment ?
>   What is your hell ?
>   What are your pains ?
>   Speak, speak,
>   That we may learn."

---

[1] Donostia : " Eskual Eres Sorta."

> " I cannot express in words
> How greatly I suffer.
> Of my terrible agony
> Were I to begin to tell
> Too weak, too weak
> Were all my words." [1]

Among the Christmas carols are one or two lovely little poems. Father Donostia, who collected the following example, writes :—" It deals with the refusal met with by Joseph and Mary on their arrival in Bethlehem to seek shelter for the child that was to be born. The words, which are incomplete, correspond probably to some primitive mumming-play :—

> " Let us go knock at the door
> Of that house over there.
> Perhaps good folk
> Will answer."

> Twice and thrice
> Joseph knocks at the door.
> A man drags himself
> Painfully to the window.

> From the window the man
> Answers them thus :
> " At this hour of the night
> What do you want ? "

> " I have a young maiden
> With me at my side.
> In her womb she carries
> Jesus as her son."

> " A virgin with child ?
> How now ! That's not possible.
> You mock me.
> Go hence."

> Take courage, Joseph,
> Take courage,
> Jesus to-day
> Shall be born.

---

[1] Donostia : " Como Canta el Vasco."

K

> And at that moment
> Midnight struck,
> And there was born
> That lovely child.[1]

The hymns are naturally a little more sophisticated, for they are usually the work of priests who have more education than simple peasants. Nevertheless they must be counted as folk-songs, for the names of their writers have been lost, and they belong to the people. In the Basque Country, the congregation takes a more active part in the service than in other Catholic lands, and, in the words of Camille Bellaigue, " the walls of the churches are alive : they sing." It is an impressive experience to hear the whole congregation, the women on the floor of the dimly-lit church and the men in the wooden galleries, sing in unison, to some ancient air, ascetic and stern as plainsong, words that have something of the spirit of the Psalms :—

> Is there aught more necessary
> In this world than salvation ?
> There is no joy that can compare
> With that of arrival in Paradise.
>
> Speak, O God, Here am I
> Come to listen to Thee.
> I long to accomplish Thy will
> Come, I pray Thee, and strengthen me.

Among the most curious of Basque folk-songs are a group which can best be described as " wassailing " songs. The English word " wassailing " is derived from the Anglo-Saxon *wes-hal* (be in health), and is applied to a custom which is undoubtedly pagan in its origins. In the British Isles the " wassailers," " guisers," " pace-eggers " or " wren-boys " are believed to bring luck and plenty into the houses which they visit. Throughout Europe the substance of their songs is the same. They announce the object of their visit, pay compliments

[1] Donostia : "Como Canta el Vasco."

to the master and mistress of the house, demand gifts of food and depart with thanks or insults according to the welcome they have received.[1]

Here are some of the verses which are sung by small boys on New Year's Eve at Saint-Jean-de-Luz :—

> God save you !
> Be you welcome !
> God give you a good night
> And grant us a good year.
>
> Beside the river stands the ash-tree
> And also in the mountains.
> The Master of this house
> Has a beard as red as gold.
>
> On the hillside the gorse
> Is all in flower.
> The Mistress of this house
> Is like the Virgin Mary.
>
> Gracious Mistress of the house
> Lovely are your eyes.
> From your hand we seek
> Bacon and sausages.
>
> Give if you are going to give :
> If not then say so.
> In the food cupboards of this house
> The mice rear their young.

Up at Larrau where the young men go wassailing on the last Saturday in January, a curiously arbitrary date, one of the complimentary verses is rather remarkable :—

> The Master of the house is on his way
> With a golden rod in his hand.
> When he speaks with the King
> He keeps his hat on his head.

There are villages in Spanish Navarre where in the early hours of New Year's Day the children draw fresh

[1] See Rodney A. Gallop : " Basque Wassailing Songs." Music and Letters. October 1930.

water from the well or collect the first rain which falls
after midnight and carry it round from house to house
singing :—

> Water below, water above,
> A good New Year to you.
> May there enter into this house
> Health with peace
> And riches with the water.[1]

It is on the eve of Saint-Agatha's Day that the children
of Vizcaya go wassailing. They mask their faces and
carry a tall pointed pole on which they impale the sausages
and bacon which are their traditional recompense. In
Basse-Navarre the gypsies have seized on this custom as
an excuse for begging. Just before Lent they go round
with a song proclaiming that Santibat, a mythical per-
sonification of Carnival, has sent them forth to seek
gifts of bacon. It is possible that they may once have
taken Santibat with them in the form of a " guy," just as
the little boys of the Bidassoa valley on Christmas Eve
take round a " guy " whom they call Olentzero or
Onenzaro, singing :

> Here comes our Olentzero,
> Silent he sits with a pipe in his mouth.
> To-morrow he will sup
> On a couple of capons
> And a bottle of wine.

Olentzero is said to be a charcoal-burner with red eyes and
a black face, and, like Santa Claus, to come down the
chimney. In common with the French *Pansard*, the
Poklad of the Adriatic island of Lastovo and our own
Guy Fawkes, he finishes his days on a bonfire.

One of the most curious forms of wassailing is found
at Laguinge (Soule), where at Carnival time masked
figures enter and ask for presents of food in dumb
show, recalling the silent masqueraders of the Roman

---

[1] Azkue : *op. cit.* The first line, rather obscure, may mark a distinction between well and rain water.

Saturnalia whose purpose was to expel the spirits of the
dead.

   Closely related to these various songs are those known
as *toberak* and *erregiñetakoak*.   The former are survivals
of a very curious custom which is observed nowadays
only in one or two villages of Navarre and Guipuzcoa.
They are special serenades sung to a bridal pair on their
wedding-night or more usually on the day when their
banns of marriage are published in church.   A band of
youths signify their intention of observing this time-
honoured custom by planting in front of the bride's
house a steel bar known as a *tobera*, which is then decorated
with flowers and lace by two unmarried girls chosen from
among the nearest neighbours.   Manuel de Lekuona [1]
thinks that the *tobera* was originally a bar of bronze used
in foundries and that the first serenaders were smiths.
Nowadays anyone may serenade the betrothed couple,
but only those who are the first to plant the *tobera* are
entitled to share in the *pregu afari*, the traditional supper,
any others being recompensed with presents of food and
wine.

   When night falls the serenaders appear outside the
house.   Two of them support the *tobera* suspended
horizontally on rings hung from a rope which they hold
over their shoulders.   It is the business of two others,
known as the *pikatzaile* and the *biya*, to beat it with small
metal rods, and the fifth sings the *koplak* (verses).   They
usually start with a curious little refrain, the first line of
which has never been satisfactorily explained :

> *San Martin de la moja, moja de la San Martin*
> Let us strike the *tobera* in good time,
> In good time and with the aid of the Virgin Mother.

After this the singer asks permission to observe the
custom of the *tobera* and proceeds to extol the virtues of
the bride and bridegroom : some of the verses are

---

[1] Manuel de Lekuona : " Las Toberas." *Euskalerriaren Alde*. No.
194.

improvised, but many are similar to those of the wassailing songs :—

> The walnut has a thick shell
> And the bridegroom is a lusty fellow.
> You have chosen a buxom maid
> Daughter of an honourable house.
>
> The bride is a flower;
> She has a laugh on her lips.
> The bridegroom who is betrothed this eve
> Is her equal.
>
> In the month of May the cuckoo sings
> In the garden of the bride;
> Ten angels have entered
> Into the bride's heart.

Each verse is followed by a solo on the *tobera* by the *pikatzaile* and his companion until finally the serenaders are invited to join in the wedding or betrothal supper.

A custom which may have some connection with the *toberak* was observed till recently at Oyarzun (Guipuzcoa). On St. John's Eve the young men used to go out into the woods and cut down a number of young poplars, of which they planted one in front of the church and the others in front of the houses of their sweethearts. All this was done without singing, however, and in the strictest silence and secrecy.

The *erregiñetakoak* are as rare and curious as the *toberak*. Clearly the remnant of a Spring Festival, they are sung on a day in May, when a tree is planted and other rites, pagan in origin, are performed, as thus described by Father Donostia :—

" They choose a young girl and dress her as a Queen. She must be able to remain serious, and not laugh. . . . They seat her on a chair, to which they fasten her arms with ribbons. Sometimes they strew roses round the Queen and decorate her hair with flowers. The women sing to the accompaniment of a tambourine. Every passer-by is called upon to place a contribution in the royal cup. In return they sing to each a verse of which the words vary according to the amount of the gift and the condition of the giver, e.g. :—

> The bean is still in flower
> And has not yet seeded.
> You are still unmarried,
> We will sing you a song.

Those who give nothing are not allowed to escape without a parting shot :—

> In the water there is a big lamprey,
> A seagull falls on it from above.
> This young man who passes by
> Keeps his money in his cupboard."

This chapter would be incomplete if it did not contain some account of the *bertsulariak* or professional improvisers, whose facility and virtuosity are little short of amazing. Nogaret writes :—" There used to be old women, homeless, living on public charity, who wandered from house to house and from village to village. Like troubadours, they were usually made welcome. For not only did they carry news from one family to another, but they passed on gossip about everything that happened in different places. These women composed poems of an infinite number of stanzas, and sang them to audiences which used to gather round during the long winter evenings."

There are no such women nowadays, but in every village there are men whose talents have won them the name of *bertsulari* or *koblari* and who are always ready to improvise a song. When two of them meet at the inn or at some wealthy farmer's well-spread table they engage in verbal combat, singing alternate verses in which each tries to score off the other. Usually their improvisations are forgotten next day, but one such meeting, that between Etchahoun and Otchalde, is remembered and the verses which it inspired are still sung.

In many parts of the country it is usual to include a competition for *bertsularis* in the programme of festivities arranged in honour of the local patron saint. After the *pelote* match, which is followed by vespers, there is dancing on the *pelote* court, and finally two *bertsularis* are given a conventional subject, and a well-filled purse is awarded to the one who is adjudged to be the winner on points. The choice of subjects is wide. Here are one or two: emigrant versus stay-at-home: miller versus ploughman : sandal versus clog.

Not long ago I came upon one of these contests in a Labourd village. The competitors, who had been billed, like boxers or cinema stars, as Mattin of Saint-Pée and Larralde of Louhossoa, were standing on a platform of wooden barrels with their backs to the ball-pitted wall of the *pelote* court. Their theme was the rival merits of land and sea. The crowd drew close in, eager not to miss a word. Larralde, a big burly man, with fair hair, stood upright and confident like the Strong Man at a circus. He started off with a string of commonplaces, sung in a loud voice to a very favourite air :—

When he had finished his quatrain, Mattin, a little wizened man with a wrinkled face and a mischievous

twinkle in his eye, hesitated the merest fraction of a
second.   Then in a cracked voice he sang his verse, and
as he started the fourth line it was drowned by a roar of
laughter from the crowd, quick to appreciate the quip
almost before it was out of his mouth.   Hardly had the
laughter died down when Larralde was off again.   This
time he had the satisfaction of drawing a laugh even
louder and longer.   But without a pause Mattin went
on, in his dry and quavering voice, with his *pince-sans-
rire* smile and his incisive wit.   For a long time honours
were even.   Verse succeeded verse, and each had a sting
in its tail.   There was no moment's interval between the
end of one verse and the beginning of the next, so that it
seemed hardly possible that the singers could really be
improvising.   Yet their theme had only been announced
to them a few minutes before.   At last, however, Larralde's inspiration began to run dry.   His retorts descended to a schoolboy's level of wit, and amid the cheers
of the crowd, Mattin was declared by the judges to be the
winner.   Having felled his Goliath, David leant back
against the wall, quietly chuckling over his victory.

CHAPTER VIII

FOLK-SONG: MUSIC

Aire zahar batean
Kantore berria.
ANON.

A new song
To an old tune.

WHEN, a century or more ago, the literary and musical
world first began to take an interest in folk-song, they
found it difficult to believe that these intensely moving
poems and melodies could possibly have sprung spontaneously to peasant lips. No country bumpkin could
have imagined and perfected the lovely airs of the Celts,
for instance, or such songs as our own exquisite " Sair
Fyeld Hinny " and " Brigg Fair." Peasants were dull,
unimaginative, materialistic folk, scarcely better than the
beasts of the field, and caring for little beyond eating
and drinking. When, therefore, it was proved beyond
doubt that these very peasants had their own literature
and music, less pretentious, perhaps, but no less perfect
in form and deep in emotional significance than those
of cultivated society, the fact seemed not to admit of
any explanation other than that of spontaneous and
collective generation.

One Irish yokel, it was argued, could not have composed the " Londonderry Air," but ten, a hundred, a

thousand Irish yokels could have and indeed had done so. How else could its existence be explained? It was not very clear, however, what the process had been. Did one peasant compose the first phrase, another the second and so on? Nothing so definite. The spirit of the race spoke through the mass of the people, and, all unconsciously, without anyone noticing, a song came into being. Its composer was anonymous, not because his name was not known, but simply because he had never existed as an individual. This theory had the advantage of being so unsubstantial that it was difficult to find any flaw in it. Only relatively solid edifices have flaws. This one eventually collapsed like an airy bubble, and the light of pure reason made people see that some time, somewhere, every song must have been sung for the first time ; and that, whatever its subsequent history, he who first sang it was its composer.

" Folk-song," writes Phillips Barry, " is song alive, a living organism subject to all the conditions and manifesting all the phenomena of growth and change." But in many countries the organism is worn out, and songs of which once there were countless variants have grown old and set in their ways. They have cooled in the moulds into which popular diffusion has poured them and have become standardized by constant repetition.

There can be few places in the world to-day where one may study the birth and growth of song so easily and so satisfactorily as in the Basque Country. Here new songs are born every day, and the old ones, with a few exceptions which seem to have attained their final form, are for ever rising, Phœnix-like, from the flames that rejuvenate and renew them.

The wonderful talent of the Basques for improvisation is probably the principal cause of this great fecundity. At any moment, in the house or in the fields, in the tavern or on the mountain side, a new song will spring to Basque lips. But the question arises : Will this song, at each subsequent repetition, remain unaltered as regards both words and tune ? When the friends of its creator pick it up, or a passer-by, overhearing it, tries to recapture its lilt a few days later, it will inevitably be altered to a greater or less degree. Those who are imperfectly acquainted with it may recall the words and sing them to some other tune, or they may remember the tune and adapt it to other words. They will forget parts of it and fill in the gaps from their own imagination or from their recollection of other songs. Thus when the original singer hears his song again, as in the old game of " Russian Scandal," he may well fail to recognise it.

Although, therefore, every song is originally composed by some definite individual, it does not at once attain its final form. Indeed many songs never do so. One can even say that not until it has been profoundly modified by singers innumerable does it usually acquire the characteristics of a race and so become, in the fullest sense of the word, folk-song.

It is obvious that this participation of the multitude in the formation of a song must influence the melody more than the words. It is difficult to alter verse without making nonsense of it. Furthermore the restrictions imposed by rhyme and metre make any departure from them immediately noticeable, and thereby help the mind to retain verse more easily than melody. The Basque peasant's sense of tonality, rhythm and musical symmetry is naturally much vaguer than his sense of rhyme and metre, and like most folk-singers he usually (and most misguidedly) attaches more importance to the words than to the air of his songs. When the words and tune conflict, therefore, it is always the tune that gives way. But music is a far freer means of expression than poetry, and a melody may be altered and transformed almost out of recognition without losing any of its beauty. In the Basque songs it is often those touches which most obviously cannot have belonged to the original tune, and which, indeed, vary with each individual singer, that lend to the melody its principal charm and character.

If an attempt were made to reconstitute an original tune from its hundred and one surviving variants (and I do not admit that it would be possible to do so), nothing would be gained. For only the skeleton, and not the warm living flesh, would remain. How could one choose any one of the lovely variants of the " Bird in the Cage " (Ex. 16), for example, and proclaim it to be the " normal " version ? And if one attempted to reconstitute such a version by cutting out all the " subtle deviations from the normal that give a continuous, convincing psychological sequence to the development of the lyrical mood," [1] there would remain something infinitely less beautiful and less Basque.

The number of possible combinations of but a few melodic phrases is almost infinite, and, taking into account the newly-improvised poems which, even if they do not give rise to new tunes, necessarily affect the old ones to which they are sung, it is easy to understand that the number of variants is enormous. In 1911, when the *Diputaciones* of the four Spanish Basque provinces offered a prize for the best collection of Basque folk-songs, Azkue and Donostia, the winner and runner-up respectively, submitted between them some 2500 songs. They must have collected at least as many again since that date, and it might be thought that they had exhausted the supply. Yet this is by no means the case. On the contrary, my own experience has been that with the exception of a small number of tunes, say fifty or a hundred, which are now sung over a wide area and in an almost invariable form, I have seldom heard the same variant twice.

Before enquiring into the origins of Basque folk-song it might be as well to dispose of certain pre-conceived ideas on the nature of these tunes, for as many wild statements have been made about Basque music as about everything else that is Basque. Borrow, with his usual

[1] Mrs. Fraser Kennedy, quoted by A. P. Graves in " The Celtic Songbook," p. 84.

erratic self-confidence, writes of " wild and thrilling marches to the sound of which it is believed that the ancient Basques were in the habit of descending from their mountains to combat with the Romans." Other writers have emphasised the gaiety of Basque song, thinking, no doubt, of imported fandango tunes, or, misled by sophisticated *zortzikos* (songs in 5/8 time based on dance music), have described it as intensely rhythmic. In actual fact the airs of Basque folk-song are neither savage nor gay nor rhythmic. Slow and poignant, they are imbued with a sadness which seems to express vague longing and nostalgia rather than sharp sorrow. In place of the tense but rather theatrical emotionalism of the Latins and the harrowing despair of Balkan folk-song, they breathe a spirit of placid and contemplative melancholy, serene and detached as is the Basque himself. The melody wanders about according to its own sweet will, taking little heed of pitch or rhythm. The whole effect is subdued and curiously indefinite and immaterial. One has the impression of something infinitely old and infinitely remote.

The origins of Basque song, like those of the race, are lost in the mists which obscure even the more recent past. It cannot be said with any degree of certainty whether these lovely airs were, for the most part, evolved out of the inner consciousness of the Basque or borrowed from neighbouring peoples. The *pastorales* show that the Basques have a way of adopting art forms not exclusively their own, and, with their intensely conservative spirit, of preserving these forms long after they have been abandoned in the lands of their origin. The point is not of very great importance, perhaps, for the Basques stamp all that they borrow with their own intensely individual imprint, so that whatever its origin it takes on an unmistakably Basque character. The manner is of greater significance than the matter, and their art, in the words of Philippe Veyrin, " mirrors both the most secret depths of the Basque soul and the long succession of external influences which have modified it during past centuries."

Basque folk-song has not remained free from these external influences. On the contrary it has been strongly affected by the music of other races. To my mind the material on which most of Basque folk-song is based was probably borrowed, and indeed the borrowing process is still going on. There is no historical record of a Basque musical tradition dating back to the sixth century as in the case of the Serbs, or earlier as in the case of the Irish and the Greeks. The cultural standard necessary for the growth of such a tradition has never existed in the Basque provinces, and the Basques have never shown themselves to be a creative race.

Yet it is not to be supposed that the Basques never had any songs of their own. Song, it has been said, existed before speech. This may or may not be the case. But it is quite certain that, just as babies croon to themselves before they can talk, every race, however primitive or isolated, will spontaneously evolve some form of song. It will begin with faltering steps, simple successions of notes and brief melodic phrases. These may be similar to or even identical with those invented independently by other races, but their very simplicity is sufficient guarantee of their originality. " Calls to cattle, street and country cries . . . strike one as among the probable beginnings of song," writes Dr. A. P. Graves. " The songs of occupation would seem to be extended instances of these primeval chants. The occupation suggests certain measures ; thus the rocking of the cradle, the blow of the hammer on the anvil, the sweep of oars through the water, the turning of the spinning-wheel, each invites a rhythmic chant, monotonous at first, but afterwards taking on melodic cadences which become tunes."

Such melodies are found in the Basque Country, and of these there is no need to seek the origin elsewhere. They are usually lullabies or nursery rhymes, and it is a happy coincidence that those airs which were born in the infancy of the race should be associated with the children of to-day.   Here is a song for dancing children on the knee :—

Ex. 1.—ARRI, ARRI MANDOKO.

<pre>
Ar - ri   ar - ri   man - do - ko   Sar - ri   I - ru - ña - ra - ko:
Han - dik zer   e - kar - ri - ko?   Za - pat e - ta ger - ri - ko:
Hek   o - ro   nor - en - da - ko? Mu - til   e - der hor - en - da - ko:
</pre>

It consists of a short two-bar phrase on two notes repeated *ad infinitum*.   This is musical thought reduced to its simplest expression, the very germ of music in fact.

The next song, a lullaby, is slightly more complex :—

Ex. 2.—BILIN BALAN.

<pre>
Bi - lin   ba - lan   Ba - le - ra - koak   e - li - zan   Nor da

hil - a?   Ma - ri - a   Lan - da   Zer jan du   bar - da?   Il - har' e - ta

ba - ba   Ho - be - cha - go   bai - tzu - en   Pa - pa e - ta   Ña - ña
</pre>

Here a phrase on three notes which occupies the first two bars is repeated several times in a more or less varied form, sometimes with the addition of a fourth note.

Then by degrees the register, which hitherto has not exceeded that of human speech, is extended, the phrase grows longer and is repeated less frequently.   New themes are invented ; foreign tunes are borrowed and imitated.   The Basques, however, seem to have borrowed only such musical cadences and melodies as appealed to them and as had some affinity with those which they already sang. Everything that savoured of Southern warmth and colour left them cold. They did not lack opportunities of hearing the songs of the Moors and the folk-music of Spain which was so strongly coloured thereby. Yet there is not the faintest trace of this oriental influence in their melodies. On the other hand, two very different forms of music seem to have made a very strong appeal to them, for their imprint on Basque song has been deep and lasting.

The first of these influences is that of plainsong. The Basques were always good church-goers, as even Aymeric Picaud was forced to admit, and it was natural that the splendid Gregorian chants should have affected the songs which they sang at home. Some thirty years ago Charles Bordes collected in the mountains of Soule a wordless melody, said to represent the soaring flight of the buzzard, which is pure plainsong :—

Ex. 3.—Belatsa.[1]

[1] Charles Bordes : " La Chanson Populaire Basque " in " La Tradition Basque."

L

Although the Basques did not imitate the music of their Southern neighbours, they had many opportunities, in the course of their distant expeditions in Northern seas, or while foreign armies were passing through their country, of hearing songs of a different type, more restrained in character than those of the Latin races. To these they did not turn a deaf ear, and there is not only an affinity of mood but often a definite resemblance between Basque airs and those of England, Flanders and Brittany. "Urzo Churia," for instance, is clearly a Basque form of the air "Ah Vous Dirai-je Maman," which is to be found among the folk-songs of several Northern nations :—

Ex. 4

Urzo Churia.

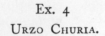

Ah Vous Dirai-je Maman.

The tune of " Iru Damacho Donostiako " (variations on which form the main part of Sarasate's " Fantaisie Basque ") is neither more nor less than a slightly altered version of " The Miller of Dee," and that of " The

Ex. 5.

Iru Damacho.

The Miller of Dee.

Little Brown Jug " has been borrowed for the French Basque song " Kaiku." The Basque mercenaries who

accompanied Edward I on his Welsh campaigns must
have heard Welsh songs, while the commercial and
maritime contact between the Basque Country and
Brittany and Flanders must have been fruitful from a
musical point of view.   When, some years ago, I played
to Alfred Cortot a quiet and delicate air, used as a lullaby,
which I had taken down from a young Basque girl, the
great pianist replied by playing the same sequence of

Ex. 6.—Ama De nean Haurrekin.

notes, in a jaunty march time, as he had heard them sung
by Breton sailors at Quimper.

Another possible source of Basque musical inspiration
is to be found in the marching songs of the pilgrims
to Santiago de Compostella, who passed through the
country in large bands.   I have been told that their
favourite song, the " Grande Chanson de Route," is not
unlike a song which I transcribed at Saint-Jean-de-Luz :

Ex. 7.—Bazterretik Bazterrerat.

The Spanish Basque musician Gaskue was so struck by the resemblances which be believed he detected between the themes of Basque and Celtic folk-song that he had the temerity to prepare an analytical table showing the precise percentage of similarity between the songs of the Basques and those of the Bretons (57 per cent.), Welsh (25 per cent.) and Manx (33 per cent.). Unfortunately, many of the tunes which he quotes are of the commonplace type found in every country, and in other cases the resemblances are purely superficial. The value of his work can be judged from the fact that, finding no resemblances between Basque and Irish or Scotch folksong, he overrides this objection by saying that in these two countries English musical influences have completely displaced the native Celtic melody !

In any case these statistical methods cannot be satisfactorily applied to so spontaneous and elusive a thing as melody, and, where Basque folk-song is concerned, definite resemblances are comparatively rare. Personally I am convinced that if the majority of Basque tunes are ever traced to their foreign sources, those that owe nothing to Church music will be found to have originated in French folk-songs, *chansonettes* and even military marches. Garat, a celebrated Basque singer at the Court of Louis XVI, is said to have acclimatised in his native land many of the popular successes of his day. Yet the Basques have transformed this material almost out of recognition, not only by taking liberties with the rhythm and melodic line, but by a variety of individual touches peculiar to their manner of singing, some of which cannot be transcribed in ordinary musical notation.

This only demonstrates the essential vanity of the scientific method when applied as it was by Gaskue. For if one dissects Basque melodies to examine in turn their tonality, their rhythm and their form, all the elements, in fact, which constitute a tune, one finds no single element definitely exclusive to the Basques. Yet

one has only to hear the song resulting from the fusion
of these elements, seasoned with that undefinable something which comes from the very heart of the singer,
to realise that Basque folk-song stands as a thing
apart.

Most Basque tunes are marked by an unexpected
perfection of form. The musical phrases, unsymmetrical and apparently illogical in themselves, are linked
together with a strong feeling for symmetry and logic.
Sense of form seems to replace sense of rhythm and
tonality, and it is easy to see the stages by which this
sense must have developed. In the beginning song can
have been no more than the monotonous repetition of
a musical phrase. Then, doubtless, the phrase grew
longer and more pretentious or was varied in order to
relieve the monotony of constant repetition. This was
not enough, however, and singers began to interpolate
a completely fresh musical idea between the original
phrase and its repetition. The form thus created is
known as " the primitive rondo form." It can be represented by the formula A B A or A A B A, A standing
for the original phrase and B for the contrasting middle
subject.

So simple a form must have been invented independently in many parts of the world, for it is used for every
kind of music from the songs of remote and primitive
peoples to the Sonata movements of great musicians.
Musical minds have elaborated many more complex
forms, but the Basques have never gone beyond the
primitive rondo form (though they have modified and
extended it in various ways), for it is the best suited to
their verses of three or four lines.

The middle part of the tune is usually distinguished
by a rise in pitch as in Ex. 7 or by a change of
rhythm. In the following example, which is typical of
a number of Basque melodies, the time changes from
3/4 to 4/4 :—

Ex. 8 —FRANTSESA DIZUT SENHARRA.

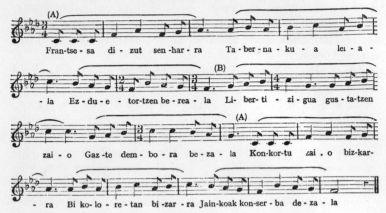

Fran-tse - sa di - zut sen -har - ra Ta - ber - na - ku - a lei - a -

- la Ez -du - e - tor-tzen be - rea - la Li - ber - ti - zi - gua gus - ta-tzen

zai - o Gaz -te dem - bo - ra be - za - la Kon-kor-tu zai . o biz-kar-

- ra Bi ko-lo - re - tan bi-zar - ra Jain-koak kon-ser - ba de - za - la

More rarely the contrast between A and B is heightened by a change of key.

Many songs show interesting and effective extensions and variations of the primitive rondo form. For cadential reasons the concluding notes of A may be modified each time it is repeated. A lovely air without words which I took down in the valley of Bertiz Arana (Navarre) corresponds to a new formula, A A^1 B A^2 :—

Ex. 9.

From here it is an easy step to the forms A A B C, A B C A, A B C B and, in the last resort, A B C D. These forms are all extensions of the four-part formula

A A B A, but there are others based on the simpler form
A B A, such as A B A¹ and A B B (Ex. 6).   Sometimes
each of the three sections is divided and there is a subtler
interbalance of the phrases.   One comes across songs of
which the form is A A B C B D, A B C D E B or, as in
the following example, A B C A C B:

Ex. 10.—Urr'Erreztun Bat.

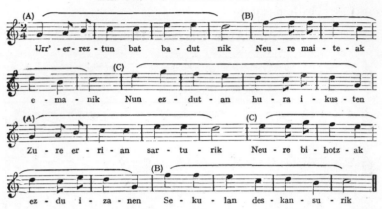

Many Basque tunes are written in the old Gregorian
modes, especially those (on the white notes of the piano)
which have as their tonic D (Dorian mode):

Ex. 11.—Anderea Ideka Dazu.

G (Mixolydian mode):

Ex. 12.—Haltzak Eztu Bihotzik.

Hal-tzak ez - tu bi - hotz-ik Ez gaz - tam- ber - ak e - zur-rik E -
ni - an us - te er - rai - ten zie - la Ai - tu - nen se - mek ge - zur- rik.

and A (Æolian mode):

Ex. 13.—Aire Delizius Huntan.[1]

A - hai - re de - li - zius hun - tan . . .

Such tunes, however, are exceptional, and the majority
are now in the modern major and minor scales. Modal
tonality persists more as an influence than as a concrete
survival, and makes itself felt in the manner of singing
rather than in the actual melodies. The peasants, I
have constantly noticed, do not sing strictly in tune, and
this very fact is responsible to a large extent for the
peculiar quality of their singing. Played on the piano,
even unharmonized, the tunes at once lose much of their
character. This is true of all folk-singing, but especially
so of Basque songs. For a long time I used to think that
this out-of-tuneness was due only to the peasant's faulty
sense of pitch, or to the fact that peasants always sing
in the " natural " scale rather than in the skilfully faked

[1] This air was given to me by M. Lebout, Organist of Saint-Jean-de-
Luz. I believe it to have been collected by Bordes in Soule.

scale of the " Well Tempered Clavichord." Both of
these explanations are doubtless partially true, but they
do not suffice to account for certain peculiarities which
are so constant and so pronounced that some further
explanation seems necessary.

Donostia and I have both found that certain notes of
the scale are affected more than others, and appear as a
result to be about half-way between one semi-tone and
the next. Two factors in my opinion account for these
doubtful notes (which it is convenient to indicate by
writing a sharp or flat above them).

In certain Northern countries peasant singers seem to
have a pronounced dislike for the interval of a semi-tone.
This at least would appear to account for the gapped
scales used in Celtic folk-song. While the Basques do
not use these scales they appear to share the dislike for the
semi-tone, a fact which may account to a certain extent
for their neglect of the chromatic Hispano–Mauresque
music. The " false " intervals are only introduced
where a whole tone is followed by a semi-tone or *vice
versa*, and their effect is to replace these by two equal
intervals of three-quarters of a tone, thus eliminating the
semi-tone, as in the following example :

Ex. 14.—Hartzen Dut Hartzen

Har-tzen dut har-tzen o - fi - zi - u - a   Ya - ti - at ul - hain ba - nu - a

Nu - la bei-tut bi - zi - u - a   oi - an - e - tan kan - ta - tze - ku - a

A - bis hu - nik e - mai-tez e - ta   E - gi - a er - rai - tez ba - nu - a

More even than from any dislike of the semi-tone,
however, these queer intervals seem to come from an

unconscious hesitation between the Gregorian tones and the modern major and minor scales. Sometimes this hesitation results in the alteration by a full semi-tone of certain notes :—

Ex. 15.—Eztut Nahi Ezkondu.

Ez - tut nahi ez - kon - du ez dis - pu - tan sar - tu Ko - men - tu
ba - te - rat se - ro - ra ni - o - a - zu Ez - in zin -
- du - en zin - du - en zu le - na - go de - li - be - ra -
- tu Be - har zi - ne - la se - ro - ra sar - tu Ko - men - tu -
- ak o - ro be - te - ak di - - tu - tzu.

Except for the last phrase, which is in the relative minor, this tune is in the key of E flat. But there are places where the fourth is sharpened and the seventh flattened. Somewhere at the back of the singer's mind is a recollection of the sharpened fourth in the Phrygian mode, and of the flattened seventh in the Mixolydian mode.

More frequently the alteration of the notes is less clearly defined, and, in the minor scale, the peasant singer hesitates whether to sharpen the sixth and flatten the leading note, and eventually sings something between the two as in Ex. 14, where the doubtful notes show Dorian influence. One of my singers has even gone up the scale from E to A, singing neither E F G A nor E F

sharp G sharp A, but dividing the rise of five semi-tones
into three equal intervals of about three-fifths of a tone.
The hesitation between the Æolian mode and the
melodic minor could not be more complete.

More than anything else this tendency accounts for
the remote and primitive atmosphere of Basque folk-song.
Sometimes uncertainty of tonality and dislike for semi-
tones result in the most unusual modulations, as in this
variant of *Choriñoak Kaiolan* :—

Ex. 16.—Choriñoak Kaiolan.

Cho - ri - ño - ak   kai - o - lan   Tris - te-rik du   kan - ta - tzen

Dia - la - rik han zer jan zer e - dan   Kam -po - a du   de - si - ra - tzen Zer -

- an   Zer - en   Li - ber - ta - te - a   zoin - en   e - der den.

Here the singer, a Labourd farmer's wife, probably
intended, on the word *Zeren* in bars 8 and 9, to sing F sharp
G, but, striving unconsciously to avoid the semi-tone, she
jumped from F sharp to G sharp.   Being then unwilling
to sing the semi-tone in the place to which she had shifted
it, she went from G sharp to A sharp instead of to A and
found herself forced to continue in the remote key of
G sharp minor.   In another song a drop of a whole tone
where a semi-tone is expected leads to the drop of a whole
tone in key.

Basque singing has two other strongly defined characteristics.   One is that of *portamento*, or scoop from one
note to another, which is, I think, partly the cause and
partly the result of an uncertain sense of pitch.   The
other, more unusual in peasant singers, is a very general

and pronounced tendency to sing sharp and to rise gradually in pitch throughout the course of a song. Madame d'Elbée, who plays the organ in Guéthary church, tells me that she is often obliged to transpose her accompaniment a semi-tone higher once or even twice in the course of a hymn in order to keep up with her congregation.

The most interesting aspect of Basque folk-song is probably that of rhythm. In this connection there remains yet another popular illusion to be shattered, namely, that of the *zortziko*, or song in 5/8 time. This type of tune is immensely popular in Bilbao and San Sebastian, where it is produced wholesale by musical hacks entirely lacking in inspiration or originality. For some reason or other the *zortziko* has come to be regarded as the only typical Basque song and has found its way into the works of such composers as Sarasate, Albeníz and Pierné. The inevitable dotted crotchet which appears in almost every bar gives all *zortzikos* a strong family resemblance. The tune of *Gernikako Arbola* is neither better nor worse than most :

Ex. 17 —Gernikako Arbola.

The origin of the *zortziko* (which is genuinely used by the Spanish Basques for their folk dances) has never been satisfactorily established. The first printed collection of Basque songs, that of Iztueta, does not contain a single tune noted in 5/8 time, while many of the tunes which appear in later collections (that of Sanesteban, for instance) in 5/8 time are noted by Iztueta in 6/8 or 2/4. Indeed the majority of *zortzikos* could be so noted, although to-day they are played in an unmistakable 5/8. "Gernikako Arbola," for example, would lose very little by the change :—

Donostia has found two songs in *zortziko* time printed in the eighteenth century, so it is possible that Iztueta noted the tunes incorrectly. Nevertheless it seems probable that 5/8 time is a mannerism which has crept into sung music within the last hundred and fifty years. Should this be the case, it may have originated, as Gaskue thinks, in a tendency in instrumentalists to hurry the second half of the 6/8 bar, a tendency which might well have been deliberately exaggerated, or it may have been borrowed from Castille, the *ruedas* (round dances) of which have been taken down by Olmeda in 5/8 time. At all events the *zortziko* is neither natural nor grateful to the voice. It is very difficult to sing accurately, and it can safely be said that not a single sung *zortziko* of the dotted crotchet type is popular in origin. Apart from anything else, the melodic line is sufficient to show this.

It is occasionally necessary to take down in 5/8 time genuine folk-songs which have the appearance of a natural 4/8 time in which one beat, either the second or the fourth, is unnaturally accentuated and prolonged. This is a good example:

Ex. 18.—Arotzak Erran Dio.

A - rot-zak er-ran di - o be - re an - dre- a - ri Hur - tu be - har di -
na - gu e - kar-ri sain-du o - ri Gi - zo - na zer- ta't zo - az Be -
- ka - tu da o - ri Et - zio - na - gu er - ra -nen se - ku-lan ni - ho - ri.

This air could certainly be sung in 4/8 time without affecting the vocal line, although it would thereby lose much of its distinction.

In taking down Basque songs one is constantly obliged to vary the time signature, not necessarily because the rhythm itself varies, but rather because the rhythmic structure of the phrase is such that the ordinary methods of musical notation are incapable of expressing it, just as they are incapable of expressing the finer shades of tonality.   The phrase has a lilt which is extremely difficult to recapture and an independent life of its own which ignores the conventions and restrictions of art music.   Sometimes therefore it is simpler to omit the bar-lines and punctuate the tune as in Ex. 9 and Ex. 11. In other songs it seems better to keep the bar-lines and change the time-signature as often as may be necessary, as in the following example :—

Ex. 19.—Konbeni Diren

Kon- be - ni di -ren ber -su ber - ri - ak Es - pli - ka -tu al ba -ni - tza A - di-

- tu -tzi - a   de - se - o   du -en   ba - ti   e - man di - ot   it - za   Mun -du-

- ko   bai -le   soi - nu   e - der -rek   en - ga - ña - tu - rik ga - bil - tza   Gu - re

a - ri - men kal - te - an da -tor   gu - re mun - du - ko bi - zi - tza.

The rhythmic structure of the phrase is greatly affected by the words of the song to which it is sung.   The Basque has a poorer sense of the rhythm of music than of that of speech, and should the words not fit the tune exactly, then the tune is bound to suffer.   He inclines strongly to giving to each note its syllable and to each

Mi - la zor -tzi e-hun e - ta ho - goi e - ta lau - ri - an Mi-sion-

- e bat - zan da Bi- dar - te - ko her - ri - an. . . etc.

II.

Jain - ko - ak oi e - gun on a - dis - ki - de - ak e -

- ta par - ti - ku - lar - zki es - pos mai - te - ak . . etc.

Indeed there are singers who allow the rhythm of the
music to disappear within the subtler measure of the
words, the finer shades of which can never be rendered
by musical notation.

No description, even aided by musical examples, can
convey to the reader the manner of Basque song, which
is so much more individual than its matter. Its essence
can only become apparent to the listener who has an
opportunity of hearing the songs sung by the Basques
themselves, without any instrumental accompaniment
but with all those delicate shades of tonality and rhythm
which none but the unsophisticated singer can give to
them.

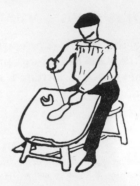

CHAPTER IX

FOLK-TALES AND PROVERBS

Zahar hitzak, zuhur hitzak.
(BASQUE PROVERB.)
Old words are wise words.

THE widely scattered Basque farmhouses have a great air of independence, standing firmly planted amid their ricks of dried bracken, their maize fields and their vineyards. This appearance is not wholly misleading, for in the main they are self-supporting as regards both their material and their social needs. In some of the wilder parts of Soule there are farms, four hours on foot from the nearest village, whose inhabitants seldom leave their homes more than once or twice a week, on Sundays and market days.

For society they are thrown back upon themselves. This largely accounts for the special relations which exist between the inhabitants of one isolated farm and their nearest neighbours. The *lehen auzo* or " first neighbour " is regarded almost as a relative. From his house the best man and chief bridesmaid are chosen if there is a wedding in the family. The relationship is even more strongly emphasised when death visits the house. If a member of the family is dangerously ill the *lehen auzo* is told as soon as the priest has been summoned and before even the near relatives are called in. He follows the priest into the house, and from that moment

160

he and his family see to the urgent work of the farm, and make all necessary domestic arrangements. Should the illness end in death the *lehen auzo* is informed before the bell is tolled, for were he to learn the news by any such indirect means he would be mortally offended.

At the funeral it is the neighbour nearest in the direction of the church who carries the Cross at the head of the sad procession, which, clad in great black mourning capes, winds slowly along mountain paths.[1] His other duties towards the bereaved family "are or were to lift a tile from the dead man's house to let out his soul,[2] to drop a cross of hot candle drops on his chest to verify his death, and to burn a wisp of hay as the coffin passes the threshold. The smoke rising to heaven is symbolical of the soul, the ashes falling to the ground symbolise the mortal remains."

The winter evenings seem long in these outlying farms. There is no inn where the men may foregather, and the women have no cronies near by with whom they can exchange the gossip of the neighbourhood. But they have one great resource—their store of legend. The whole family congregate round the wood fire. Someone lights the spluttering candle of solidified resin, and uncouth shadows are thrown on the whitewashed walls and massive cupboards of sombre walnut. A small boy is sent to invite the *lehen auzo* with his family and the rest of the evening is spent in the telling of folk-tales, humorous or eerie, which have been handed down from generation to generation and which form part of the treasured traditions of the race.

This is the right setting for fairy tales : wild weather

[1] In many villages in the Spanish provinces the funeral must follow an appointed route, not necessarily the shortest, known as *andabide* or *gorputz-biri*. This route may even pass through the interior of houses on the way. Any path by which a funeral has once passed is regarded for this purpose as a right of way and cannot be fenced off.

[2] Ormond : *op. cit.*, p. 77. This is still done at a number of villages. Alternatively it is not unusual for the window to be thrown open for the same purpose.

M

outside, gusts of wind that drive the smoke down the
chimney, dark shadows in the corners of the room and
the respectful expression of those earnest faces, lit up by
the ruddy glow of the fire. One finds oneself almost
ready to believe that even now the *sorgiñak* are off to the
Sabbath on the heights behind Zugarramurdi, or that at
any moment a gaunt *lamiña* may come slithering down
the chimney. Amid tense silence *Amachi* begins some
such tale as this :—

" As is usual in this world there were once two mule-
teers. Each owned seven mules, and having laden their
mules they went to market. They made a wager, and
he who lost the wager would lose his seven mules. One
of them won the wager, but not fairly, for he cheated the
other. But the latter gave him his mules. He who
lost the wager was the father of a family and burdened
with children. He did not know what to do nor how to
return home for the great misfortune which had fallen
on him. This is what he did. In order to reach his
house he had to cross a bridge, and he stood on the bridge
trying to make up his mind to cross it. At midnight
he heard voices. The witches were arriving at the
Sabbath. Some said *fuzta* and some said *huzta*. They
danced there to the sound of the tambourine. When
they had disported themselves for a time one of them
said : ' The lady of such-and-such a house has been ill
for seven years, and nothing they can do can cure her :
but they do not know that to cure her they must find a
piece of holy bread in the mouth of a toad at the church
door and give it to the lady to eat.' Our muleteer
listened carefully to what the witch said, and when they
had left the place he went home. He said nothing to his
wife about having lost the mules. He threw on a cloak
and went off. He walked and walked towards the house
of the lady until he came upon it. At last he came to
the place he was seeking and asked if they would give
him shelter. He said that he was on foot and begged
them to let him stay there a few days. They agreed.

A Biscayan Farm.

Houses in Basse-Navarre.

He learnt that the lady of the house was ill and that they
had tried every means of curing her. But all in vain.
Our muleteer said : ' Let me see her too : perhaps I can
do something.' They brought him in, and he examined
the lady carefully and said to her : ' Do you remember
that seven years ago you contemptuously threw away a
piece of holy bread at the church door ? ' ' Yes,' she said.
' Well, since then, a toad sits there with the piece of holy
bread in its mouth, and until you eat that bread you will
not be cured.' Her husband went off at once with the
muleteer. Just as the latter had said they found the toad
under a stone with the bread. They took it and brought
it home, cleaned it carefully and gave it to the lady to
eat. And she was cured at once. You can imagine
their joy." [1]

These fireside tales of the Basques are a strange hotch-
potch of legends which must have reached them from
East and South and North, and—who knows—perhaps
even from the West, if there is anything in the Atlantis
theory! For the themes are all borrowed,[2] and only
the settings and the picturesque details are definitely
Basque. One may recognise scraps of Greek mythology,
and memories of pagan divinities which the Romans
never knew, intermingled with miracles and parables
from the Gospels, magic gifts from the Arabian
Nights, fairies from the Far North, Cinderella, Tom
Thumb and all the *dramatis personæ* of Perrault, Grimm
and Hans Andersen. This motley variety of themes
is given individuality and uniformity by a multitude of
local allusions and touches of realism.

[1] I have translated this story almost literally from the Basque as I
heard it narrated by Joseph Suhas of Arcangues . . . through Professor
Urtel's gramophone.

[2] Wentworth Webster quotes as a particularly interesting example
the Basque story of Juan Dekos (Jean d'Ecosse). This is neither more
nor less than a variant of a Highland tale " The Barra Widow's Son,"
in which the hero is called Iain Albanach or John of Scotland (" Basque
Legends," p. 146). This is, however, the only example which could
possibly justify Webster's contention that Basques and Celts borrowed
folk-tales from each other.

All the details of setting or action are filled in with the conscientiousness and the care of a Van Eyck " Adoration." Just as in the paintings of the Cuatrocento the life of Christ is translated into terms of the Middle Ages, so in the Basque tales " the reader must not be startled by the introduction of maize and tobacco, of cannon and gunpowder, of dances at the *Mairie* and the use of the Guillotine in stories which, perhaps, originally told of the movements of the stars, of the wars of the forces of the atmosphere, of the bright beauty of the rising or of the gleaming glory of the setting sun." [1]

This delight in and conscientious attention to every traditional point of detail testify to a naïve belief in the essential truth of these tales. Webster remarks that " the problem of reconciling religion and science presents itself to their minds in this strange guise . . . how to reconcile these narratives with those of the Bible and the Church. The general solution is that they happened before the time of which the Bible speaks or before Adam fell. They are *lege zaharreko istorriguak*—(histories of the ancient law)."

Here is a story which breathes implicit faith, not only in the existence of powers of evil and their ascendency over human beings, second only to that of God, but in the truth of the events it narrates :—

" One evening, long ago, at the house of Inhurria at Beyrie, they were stripping the maize stalks. Suddenly the servant noticed that he had left his two-pronged fork in the fields : as he needed it for breaking up the maize stalks, he exclaimed out loud that he would give ten sous to whomsoever brought it in.

" A young girl, a servant of the house, attracted by the money, told him at once that she would go and look for it. So she went out. Hardly was she outside the door when the manservant regretted his promise and, being in an ill-humour, began to swear saying : ' May the Devil make off with her.'

[1] Webster : *op. cit.*, p. ix.

" At that very instant they all heard a heartrending cry in the distance, and barely a moment later, close by the chimneys of Inhurria, no higher, passed the poor young girl, who had been seized and carried off into the air. And as she passed she threw the fork into the house saying : ' There is your fork. As for me, because of my cupidity, I am seized and carried off into the air by the Evil One.'

" The people of Inhurria and all their neighbours set off in pursuit of the poor girl. All out of breath they reached Larceveau, and there they stopped unable to go any further. But from Larceveau the people of that village set off in turn to follow the young girl.

" The girl was swept ever onwards, borne through the air, and so came to a point beyond Mendive opposite Saint-Sauveur-d'Iraty. Recognising the holy church she began to cry : ' Holy Saviour, I pray Thee, have pity upon me.' And hardly had she spoken these words when she alighted gently on the ground, delivered out of the hands of the Evil One." [1]

The Abbé Barbier, who took down this legend, adds that at Beyrie (near Saint-Palais) the house of Inhurria can still be seen, and that he was shown the field where the fork was left. In a small building close by the chapel of Saint-Sauveur there is a wooden image of the girl with the fork in her hand, and every year when the *Fête-Dieu* pilgrimage to Saint-Sauveur-d'Iraty takes place the people of Beyrie send representatives to pay their respects to the image. Moreover, each year they send (by postal order !) a special contribution to the chapel. Could conviction be carried further ?

Many of the stories resemble that of " Chaindia " in that they describe the adventures of human beings with the forces of evil, which are for ever struggling to obtain possession of human souls or bodies, and can only be vanquished by the power of Christ. These tales seem to be symbolical of the eternal struggle between the powers

[1] " Chaindia," *Gure Herria*, 1921.

of good and evil, and of the triumph of Christianity over the pagan gods and forces of nature. Virtue is usually victorious, and, in place of our conventional ending : " And they all lived happily ever after," many of the Basque tales end : " And if they lived well they died well."

The first of these supernatural powers is the Devil himself, or, as he is usually called, the Red Master, who is shown in ceaseless pursuit of the human soul. I will leave to another chapter the tales in which he appears at the Witches' Sabbath, but there is a curious story of how he was tricked by Axular, Curé of Sare and author of the " Guero " :—

" In olden times they say that there were three brothers called Axular. All three were remarkable men, especially one of them, the youngest. One day they agreed among themselves to take lessons from the Devil. In talking to the Devil the eldest Axular asked him what he would charge for teaching them. The Devil, never a fool, answers : ' I will teach you for a year and a day, and after a year and a day he who is the last to leave my cave is the one whom I shall keep in payment. Will that suit you ? ' ' That will suit us very well.'

" The very next day they began to learn : and, since they learnt everything, a year and a day passed as though by magic. The last night our three brothers did not sleep a wink ; the one hoping that he would not be the last ; the other also hoping that it would not be he ! The two elder brothers went so far as to agree on a way of leaving the youngest to be the last. The youngest slept lightly too, thinking things over. All three got up early next morning. As early or earlier the Devil had risen and was very much awake. Suddenly without a word all three rushed for the opening of the cave, the two eldest in front and the youngest behind them. With arms outstretched the Devil made a grab at the hindermost : ' My payment, the last one of you ! '

" Young Axular jumped outside and, pointing to the shadow behind him, exclaimed : ' Take that one : he is the last.' So the Devil seized the hindermost, and it was the shadow of Axular that remained in his arms. And ever after Axular was the man who lived in the world without a shadow."[1]

In another story we find Axular taking flight on a demon's back, and, like the hero in a Wild West film, arriving at Rome in the nick of time to save the Pope from falling into the power of the Evil One.

In addition to the Devil the supernatural powers are represented in Basque folk-lore by various monsters such as the *Tartaro*, the *Basa Jaun* and *Basa Anderea* and the *Lamiñak*.

The *Tartaro* is neither more nor less than our old friend the Cyclops of the Odyssey, although Chaho prefers to see in him the Basque's ancestral recollection of the orang-outang. In the words of Webster he is " a huge one-eyed giant, occasionally a cannibal, but not without a rough bonhomie when satiated with food and drink. Intellectually far below the feebler race of mankind he is invariably beaten in his contests with them, notwithstanding his enormous strength : he loses all his wagers and is generally lured on to commit involuntary suicide." He is often accompanied by an *olano*, a mythical monster described as " an animal of some sort which serves the *Tartaros* like a dog but is terrible to other people."

The *Basa Jaun*, or " Wild Man," sometimes called *Ancho*, differs from the *Tartaro* in that he has two eyes instead of one. He is a cross between the classical satyr and the ogre of our fairy stories, with his cave in the mountains or in the depths of the forest, his taste (and nose) for human flesh, his giant strides, his limited intelligence. The imaginative Chaho describes him as being " tall and of prodigious strength : his whole body is covered with a long smooth coat resembling hair : he walks upright like a man, surpassing the stag in agility." His foot leaves a circular imprint on the ground. Sometimes he may be successfully duped, but at other times divine intervention is necessary for the rescue of his

---

[1] " Axularren Itzala," *Gure Herria*, 1925.

victims. At all times, however, a handful of salt is a
sure protection against him, as it is also against the
Lamiñak.

Sometimes the *Basa Jaun* shows himself willing to give
his victims a sporting chance, as in the tale of the *Basa
Jaun* of Musculdy who promised to let a shepherd go
free if he could state three irrefutable facts. The peasant
replied : " People say that when the moon is full night
is as clear as day. That's not true. Then people say
that maize bread is as good as wheaten bread. That's
not true either." The *Basa Jaun* approved these two
answers, and the peasant pondered a moment. Then
he said : " If I'd known you were here I shouldn't have
come." The *Basa Jaun* was unable to deny the truth
of this, so he let the lad go.

The *Basa Anderea*, or " Wild Woman," is a very
variable quantity and never plays a leading rôle. She
is the daughter of the *Basa Jaun*, and is sometimes portrayed as a siren assiduously combing her golden hair.
Sometimes she is a kind-hearted soul who hides those
who have strayed too near her father's cave, or helps his
captives to escape.

In Spain the *Basa Anderea* tends to be replaced by
Mari, also known as the Lady of Anboto or of Muru-
mendi, according to whether her residence is thought to
be the Cave of Anboto or the summit of Mt. Muru-
mendi, where she is usually to be found making golden
pots or spinning golden thread. The Lady of Anboto,
who commands all the witches, flies over the mountains
between her own cave and that of Aizgorri, but seldom
descends to the towns and villages. On the day of
Holy Cross, the Guipuzcoan peasants climb up to her
cave and solemnly pronounce a blessing on her, for they
believe that if they catch her at home she will have no
power to loose storms upon them for the rest of the year.
A farmer from near Oñate declares that he once set eyes
on her. First he heard a noise, he said, like a squadron
of cavalry at the trot. Looking up he saw that his neighbour's house appeared to be on fire. To his astonish-

ment the flame, which was like a blazing bracken stack with a very long tail, moved away, passed through the air above his house and disappeared in the distance. The heart of the flame was the *Anbotoko Dama*.

The *Lamiñak* seem to be a cross between the fairies of Celtic legend and the English goblins or Scandinavian kobolds. Colas sees in them the descendants of the Phœnician *cabires*, who were the protecting genii of mines. Their name is thought to be derived from the *lamiæ* of the Ancients with which, according to Tertullian, the little Roman children were frightened into obedience, as are the Basque children with the *Mamou* to-day. But whereas the *lamiæ* were wholly evil, the *Lamiñak*, apart from one or two lapses from virtue, are on the whole benevolent.

Every evening before they went to bed, runs one story, " the people of Bazterretchea used to leave a bowl of milk by the fireside together with crusts of toasted maize bread and some bits of bacon in the grease that was left in the pot. When they were all asleep the *Lamiñak* came down the chimney and *murtcha-murtcha* with little grunts they fell to, until they had finished all the scraps by the fireside. Then they made off again up the chimney. The next day the people of Bazterretchea used to find all the manure spread, the gutters cleaned, the fields ploughed and the maize-stalks stripped.

" One night they went to bed without remembering to put the bowl of milk and the scraps of bacon and toasted maize bread by the fireside, and the *Lamiñak*, deeply hurt, went to another village far, far away, and never returned to help in the work of Bazterretchea." [1]

---

[1] *Lamiña Bazterretchean, Gure Herria*, 1925.
      Cf. " . . . tells how the drudging goblin swet
         To ern his Cream bowle duly set,
         When in one night ere glimpse of morn
         His shadowy Flale hath thresh'd the Corn
         That ten day-labourers could not end,
         . . . And crop-full out of dores he flings
         Ere the first Cock his Mattin rings."
                      (MILTON : " L'ALLEGRO ".)

The benevolence of the *Lamiñak* seems to be largely a matter of cupboard love, for they are dependent on human beings for certain services and are generous only when these are rendered. No *Lamiña* can die until a human being has said a prayer for his soul, and in one tale a female *Lamiña* is shown as requiring the services of a human midwife. Such services are usually rewarded with gifts which, like fairy gold, have a way of melting into thin air. Sometimes the *Lamiñak* are definitely malevolent. In the story of the " Black Hen " there is a wicked *Lamiña* whose wife tries to atone for his misdeeds. They have power to make away with young babies unless there is somebody to say *Dominichtekun* (*Dominus tecum*) when the infant sneezes. Sometimes, like the Devil, they are not averse to speculating in human souls, but they can always be driven away if necessary, by ploughing the land near their habitation with a pair of fawn-coloured yearlings born on St. John's Day.

Needless to say the appearance and habits of the *Lamiñak* differ considerably in the different stories. Their size in particular seems to vary. In one or two legends they appear to be as big as human beings, while in others they are as small as the orthodox fairy, that is to say, almost small enough to pass through the holes of a sieve. They live in caves in the hill-side or beneath the river-bed under a bridge. There were *Lamiñak* dwellings at the top of Mondarrain, a mountain just behind Itxassou, whose curiously rocky summit is visible as far away as the coast. Another colony lived beneath the lovely stone bridge of Utsalea, which spans the Nivelle at St. Pée. In their mysterious dwellings the *Lamiñak* guard untold treasure, but although human beings may be taken to visit them underground and may even partake of their wonderfully white bread (a Celtic touch) they may take nothing away, or their return to earth becomes impossible. They themselves do not appear on earth except at night, and they must be gone by cock-crow. This fact coupled with their marvellous building powers is responsible for a tale which is particularly popular, probably because it depicts a Basque getting the better of them by a ruse :—

"Long ago the Lord of Laustania, finding his house too poor, asked the *Lamiñak* to build him a new one. The *Lamiñak* said that they would do so willingly, and finish it before the first cock-crow after midnight, on condition that he gave them his soul as salary. This the Lord of Laustania promised to do.

"That very night the *Lamiñak* began their work and laboured hard with the fine red stone of Arradoy (a mountain near Ispoure in Basse-Navarre). They passed the blocks of stone from one to another whispering : 'Here, Guillen,' 'Take this one, Guillen,' 'Give it to me, Guillen.' So the work went on apace. The Lord of Laustania watched the *Lamiñak* from the ladder of his hen-house with a certain little grey packet in his hand. The *Lamiñak* came to the last stone. 'Here, Guillen,' 'Take it, Guillen,' 'It's the last, Guillen.' At that very moment the Lord of Laustania set fire to a big lump of tow, and a great glare shone in front of the chicken-run so that a young cock, scared into thinking that the sun was up before him that morning, began to crow 'cock-a-doodle-doo ' and to beat his wings.

"With a shrill cry the last *Lamiña* threw into the depths of the river the stone which he held in his hands. 'Accursed cock ! ' he cried, and disappeared into the ravine with his companions. Nobody has ever been able to recover that stone from the depths. It remains there beneath the water, for the *Lamiñak* grasp it with their claws, and the mansion of Laustania has lacked a stone ever since." [1]

In Navarre a similar story is told concerning the bridge of Torre-auzo, which is said to have been built by the Moors on condition that the Lord of Torre-auzo gave them his daughter if the work were completed by

---

[1] "Laustaneko Jauregia," *Gure Herria*, 1924.

daybreak. As they were about to lay the last brick the Lord of Torre-auzo himself imitated the crowing of a cock, and the Moors, thus easily duped, made off, leaving the bridge complete save for one stone.[1] The confusion between the *Lamiñak* and the Moors is curious. In one of the stories in the Cerquand collection the narrator, Jean Sallaber of Aussurucq (Soule), speaks of " wild men, handsome, big, strong and rich, who were called Moors and whom Roland drove out later. Every week the Moors and the *Lamiñak* used to meet in the field of Mendi to amuse themselves." The *Lamiñak* are sometimes confused also with the " Gentiles " concerning whom many of the same stories are told. These " Gentiles " are described by the peasants as a race of giants who disappeared with the introduction of Christianity, but they are more probably a dim folk memory of forgotten pagan divinities. Their name is connected with various freaks of nature such as caves, giant stones and imprints in the rock, and the construction of some of the older churches is attributed to them. Curiously enough a number of recently discovered dolmens and cromlechs were already known to the peasants as " Gentile houses " and " Gentile gardens." There is also a series of rather quaint stories concerning the wanderings of Our Lord and Saint Peter through the Basque Country. These tales are not absolutely peculiar to the Basques, for similar legends have been found in Spain, in Brittany and other parts of France, and even so far afield as Czecho-Slovakia. Yet they are thoroughly Basque in character, blending incongruity and humour with essential reverence like Negro spirituals, and breathing throughout a sound matter-of-fact morality. They are full of reminiscences of Gospel stories and parables, mixed up with such familiar ingredients as trios of sons who set forth to make their fortunes, magic gifts and all the paraphernalia of ancient fairy tale.

[1] " Anuario de la Societad de Eusko Folklore," 1921, p. 9. " Torre-auzoko Zubia."

The rôle played by Saint Peter is very curious. He is by turns a sort of Sancho Panza, getting a double drubbing of which half was intended for his Master; an honest duffer puzzled by the apparent injustice of Our Lord's acts and having to have the moral carefully explained to him; the impetuous Peter of the New Testament, cutting off the heads of a woman and a devil who were quarrelling (a reminiscence of the centurion's ear, perhaps); and then, when reproved by Our Lord, he becomes the buffoon once more, putting the heads on again the wrong way round (which, says the narrator, explains a lot of things). Yet he is essentially good-natured, for in one tale Christ tells him that a party of reapers will garner as many quintals of corn as they make sheaths, and Saint Peter hangs behind to tell them secretly to make small sheaves and many of them. When an old soldier (the *Jean Soldat* of French legend) is offered the alternative of an inexhaustible sack or a place in Paradise, Saint Peter hastily prompts him to make the right reply.

I will quote in full two of these tales, in both of which Saint Peter gets the worst of it :—

" One day Our Lord Jesus said to Saint Peter, ' I will give you a horse if you will recite the Paternoster from beginning to end without letting your thoughts wander.'

" ' Bah! That's an easy thing you're asking me to do.'

" And, *tarrapatan*, Saint Peter began : ' Our Father, Which art in Heaven, Hallowed be Thy Name. . . . But, Lord, will the horse have a saddle or not ? '

" And Jesus said : ' Now you will get neither saddle nor horse.' "[1]

" At that time our Lord Jesus was still wandering through *Eskual-Herria* with Saint Peter. One day it was very hot and they were thirsty. Passing near a spring, Jesus having asked her, a woman gave them a

[1] " Don Joni Petriren Zaldia," *Gure Herria*, 1923.

drink of water in a very dirty glass. After drinking the water Jesus gave the glass back to the woman, saying : ' God give you a good husband.'

" When they had gone further they grew thirsty again, and another woman gave them a drink of water in a very clean glass. Jesus said : ' God give you a slovenly husband.' When they had gone a few steps Saint Peter said rather crossly to Jesus : ' Lord, what had You in mind when You promised a good husband to the first woman who was so dirty and a slovenly husband to the second who was so clean ? ' And Jesus replied : ' The first woman, even with a good husband, will have enough work to do : the second will be capable of keeping even a slovenly husband in order.' " [1]

In 1764 there was born at the mountain village of Amezqueta in Southern Guipuzcoa a child who was destined to earn peculiar fame. This was Fernando Bengoetchea, better known as *Pernando Amezketa*, a shepherd and *bertsolari*, who became famous throughout the province for his quick wit, his apt retorts often in rhyme and his ingenuity in getting something, usually to eat, for nothing. What Nasreddin Hodja is to Turkey, Pernando is to the Guipuzcoans, and many exploits are attributed to him for which he was probably never responsible.

One day Pernando is said to have been asked to eat with the village priest. His son, however, was not included in the invitation. But he did not despair of getting a free meal for the latter and told him to wait outside the priest's house until he was summoned in. Before the meal began Pernando announced that he himself would say grace instead of the priest. His host consented with a smile, for piety was not usually Pernando's strong point. So Pernando began : " In the Name of the Father and of the Holy Ghost. Amen." " But what have you done with the Son ? " asked the priest. " Oh he's outside," said Pernando, " I'll call him in

[1] " Emazteki Zirtzila eta Emazteki Garbia," *Gure Herria*, 1922.

at once." So the priest had no option but to feed Pernando's son as well.[1]

It is the custom in every Basque village for a farmer who kills a pig to make presents of sausages to all his friends, including, of course, the village priest. One day the priest of Amezqueta sent for Pernando. " I want your advice," he said. " I'm going to kill my pig, but it's only a little one, and if I give away sausages to all those who have given theirs to me there will be nothing left for me. What shall I do?" Pernando pondered a moment; then he said: " You must hang the carcase from the first floor balcony of your house for all to see, and at ten o'clock to-night you must cut it down and hide it. Then you must raise a tremendous hullaballoo and pretend that your pig has been stolen." The priest agreed to this, and at ten o'clock that night Pernando took care not to be far away, so that when the priest started his noise he was the first on the scene.

" They've stolen my pig! They've stolen my pig!" cried the priest.

" Bravo, that's the way!" said Pernando encouragingly.

" But they really have stolen it!" protested the priest.

" Splendid," said Pernando. " You're a wonderful actor! Why I almost believe you myself!"

And well might Pernando believe him, for it was he who had stolen the pig only half an hour earlier.

Like every other race the Basques have innumerable proverbs. One might add that more than other races they respect them and are guided by them, one of their favourite sayings being: *Zahar hitzak, zuhur hitzak* (Old words are wise words). Basque proverbs are not strikingly original. Indeed it is unlikely that they would be so, for these ancient truths (or fictions) are the common property of mankind. Although many are obvious

[1] G. Muxika : " Pernando Amezketarra. Bere Ateraldi ta Gertaerak," p. 50.

translations from other languages some succeed none the less in expressing an old thought in a new and often diverting manner.

Here are a few taken mostly from the collections of Garibay (1596) and Oihénart (" Atsotizac eta Refranac," 1657):—

" A fish and a guest go bad on the third day and must be thrown out."

" I command the dog and the dog commands his tail."

" Satisfy a dog with a bone and a woman with a lie."

" Gold, women and linen should only be chosen by daylight."

" When the fox starts preaching look to your hens."

" When the shepherds quarrel the cheese shows it."

" One eye is sufficient for the merchant, but a hundred are scarcely enough for the purchaser."

Proverbs are usually laconic, and since Basque is an extremely concise language these examples are still more brief and forceful in the vernacular. It will be noticed too that they are very different from our own sanctimonious sophisms about honesty being the best policy and virtue its own reward. Basque proverbs are strictly practical and objective, if not actually cynical. Some indeed are worthy of La Rochefoucauld. The author of the " Maximes " would not, I think, have disowned these :—

" There is never trust without loss."

" Ancho is very charitable : he gives a poor man the trotters of a stolen pig."

It is difficult to determine the age of these proverbs. One of them seems to go back to the days when fire was the object of a household cult:

" A house without fire is a body without blood."

Another clearly dates from the days when bread was baked among the embers :

" Every man pushes the ember near to his own bread."

The earliest adage that can be dated with any certainty is this :

" Rodrigo de Villandran,
    Here to-day, there to-morrow."

Rodrigo de Villandran was a 15th century adventurer, whose brutality was such that a contemporary Gascon author quotes his name as having passed into proverb during his own lifetime.

There is also a whole series of proverbs fastening particular qualities on to certain villages and districts. " At Cambo," they say, " tongues are more active than brooms." The foreign visitor might not be surprised to hear the people of Sainte-Engrâce described as " smugglers and savages," but he would surely be astonished to learn that local opinion stigmatises the inhabitants of Saint-Jean-de-Luz as " drinkers of chocolate " and those of Biarritz as " sorcerers."

The children have a number of catch stories like the oriental " Another little ant brought another grain of sand," or our own " I'll tell you a story of Jack and Manory." Here is one :—

" As often happens in the world there were two crows. One had a long tail and the other had a short one. If the one that had the short tail had had the long one then my tale would have been long, but it had the short tail so my tale is short."

It is the children, too, who take the greatest pleasure in riddles. These are introduced by a special formula. One child begins : " *Zuk papaita nik papaita*, you a riddle, me a riddle ; I know a little thing, you perhaps know another. What is it ? " Then comes the riddle : " A short skirt and a long leg ? . . . A bell " : or " That which looks at the house when it goes to the woods, and looks at the woods when it returns to the house ? . . . The horns of a goat." Some of these riddles take the form of poetical comparisons ; for instance, " a white mare in a stream " is the flour in the kneading trough ; and the mist is " a white horse which rides from crest to crest."

N

CHAPTER X

FOLK-DANCE

Haurrak ikasazue
Eskuaraz mintzatzen,
Ikas' pilota eta
Oneski dantzatzen.
ANON.

The child must learn
To speak Basque,
To play *pelote* and
To dance properly.

THE Basques have always been famous dancers. To the strains of flute and trumpet Strabo's Vascones danced after drinking " either together or singly, competing amongst themselves as to who should leap highest and fall on his knees with most grace." Silius Africanus describes a war-dance performed by Hannibal's Galician recruits which bears a strong resemblance to the Guipuzcoan *Brokel-dantza* of to-day.

Among more recent writers Le Pays wrote in 1659 that in the Basque Country " a child knows how to dance before it can call its father or its nurse by name," while the Comte de Guiche, who was sent to Labourd in 1671 to suppress an insurrection, found that " during the Carnival it is impossible in the *Pays Basque* to do aught but dance." There is also that popular and frequently misquoted allusion of Voltaire to " *les peuples qui demeurent ou plutôt qui sautent au pied des Pyrénées et qu'on appelle*

Vasques ou Vascons." Abel Jouan, who accompanied Charles IX on his voyage through the South of France in 1557, describes how the Queen of Spain came to meet her brother at a place called " *Endaye ou Boyvie* " (Hendaye or Béhobie), and then spent eight days at Saint-Jean-de-Luz, where she took great pleasure in seeing " girls dancing in the Basque manner, who are all shaven, those that are unmarried, and who have each a tambourine shaped like a sieve on which are many bells, and they do a dance which they call *les Canadelles* and another called *le Bendel.*"

Nothing more is known of the *Canadelles* and the *Bendel*, for these early writers give no detailed description of such dances as they mention. De Lancre, the witch-hunter, alone is a happy exception. In the " Table de l'Inconstance des Mauvais Anges et Démons " he refers to the Basques' " love of the dance, which they practise both night and day with that same tambourine to which they are accustomed to dance at the Sabbath." He also mentions " the evil and pernicious proximity of Spain whence come all the . . . Morisques, Cascata, etc." Some of de Lancre's victims told him that they attended the Sabbath merely for the pleasure of dancing, and his account of their dances indicates that he is describing what he saw with his own eyes, if not at the Sabbath, then perhaps in front of the church of Saint-Jean-de-Luz. He even mentions the musicians by name : Gastellure, the little blind man of Ciboure, Ausugardo of Hendaye and Ausuperomni, playing the violin, tambourine, flute, trumpet and " that long instrument which they place on the ground and beat with a little stick." [1] Then follows his description of the three kinds of *branle* danced at the Sabbath. The first he calls *à la Bohémienne* and the second *à sauts.* The third appears to be a kind of faran-

---

[1] The text uses the word *col.* I have followed Commandant Boissel in translating this by " on the ground." But may it not rather mean round the neck ? The rest of the sentence is equally obscure : " . . . *posent sur le col, puis s'allongeant iusqu' auprès de la ceinture ; il le battent auec vn petit baston . . .,*" etc. This might be the *ttun-ttun*, but it might equally be some kind of zither or xylophone.

dole. All three dances can be identified with those danced in the Basque Country to-day, and de Lancre seems to have been able to describe with a fair measure of accuracy what he himself saw. It is all the more regrettable that he showed such credulity in accepting the evidence of others who testified, for example, to having seen "the lady of Martibalserena dancing with four toads, one clothed in black velvet with bells on its feet sitting on her left shoulder, another without bells on her right shoulder and, in each fist, another like a bird, these last three unclothed and in their natural state."

Two sorts of dance are performed in the Basque Country to-day : recreational dances which are usually of recent and extraneous origin and may be danced by men and women together : and dances of a spectacular or ritual character performed only by men. The *sauts basques* do not properly fall into either of these categories, but although their performance nowadays is principally recreational their origin is more probably ritual. All that need be added in this chapter is that they are danced in all three French provinces and in Navarre, where they are known as *mutildantzak*.

There is relatively little of interest in the recreational dances, which include the quadrille and the farandole. These are charming to watch at a country wedding or village *fête*, but there is really nothing to distinguish them from the quadrilles and farandoles of the rest of France. Occasionally a touch of originality is imparted to the latter dance when the first and last dancers hold bouquets in their hands and perform more complicated steps as do the peasants of Serbia and Greece.

Similarly there is nothing really Basque about the *fandango* and its *suite* the *ariñ-ariñ* which *Syndicats d'Iniative* and organisers of pseudo-Basque *fêtes* have conspired to impose on the foreigner as original Basque dances. The *fandango* is both spirited and graceful, but as danced in the Basque Country (there is an Andalusian dance of the same name) it is no more than a variant of the Aragonese *jota* and was in all probability introduced into France by Aragonese workmen who crossed the frontier in large numbers during the nineteenth century. Although it is said to have been danced in the Spanish Basque provinces a hundred years earlier, there is every reason to believe that it did not reach its present home of Ciboure until about 1870.[1] Even now it has scarcely penetrated into the villages of Basse-Navarre, and in Soule it is unknown.

In Spain one of the principal dances of the recreational type is the *aurresku*, which, however, is quite definitely Basque, and, moreover, is partially spectacular, not to say erotic in character.[2] It can be described as a complicated farandole in which both men and women take part. The leader of the line, who himself is called the *aurresku* (first hand), sends four men to fetch from among the spectators the maiden of his choice. He then dances in front of her and finally carries her off into the dance. This performance is repeated by the *atzesku* (last hand), who brings up the rear, and by one or two of the best dancers. The *aurresku* and the *atzesku* then take it in turns to direct the complex evolutions of the long chain until the end of the dance. The invitation to each lady is danced to this beautiful air:

Ex. 1. *Very slow.*

etc.

---

[1] Cf. Philippe Veyrin : " Le Fandango." *Bulletin du Musée Basque,* Nos. 3 and 4, 1927. Veyrin quotes Webster as having written in 1904 :—
" I remember quite well having heard said some thirty years ago : ' The *kaskarrots* of Ciboure are beginning to dance the fandango. They have learnt it from the Spaniards, and the others have learnt it from them. The real Basque dances are now completely forgotten.' "

[2] It proved too much for the rather delicate susceptibilities of the English Folk Dance Society, who prevailed on the Basques to omit it from their programme at the Lyceum Theatre and Albert Hall in November 1927.

It will be noticed that there is nothing Basque, and indeed nothing " folkish " about this tune, which has rather the sophisticated grace and delicacy of an eighteenth century *Andante*. It may well have been composed by some Court composer, for there are but few original airs in the music of Basque folk-dance. Not only are most of the themes borrowed, but, unlike the song-tunes, they have not been absorbed and transformed by the people to the point of being almost or wholly unrecognisable. This need not appear unnatural. For whilst all sorts of people sing, only professional or semi-professional musicians play the *chirula* or the brass instruments which have superseded it in many villages. Sometimes, even, there are regular dynasties of *chistularis*, like the Amezuas of Berriz, who have been musicians for two centuries. Now your professional musician has a special outlook of his own. First of all he has a definite *repertoire* of pieces which, in many instances, he commits to paper and which will never be modified by either himself or his successors. Secondly, a misguided sense of professional pride will lead him to seek out novelties for his hearers' delectation and to introduce sophisticated tunes from abroad. The consequence is that, thrilling and exciting as are these airs when played on the pipe and drum or tabor in the accentuated 5/8 or 7/8 time which, in Spain at least, has become traditional, there is no real musical interest in the commonplace cadences which they derive from their original models. Glancing through them in the collections of Iztueta,[1] Azkue,

---

[1] The full title of Iztueta's work, published in 1824 and 1826, is : " Notice or History of the most memorable dances of Guipuzcoa, with the ancient airs and words in verse and also with instructions for dancing them properly. A useful and very necessary work in order to preserve the innocent amusements of the Guipuzcoans and the customs so cherished by the aboriginals of Spain, distinguished by their distinction (*sic*) and the purety of their habits, of which the author is Don Juan Ignacio de Iztueta, born at Zaldivia, loyal town of Guipuzcoa, etc." In spite of the title, the first edition appeared without the airs, which, for some reason, were forbidden by the censor. They were printed in the second edition, however, and have recently been reprinted by the *Eskual Ikaskuntza*.

Donostia and others, one is struck by their extreme
banality. Foreign tunes are necessarily accompanied by foreign
instruments and in the Spanish provinces one hears the
Galician bagpipes, the accordion and a peculiar pipe called
alboka, derived, no doubt, from the Hispano–Moresque
albogón (shawm ?). This instrument, which survives
only in the Guipuzcoan Goierri and in one or two remote
villages of Vizcaya, consists of two reeds, one with five
holes and the other with three, set on a small wooden
frame and made fast at each end with wax to a hollowed-
out ram's horn. One of these horns, used as a mouthpiece, contains two smaller reeds leading into the larger
ones. The *albokari* takes a deep breath and then blows
into the mouthpiece, using one reed as a drone and the
other as a pipe. The effect is that of a very shrill
bagpipe.

The dances themselves fully atone for any lack of
distinction in the tunes. Those which are spectacular
and ritual in their origin have kept some of these characteristics down to the present day. The *fandango*, the
aurresku, the *farandole* and the *sauts* are looked upon as
everyone's property, but the Sword Dances of Guipuzcoa
and Vizcaya and the *kaskarotak, volantak* and *maskarada*
dances of the French provinces are only performed by a
chosen few, who from childhood are trained to execute
their difficult and intricate steps. These young men are
called *dantza-tchikiak* and *ezpata-dantzariak* in the Spanish
provinces and *pimpiriñak* (butterflies) in the French
Basque villages. Their teachers are the *maîtres de danse*
who live in the towns and larger villages, men such as
Bernard Elgoyen of Tardets, Faustin Ventaberry of
Ispoure and Pujana of San Sebastian. Their dances are
not a mere diversion in which the public take part, but,
like the Satan Dance, a spectacle at which they assist
with the critical eye of the *aficionado* (" fan "). Moreover, although some of them are now danced at village
fêtes and on other special occasions, the majority are

associated with the Carnival, as are sword dances throughout Europe, a fact which probably indicates that their
origin is to be found in the ritual of the Spring Festival.
It is a well-known fact that the Early Churches,
despairing of eradicating pagan practices among their
flocks, preferred to adapt them to religious ends. By
absorbing them into ecclesiastical ritual they preserved
them intact whilst consigning to oblivion their original
purpose. In this way the Church of Rome adopted and
consecrated Basque dances, which are doubtless of pagan
origin and may date from the earliest infancy of the race.

In 1682, on the day of Corpus Christi, fifty-one dancers
performed the Sword Dance before the High Altar at
Oyarzun (Guipuzcoa), and a century later Larramendi
could still write that " the Sword Dance is for grave
occasions such as Corpus Christi processions." His
account vividly reflects the essential reverence of the
ceremony. The dancers, he writes, " enter in silence
without shouting or noise other than their music ; nor
do women take part in the dance, nor any other thing
which might make it less worthy of the Church or of the
presence of the Lord." Nevertheless the Church seems
to have had doubts of the propriety of such rites. As
early as 1539 the Bishop of Calahorra prohibited
religious dancing, and during the seventeenth and
eighteenth centuries many customs which had hitherto
been tolerated were attacked as savouring of idolatry.[1]
Not only religious dances but even the innocent *toberak*
and *erregiñetakoak* were suppressed on the pretext that
they gave rise to civil disturbances. Yet Saint Michael
still dances in the Good Friday procession at Andoain
and Ernani (Guipuzcoa), and there are villages in Basse-
Navarre, where on the two Sundays after Corpus Christi

---

[1] In some cases this policy seems to have been introduced at a still
earlier date. A municipal decree of the city of Vitoria (Álava) dated
September 28th, 1486 (quoted by Miguel de Rodriguez-Ferrar in " Los
Vascongados," Madrid, 1873), alludes to the " fine of sixty maravedis
incurred by those who performed sword dances, owing to the disturbances
and bloodshed which they caused."

the " National Guards," who are young men clothed in old-fashioned uniforms, dance in procession into the church and there, with the utmost gravity and fervour, execute their complicated steps before the High Altar, as do the Seises in the Cathedral of Seville.[1]

At Lequeitio, on the sea-coast of Vizcaya, the picturesque custom of the *Katcha-ranka*, or Dedication of the Coffer, is still observed. On St. Peter's Day (June 29th), the members of the Fishermen's Guild elect their officers for the ensuing year and march round the town in procession bearing a vast wooden chest containing their archives. On this coffer there used to stand in bygone days a statue of Saint Peter, who was escorted by two fishermen dressed to represent Saint John and Saint Andrew. After the last of the ceremonies Saint Peter was taken down to the sea and beaten as an earnest of what he might expect should he fail to provide good catches of fish. Latterly the Church has prohibited this manifest disrespect towards the saint, and Saint John and Saint Andrew, whose conduct was too often of an unseemly nature, have been banished from the procession. Nowadays Saint Peter is replaced by a dancer wearing a top-hat and carrying a red banner worked with Saint Peter's keys to denote his origin. Balanced precariously on the coffer, he is carried through the streets on the shoulders of eight stalwart fishermen and dances before the houses of the Mayor and notables of the little town.

The most interesting dances of the Spanish provinces are the Sword Dances of Guipuzcoa and Vizcaya, which are performed on special occasions by traditional dancers, the best of whom are to be found at Renteria and Berriz.

The Guipuzcoan dancers are dressed quite simply in white shirt and trousers with red béret, sash and *espadrilles*. Their dance consists of a series of figures, all of which closely resemble one another. They arrive to the tune of a lively march and then line up two or four

---

[1] To judge from Blanco White's " Letters from Spain " (1825) the Dance of the Seises was a sword dance only a century ago.

abreast, standing stock still while their leader dances alone before them leaping high into the air and embellishing his step with high kicks and complicated variations. When he has finished the dancers repeat the step in its simplest form, which nevertheless includes entrechats, pirouettes and, most astonishing of all the " galley " of English morris, a difficult step in which the dancer stands on one foot and twists the other in the air. All this is usually done to a slow and heavily accentuated 5/8 rhythm such as the following :—

Ex. 2.

but now there comes a curious phrase in a slower time :—

Ex. 3.

Till this moment the dancers have not moved an inch from their places, but suddenly the pace quickens and they begin the figure of the dance. They " hey " with a light running step or change places with great bounds in such a way that the line is now sideways and now endways. As they meet one another they clash the instruments they hold, which vary according to the names of the figures :—

(1) *Arkuak* or *Arcos Grandes* : resembling great croquet hoops four or five feet high, decorated with red and blue rosettes and ribbons.

(2) *Makil tchikiak* or *Palitos* : little sticks with which the dancers tap, behind and before or under each leg as in " Shepherd's Hey " and many another Morris Stick dance.

(3) *Makil aundiak* or *Palos grandes* : bigger sticks.

(4) *Ezpata-dantza* or Sword Dance : the figure from

which the whole dance takes its name. The dancers hold a sword in each hand the hilt covered with a clean handkerchief. This is the only figure in which they do not tap with one another.

(5) *Brokel-dantza* or *Escudos* : small hoops. There is also an obsolescent figure called *Zinta-dantza* (Girdle Dance) which is neither more nor less than a Maypole dance.

The Biscayan Sword Dances, performed only in a few villages round Durango, are somewhat similar, but are danced to a livelier rhythm and a more vigorous step. The morris-like figures reappear with the pirouette and a double galley, and the whole effect is more thrilling and more martial. The dancers are dressed like the Guipuzcoans with the addition of bell pads round their trouser-legs like the " ruggles " worn by morris men. Preceded by a Standard-bearer, they arrive to the tune of a Processional, at the end of which seven of them suddenly crouch down on one knee while the eighth sweeps the standard round and round so that it swirls low over their bent heads. The *Zortzikoa* and *Ezpata Jokua* which follow are both danced with swords, but the *Makil Jokua* is a variant of the Guipuzcoan *Makil Aundiak* danced with heavy clubs.

In the *Banakoa* the dancers are drawn up in double file while each of them in turn comes forward to execute a solo full of amazing high kicks in which the body remains stiffly poised while the entire foot and ankle appear above the level of the head. As soon as each soloist moves forward to begin his step the next in turn comes spinning out of the ranks to take place behind him. This is the tune :—

Ex. 4.

The *Binakoa* is similar except that the dancers come forward two at a time, while the *Lauakoa*, which is danced in fours, has figures which strongly resemble those of the morris. The performance works up to a tensely dramatic climax in the last figure, the *Chonchanguillo*, at the end of which two dancers suddenly hoist their captain into the air and hold him like the stiffened corpse of a sacrificial victim, horizontal and motionless above their heads. The *Chonchanguillo* is done only at Berriz and Yurreta, each of which claims to have originated it. The Berriz men hoist two dancers and have done so for at least fifty years, but the tradition remains that originally only one was hoisted.

Another of the Spanish Basque dances, the *Jorrai-*

dantza, or Hoe-dance, is related to the Sword Dances.
The performers line up two by two with hoes in their
hands and advance and retreat with a hoeing motion to
this catchy little tune:

Ex. 5.

Then comes the slower phrase of the Sword Dances,
during which a dark-clothed figure appears and crouches
down between the two files, bearing on his back a huge
leather wineskin. He is said to represent the Devil
tempting the men from their work. But his wiles are
vain. The dancers tap with their hoes in the same way
as they tap with their sticks and hoops in the other
dances, and on the last beat of each phrase they bring
the hoe down with a thump on to the wineskin.

In Labourd bands of dancers form in the villages at
Carnival time and wander about the countryside, dancing
as they go. They call themselves *Kazkarotak* and their
dance the *Kazkarotak Marcha.* The use of this name in
connection with dancing is most intriguing, for, although
it is usually stated that the *cascarots* of Ciboure and
Ispoure are a cross between Basques and Gypsies, there
is also a theory that they are the descendants of Moors
expelled from Spain at the same time as the latter. The
majority of the Moors left Spain by the South, but some
came North and took ship to Morocco from Bordeaux,
so that a few may well have remained in the Basque
Country. " The appearance of the Cascarot population," writes Miss Violet Alford, " is far more Moorish
than Romany. Their skins are brown, their eyes are
large and flashing, and their faces oval without the
strongly marked cheek-bones of the gypsy." Now
Hérelle cites Duvoisin as stating that the " dance of the

Cascarots is . . . the *morisque*," and himself adds that
" little bells used to form part of the conventional costume
of the Moors " (*e.g.* at Lyons in 1578), which is interesting, for the word " cascarot " comes from the Spanish
cascabeles (bells). If the *cascarot* folk are indeed a relic
of the Moors we find that the names of the English morris
(Mauresque) and Basque *Kazkarotak Marcha* are in
effect the same.[1]

The Labourd dancers are dressed in white, with sash,
sleeve-knots, zigzag trouser-braid and fluttering ribbons
of red and blue. The béret is red with a white tassel
and the trousers are nearly always hung with bells.
Their Captain, who will probably wear a uniform coat of
scarlet and gold, bears a flag. The *kazkarotak* often
carry decorated sticks with which they tap like the
ezpata-dantzariak of Spain. At Uztaritz, Miss Alford
saw them accompanied by " two or four men dressed in
red skirts and Basque shawls " who are " decorated with
ribbons, wear a leather belt with small cow-bells attached,
and, on their heads, a high erection made of bent lathes,
a mirror flashing in front." These men-women are
called *marikak* or *kotilun-gorriak* (red skirts). Some
forty or fifty years ago the Carnival procession in a
Labourd village was a much more pretentious affair.
The dancers were preceded by a Lord and Lady dressed
in the Basque notion of finery, and in addition to the
kazkarotak there were a number of *besta-gorriak* (red
waistcoats), masked figures in red uniforms. If the
spectators were lacking in respect to the Lady, who was,
of course, a man in disguise, the Lord brandished his
stick in impotent fury while the *marikak* restored order
with the little whips or cows' tails which they still carry
to-day.

There are similar men-women in the *Cavalcades* or
dance processions of Basse-Navarre. They are called

---

[1] The Sword Dance of the island of Korčula (Curzola) in the Adriatic
is called the *Morisca*. There are two Kings, a white and a black, the
second of whom is eventually killed.

THE DANCE OF THE VOLANTS.

A CAVALCADE AT ASCARAT (BASSE-NAVARRE).

basa-andreak (wild ladies) and are exotic figures clad in rich robes of many-coloured silk with bright shawls and long black hair crowned with a queer headdress profusely decked with flowers or goose feathers. They dance in company with the *kazkarotak*, the pick of whom, six or eight in number, wear tall mitres of scarlet and gold and are called *volantak* (flyers). Their step, called *Volantak-dantza*, does not differ essentially from the *Kazkarotak Marcha*.

In addition to the dancers the procession always includes a number of other figures. Some of these may be found in an ordinary *Cavalcade*, but they are most numerous at the performance of *tobera-mustrak* or acted charivaris. These are farcical " shows " which may be either the culminating point of weeks of nocturnal " rough music," or the spontaneous manifestation of village malice or disapproval. In either event these farces are always based on a real incident which has taken place in the village ; so much so, indeed, that it is not unknown for the protagonists to be present in person. A typical scandal which provoked *tobera-mustrak* at Ester-ençuby in 1926 concerned a man who deserted into Spain during the war and, profiting by an amnesty, returned to the village to marry a widow whom, to make matters worse, he maltreated. In 1929 the Spanish authorities prohibited at the last moment *tobera-mustrak* which were being prepared at Valcarlos at the expense of an unwelcome suitor who had been set upon and beaten by the lady of his choice and her sister. The prohibition was unavailing, for the performance was held at Arnéguy in French territory, although all the participants were heavily fined on their return to Spain.

When a village has decided to organise *tobera-mustrak* a rough stage is set up in the centre of the village or on the *pelote* court as for a Pastorale. The whole morning is devoted to a procession which may travel as far as fifteen or twenty miles and of which the participants fall into five groups. First of all there are the actors in the

farce, those who are to represent the villagers whose
conduct is satirised, accompanied by a Judge and Lawyers
to try them and an Usher whose rôle is that of a Fool or
Jester.   Then there are the dancers, from twenty to
sixty of them, Wild Ladies, *kazkarotak* and *volantak*
with scarlet ribbons, gold braid and little blue and red
sticks like miniature barbers' poles.   Another group is
formed by a Horse-guard and Foot-guard with their
Captain, Lieutenant, Standard-bearer and Drum-major,
and by Gendarmes and skirted *sapeurs* in cocked hats
and tall black busbies of lamb's wool faced with mirrors
and surmounted each by two tall feathers.   At Ascarat
in 1930 the *volantak* wore bérets, the *sapeurs* had borrowed

firemen's helmets and the Wild Ladies wore little girls'
pink frocks, veils and long red tresses.   The next group
consists of carnivalesque figures of every type, including
a Lord and Lady dressed in smart modern clothes and a
couple of *giranteak*, cardboard women ten feet high
with straw hats, pink veils, diminutive bodices and
enormously long skirts through which peer the faces of
the men who carry them.   Last of all come a disorderly
horde of beggars and sluts, known as *zirtzitzak*, some of
whom seem to be intended to caricature the more respect-
able figures who have preceded them.

The play, which is never committed to paper, is
improvised by a local *bertsolari*, usually by Martin Larra-
mendy of Saint-Michel, who, however, will not consent
to lend his services unless he is satisfied that there are

good moral grounds for the performance.   It invariably
takes the form of a mock trial, preceded sometimes by a
sort of Greek chorus of *bertsolariak*, who acquaint the
audience with the details of the scandal.   Sometimes,
on the other hand, the protagonists, or rather those who
play their part, re-enact on the stage the events for which
they are to be tried.   When the trial begins the Judge
listens to the speeches for the prosecution and defence
and then despatches a mounted messenger ostensibly to
gather fresh evidence but in reality to afford a pause
during which the *volantak* dance or a farcical interlude
is played.   Again and again the Judge, who pretends
to be confused by the conflicting evidence, sends out
his messengers, and during one of these intervals there is
often a curious little episode in which the Usher is accused
of some petty offence, makes off on a donkey and is
pursued by the gendarmes at full gallop and shot.
Another frequently performed interlude consists of the
wholesale trial and sentence of the unruly *zirtzitzak*.
At the end of the play the Judge pronounces a humorous
sentence, for the accused are invariably found guilty,
and a final dance concludes the programme.

In Soule *tobera-mustrak* give way to *asto-lasterrak*
(donkey-rides).   In Ancient Greece a woman convicted
of adultery was sometimes made to ride through the
streets backwards on a donkey, and this custom persisted
in Soule till a hundred years ago.   Nowadays, however,
it is the villagers and not their victims who ride the
donkeys and who, clad in a variety of disguises, parade
outside the homes of the guilty persons.   At Larrau
the traditional occasion for this practice is after Mass on
Whit-Sunday.   The term *asto-lasterrak* is also used by
extension to denote what Hérelle calls *farces charivariques*,
farcical comedies of which the plots are always similar
in origin to those of the *tobera-mustrak*.   Although the
characters are given fictitious names the performance of
these farces is forbidden by the authorities, principally
on account of the Rabelaisian quality of their humour.

o

But, just as for *tobera-mustrak*, this prohibition is often evaded in an ingenious manner. Permission is sought for the performance of a serious Pastorale and the farce is sandwiched into it. *Astyage Roi de Perse* or *Alexandre* is cut down so as to permit of the interpolation of *Petitun et Petik Huni* or *Ardéatine et Ludovina*. Sometimes the *tragérie* and the farce are welded together, and the characters of *Roland*, for example, hold conversation with those of *Recoquillard et Ariéder*.

Asto-lasterrak are staged and acted in the same manner as Pastorales, and the only dance associated with them is that of the Satans. The most interesting dances of Soule are those of the *Mascarades* which might be described as a ballet grafted on to the remains of a mumming-play. The dancers, who vary in number between twenty-five and eighty, are divided into two groups, the " Reds," or *les Beaux*, and the " Blacks." For this reason *Mascarades* are always spoken of in the plural, since there are, strictly speaking, two of them.

The " Reds " are headed by the five principal dancers who are called *Enseñaria, Kantiniersa, Gatuzain, Zamalzain* and *Cherrero*. The first of these is the Standard-bearer. He is usually older than the rest and is dressed in black cloth with white braid. The *Kantiniersa* or *Cantinière* is the Souletin equivalent of the *marika* of Labourd. This man-woman wears a blue coat braided in a herring-bone pattern with silver and gold, a small white apron and a red skirt. On her head is a blue straw hat with a flat brim and a big bow. She is a comparatively modern figure, for it is only forty years since she superseded the *Bohémienne*, or Gypsy-woman, a rôle which was suppressed for its obscenity. The *Gatuzain*, or Cat, wears the scarlet tunic and yellow breeches of a dancer. His béret is white and he holds a wooden trellis which springs out on the lazy-tongs principle and is well-suited to his rôle of Jester.

The most beautiful of *les Beaux* and invariably the best dancer is the *Zamalzain*, or Horseman, who wears the

LES BEAUX DANCING BEFORE A BARRICADE.

koha, the tall flowery headdress, and the scarlet tunic of the dancers' costume. Strapped about his waist is the hobby-horse, an oblong wooden frame, brass-studded, decked with ribbons and draped with scarlet cloth and a white lace flounce down to the dancer's knees. The ridiculous little head, like that of an ostrich rather than a horse, is harnessed with a miniature silver chain in guise of reins.

The hobby-horse is by no means peculiar to the Basque Country, for he is still to be met in one or two English villages where the old traditions have not died out, such as Padstow and Abbots Bromley. He is, or was, a familiar figure in France and Germany, and I have seen him in the streets of Athens at Carnival time, dressed in bolero and *foustanella*, prancing and pirouetting to the sound of pipe and drum. There seems little doubt, too, that he was once to be found all over the Basque country. As recently as 1926 he was brought out at Saint-Jean-Pied-de-Port, and he used always to dance at Pampeluna during the celebrated festivities in honour of San Fermin.[1]

He was thought to have disappeared for ever from the Spanish provinces until Miss Alford and I discovered that at Lanz, a village on the further slopes of the Col de Velate, he runs through the streets for the last three days of Carnival in company with a Giant, a Man-woman and a mysterious being called *Mil Ochin*, whose legs are clad in sacks stuffed with grass. The *Zaldizko*, as the Lanz hobby-horse is called, is shod on the third day and finally slain with a musket shot fired into the air.

The Soule hobby-horse is preceded by the *Cherrero*, who sweeps the ground before him with a horsehair tail on a stick, like those used by the sweepers of English

---

[1] The importance of the Horse in folk-lore and mythology can hardly be overestimated. In parts of Basse-Navarre when the peasants meet on November evenings to strip the maize they are visited at midnight by a " White Mare " enacted by two men under a sheet. It is not difficult to see in this an animal representation of the Corn Spirit.

Morris and Sword Dance. *Cherrero* means "swine-herd," but this dancer is no more a swineherd than the *Gatuzain* is a cat. He wears a dancer's costume with black velvet breeches.

The five principal characters are accompanied by a number of *kukulleros*, scarlet and white attendants on the horse, and *manichalak*, leather-aproned blacksmiths bearing the tools of their trade. The " Red " mascarade is completed by the inevitable *Jauna* and *Andrea* (Lord and Lady) and a *Laboraria* and *Etchekandrea* (Peasant and Housewife). The Lord is resplendent in dress clothes and a top-hat, with a blue ribbon across his chest and a sword at his side. His Lady is clad in white with a white veil. The Peasant is dressed like the Standard-bearer, with a *makhila* (Basque pointed stick) in his hand, and his wife is in ordinary female attire. At Laguinge in 1930 she wore a béret and a jumper.

The " Blacks " are as dingy, dirty and ragged as the " Reds " are bright and clean. They include *kauterak* (tinkers), *tchorotchak* (knife-grinders), *kherestuak* (horse-gelders) and *buhameak* (gypsies), these last for no known reason being dressed in flowing garments of coloured cretonne and armed with wooden swords. The " Blacks " used to have their own Standard-bearer, Hobby-horse and *Cherrero*, who parodied the " red " dancers, but these and a number of other characters have disappeared from the *Mascarades* within living memory.

This double troupe of dancers is formed early in the New Year in more than one village of Soule. For a few weeks they practise their steps. Then, as Lent approaches, they are invited to perform in surrounding villages, and on one special day they all meet at Tardets, where they go through their performance together. *Mascarades* cannot, however, enter any village without an invitation. This tradition is most strictly observed, and I have heard of only two cases in which it was broken. On one such occasion the inhabitants of the invaded village hemmed in the dancers so closely that they were

unable to dance : on the other they solemnly " burned
the traces " of the invaders with straw, an ancient and
mortal insult.   The last performance, on Shrove Tuesday,
is in the dancers' own village.   The following day they
put on their mourning clothes, and with mock tears and
lamentations they burn an effigy of Carnival.

When they are invited to a neighbouring village the
two *Mascarades* march out in full array, the one separ-
ated from the other by the musicians, who play a traditional tune called *Maskarada Marcha*.   The receiving
village places " barricades " in the way of the oncoming
troupe.   These barricades used to consist of a rope drawn
across the road, but now they are usually formed by two
or three men armed with bottles and glasses.   There
may be one barricade or a dozen : but tradition dictates
that they shall only be crossed in a particular manner.
The musicians strike up a special air.   The principal
figures dance up to the barricade one after the other,
and pass to the other side, where a glass of wine awaits
them.   Then the " Blacks " burst rowdily through.
When the dancers have passed the last barricade they
make for the village square or the *pelote* court and celebrate
their arrival with a *saut basque*.   Then they re-form their
procession and visit the Mayor and other local dignitaries,
dancing in front of their houses.

All this is extraneous to the actual performance, which
does not take place till the afternoon.   It falls into two
parts ; the *bralia* or *branle*, danced by the " Reds " alone,
and the *fonctions* in which the " Blacks " figure as well.
When everything is ready the " Blacks " clear a space
by the simple expedient of running a cart round the circle
of spectators, and the principal " Reds " dance a *saut
basque*, after which they choose girls from the receiving
village to be their partners in the farandole which follows.
Laughing and struggling the girls are dragged into the
circle, and there follow the three parts of the *bralia* danced
in honour of the Lord and sometimes repeated in honour
of the Peasant.   They consist of a Gavotte performed by

the *Cherrero*, Cat, Hobby-horse and *Cantinière*; the *Branli Haustia*, a series of solos by the Standard-bearer and the four dancers of the

Gavotte, who in turn go through all the elaborate steps of the Satan Dance before passing out of the circle under a handker-chief held by the Lord and his partner; and, lastly, the *Kakoil-latoia* (Snail-dance), a simple chain-dance in which the line, directed by the *Enseñaria*, winds in and out in an ever-narrow-ing circle. At one point the Standard-bearer breaks the chain between the Lord and the Lady, and leads the line him-self before restoring it to the Lord. He then does the same thing with the other end of the line which is led by the Peasant, and the dance culminates in a *pas de trois* for the Standard-bearer, Lord and Peasant.

The first of the *fonctions* is the *Godalet Dantza*, or Wine-glass Dance. A glass half full of wine is placed on the ground, and the principal " Reds " begin to dance round it. In turn they leap over the glass with double and triple *entrechats* and yet contrive not to kick it over. The crowning point of the whole performance comes when the *Zamalzain*, whose " horse " prevents him from seeing either the glass or his own feet, mounts upon it on one foot, describes the Sign of the Cross with the other, and then with a mighty bound springs clear. Woe to him if, as very rarely happens, he spills a single drop of the wine, for his reputation as a dancer will be sadly diminished.

The *fonctions* of the Knife-grinders, Tinkers and Gypsies are clownish knockabout scenes, and the Hobby-horse is again the central figure of the only other *fonction* of real interest. Dancing and pirouetting, he enters the circle accompanied by the *Cherrero*, Cat and *Cantinière*

and followed by the Blacksmiths. The latter pursue
the Horse who, for some time, eludes them. To entice
him the *Cantinière* offers him oats in her apron, and it is
only through the combined efforts of the Smiths, Tinkers
and Gypsies that he is at last caught and shod. But his
troubles are not yet over. The gelders then enter the
circle, and after many futile attempts the Horse is again
caught and forced this time to submit to the most
humiliating of operations. All his strength seems to
leave him and, exhausted, he staggers round the circle
supported by those who have outraged him. Gradually,

however, his strength returns to him. He draws himself
up and begins to leap higher and higher into the air
until, " aided by his retinue who take him beneath his
arms, the final leap is so prodigious that it becomes a
veritable hoisting and for an instant he appears in all his
splendour high above the heads of the crowd." [1]

After the last of the *fonctions* the inevitable *sauts
basques* conclude the spectacle, and the dancers return to
their own village, passing the barricades with the same
scrupulous ritual as before.

A number of writers have discussed the origin of the
Mascarades. Led by Chaho, some have seen in them a
picture of the feudal life of Soule, in which the Lord

[1] Violet Alford : " The Basque Mascarades," *Folk Lore*, April 1928.

and Lady of the Manor make merry with their serfs and domestic animals. This interpretation is manifestly absurd. Apart from the fact that the feudal system was never general in Soule, it leaves unexplained many significant details of the performance as well as the numerous points which it has in common with the dances of other lands. Nevertheless Hérelle subscribes to it, albeit rather half-heartedly, indicating the mediæval *Sociétés Joyeuses* as the inventors of what to him is only a form of merry-making. In his opinion the *Mascarades* offer a complete picture of the mediæval life of Soule. The " Reds " are the Basques and the " Blacks " are the despised foreigners. The attack on the barricades symbolises the wars of which the province was so frequently the scene ; the *bralia* represents the merry-making which went on in times of peace ; and the *fonctions* are scenes of everyday life and labour.

A more convincing theory is put forward by Miss Violet Alford, who holds that the *Mascarades* and most of the Spring dances not only of the Basque Country but of the rest of Europe, are the deformed relics of a forgotten Spring rite. In her book on English Folk-Dances Miss Alford recalls how in prehistoric times, when winter was nearing its end, our remote ancestors used to meet in sacred groves to awaken the deities of nature and propitiate them with a sacrifice. On their return to their homes they were firmly convinced that they brought with them the Spring or, as the English dancers call it, the May. The sacrifice was sometimes animal or vegetable, but often it was human. Sometimes, even, " the King-priest, King because he is Chief of the community, Priest because as Headman he bears the burden of the ceremony and acts for the people," himself impersonated Winter and was put to death in order that Spring might come again. He was the " priest who slew the slayer, and shall himself be slain." The sense of continuity which this practice implied corresponded to the conception of death and resurrection

THE CANTINIÈRE DOES AN ENTRECHAT.

THE WINE-GLASS DANCE AT TARDETS.

which was engendered in men's minds by the never-ending recurrence of the seasons, a conception which, allied later to the idea of redemption by sacrifice, has become one of the guiding principles of religious thought.

There is good reason to believe that these Spring processions, ceremonies and sacrifices survive in the Spring and Carnival dances of to-day. This explanation alone would account for the many factors common to the *Mascarades* and *Ezpata-dantzak* of the Basque Country, the Sword Dances and Mumming-plays of England and the Spring Dances of countless other countries, the majority of which embody a ritual death.

In England the Sword Dances end in the death of the Captain or in a " lock," a figure in which the swords, interwoven to form a hexagon, are placed over the head of the Leader and drawn sharply away, thus symbolising his execution. At Marquina (Vizcaya) some forty or fifty years back the Leader was hoisted on just such a " lock." At Yurreta and Berriz, in the same province, the dead Captain is hoisted by his comrades, even as, according to Chaho, the *Zamalzain* was hoisted a century ago. The *Zaldizko* of Lanz, symbol of animal sacrifice, is shot on Shrove Tuesday. At Oyón (Álava) the *Katxi*, or Fool, is put to death by the *Alcalde* waving a flag over him. Of old the sacrificial slayers were usually disguised to perform their grim task, and in the same way the dancers of to-day are dressed up or masked. The Man-woman, who seems to be inseparable from these performances both in England and in the French Basque provinces, may well, in Miss Alford's opinion, represent a Priestess or Spring-Bride to whom the King-Priest was married before his death. Certainly in Soule the *Cantinière* is the inseparable companion of the Hobby-horse throughout the performance, and it has occurred to me that she may originally have been the Mother-Goddess who was so closely associated with Dionysos the God of Death and Resurrection.

In the light of this interpretation many apparently

meaningless details of the *Mascarades* acquire a new and important significance. At the end of the Wine-glass Dance, for instance, there is a moment when the dancers suddenly converge on the glass with such swift intensity of purpose that the onlooker is irresistibly put in mind of ritual slayers in some remote age stabbing their victim, whose blood the wine may symbolise to-day.

The gelding of the Horse, too, far from being merely a coarse and senseless piece of fooling, reveals itself to be at the least an animal fertility rite, if not something more. It will be recalled that since the dawn of civilisation it has been a guiding principle of religious thought that spiritual power is a sublimation of sexual power. By the renouncement of the sexual function man gained a proportional increase of spiritual virtue. The voluntary castration of priests was one of the principal tenets of the Astarte cult, and in the form of priestly celibacy this belief has found its way into many of the world's greatest creeds. May not the ritual gelding of the Horse-god be one of its earliest manifestations?

Naturally the Spring Dances have suffered modifications and accretions, many of which are directly traceable to the buffoonery of the Middle Ages. It is by no means impossible that Hérelle's *Sociétés Joyeuses* gathered up the few surviving fragments of the Spring Rite, welded them into their present form and endowed them with new life. Nevertheless there still runs through them a strain of sinister purpose, of long-inherited instinct working itself out unconsciously in the actions of the dancers. One has only to see the air of solemnity with which these performances are invested to be convinced that, whatever their subsequent history may have been, they sprang originally from the vast issues of Life and Death.

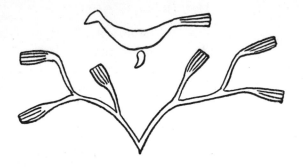

CHAPTER XI

THE BASQUE HOUSE

Ikusten duzu goizean　　　Do you see, in the morning,
Argia hasten denean,　　　At the first light of dawn
Menditto baten gainean,　　On a little hill,
Etche ttipitto aintzin churi bat,　A small house, white-fronted,
Lau haitz ondoren erdian,　　In the midst of four oak-trees,
Chakhur churi bat athean,　　A white dog in the doorway,
Ithurriño bat aldean?　　　A little fountain at the side?
Han bizi naiz ni bakean.　　It is there that I dwell in peace.

ELISSAMBURU.

Adichkidentzat lehenic,　　To friends first of all,
Heltcen denean pobreric,　　To the poor when they come,
Etsaier, nor gabe denic,　　To enemies, for who is without them?
Dener nago zabalduric.　　To all I am open wide.

LINTEL INSCRIPTION AT IBARROLLE.

THE oldest houses in the Basque Country are those known as *dorreak*. The word is derived from the Spanish *torre*, and the houses are closely akin to the *casa-torre* of Spain. They are tall stone towers built on a narrow foundation, dating often from the twelfth century or even earlier. A splendid example of this style of architecture is the *Torre del Conde* at Oñate (Guipuzcoa), a gaunt building, the uncompromising lines and grim bare walls of which are unrelieved by any exterior decoration. The windows are but narrow slits. The low pyramidal roof does not project so much as a foot beyond the outside wall.

Access to these early strongholds was obtained by an

outside stairway leading to the first floor. This stairway, being of wood, could be burnt in times of danger. Some of them were provided with courtyards, enclosed within a continuation of the outside wall of the main building. The later *dorreak*, built in the fourteenth and fifteenth centuries, are less slender and more substantial. They tend to become cubical in form. Some are provided with turrets at the corners or with one or more cylindrical towers.

In the Middle Ages special permission was necessary for the construction of these formidable strongholds, and in the French provinces a number of those which had been illegally built were destroyed by the English. This was a wise precaution, for the country suffered greatly from disputes between the nobles (*parientes mayores* in Spain), who could always take refuge in their fortresses. In Labourd, for instance, there was a long and bitter struggle between the " Red Bellies " and the " White Bellies," adherents of the respective Lords of Urtubie and Saint-Pée. Basse-Navarre was ravaged alternately by the warring factions of Luxe and Gramont. The most sanguinary of these petty wars was that which raged for thirty years in the Spanish provinces between the *Onazinos* and the *Gamboinas*. Henry IV of Castille organised a militia called the *Hermandad* to deal with this evil, and in 1456 a general order was issued for the destruction of all *dorreak*. Those which were not razed to the ground were converted into peaceful dwellings, and a new era in construction began, that of the *jauregiak* or manor-houses.

In the French provinces it was laid down by law that the height of a *jauregia* must not exceed that of the upraised lance of a mounted horseman. In Spain the buildings of this epoch were more massive and more palatial, but there was little uniformity in their style. Gothic, Mudejar, Renaissance, Plateresque, and Baroque influences made themselves felt in turn. Apart from the fact that they were unfortified, other buildings were a passable imitation of the proscribed *dorreak*. The courtyard disappeared, *ajimez* windows replaced the loopholes, and the turrets, the value of which was henceforth decorative rather than utilitarian, dwindled in size until they became meaningless pinnacles projecting above or below the roof. In some cases they projected both above and below as in the Casa Moyua at Vergara, where the two sections do not coincide vertically, showing that the architect had lost sight of the original purpose of this feature. These great square houses with narrow iron balconies, romanesque doorways and heavy stone escutcheons, are to be found in every Spanish Basque village, and their relationship to the later *dorrea* and to the *casa solar* of Spain is unmistakable.

It is not, however, the fortified tower or manor-house but the simpler farm-house which constitutes the type of Basque architecture. At first sight it might seem as though this low spreading dwelling with its whitewashed front and gable roof had little in common with the grim *dorrea*. Unfortunately, nothing is known of the farms which were contemporary with the latter, for none of those which stand to-day can be stated with certainty to have been built earlier than the end of the sixteenth century. To judge from an inscription over the door, the oldest existing farmhouse (at Caro in Basse-Navarre) dates from the year 1572. A house at Harambels bears an inscription to the effect that it was constructed on the site of a previous building dating from 984, and the old mill at Ascain is the reconstruction of one that was built in 1302. But the majority of the older houses in Labourd date only from the seventeenth century, and those in Basse-Navarre were either built or reconstructed in the eighteenth. It is quite possible that their predecessors were built of wood, for Henry IV of Castille once declared that the whole of Durango was at the mercy of any madman armed with a torch, and in the following reign Fuenterrabía was burnt to the ground with the exception of seven houses.

I have always thought, however, that the modern farmhouse, like the *jauregia*, derived directly from the *dorrea*, or was at least considerably influenced by it.   It does not seem unreasonable to suppose that when the Basques began to use stone instead of wood for their farms they turned their eyes to the nearest stone buildings which they could use as a model.   Indeed many of the *dorreak* were never more than farms, the owners of which were wealthy peasants who adopted this style of architecture for security.   The pyramidal roof of the *dorrea* admittedly has nothing in common with the broad gable-roof of the modern farmhouse beyond the brown tiles of which it is made.   It is easy, however, to imagine how the evolution from the one to the other may have occurred.   The original pyramidal roof was intended for a building constructed on a square foundation (Fig. A).   As public security improved, the square ground-plan, essentially defensive in purpose, was elongated into a rectangle (Fig. B).

   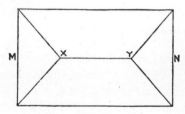

Fig. A.   Fig. B.

Simplicity and economy dictated the prolongation of the line XY until the points X and Y came to be vertically above M and N, and the two smaller pents disappeared. That at least is my own personal theory and is borne out by the fact that roofs of every stage of transition are still to be found all over the country.   Sometimes, indeed, the transition was dispensed with.   In many of the *dorreak* which were transformed into peaceful dwellings the top story was removed and the truncated body crowned with a gable-roof.   On the other hand, in the Arratia district of Vizcaya the farmhouses are exact reproductions

DORREA TOWER AT DONAMARIA (NAVARRE).

THE VILLAGE OF ECHALAR (NAVARRE).

on a smaller scale of the square *dorreak*, including even the outside staircase.

It must be admitted that Philippe Veyrin, who has made a close study of Basque architecture, does not share my opinions in this respect. In his view the peasant dwelling and the *dorrea* are two distinct architectural types which have always pursued an independent existence. The *dorrea* may perhaps have been a development of the earliest type of farmhouse, but it is more likely that it was copied from French or Spanish models. The roof with four roof-slopes, which affords better protection against the wind, is architecturally an advance on the gable-roof, and any evolution would naturally be in the direction of four roof-slopes rather than the reverse. He points particularly to the *miru-buztana* (buzzard's tail), a modification of the gable-roof frequent in Vizcaya and Basse-Navarre in which the gable is cut off at an angle at either the front or the back to form a small third roof-slope (hooded gable) with the object of breaking the prevailing wind.

It is not impossible that the original Basque farmhouse was of a type still to be found in parts of Guipuzcoa, particularly in the neighbourhood of Ataún. In these farms a ground-floor, stone-built, contains not only all the living-rooms, but also the cattle-sheds and stables, and is covered by a gable-roof of the ordinary châlet type. The space between the ground-floor and the roof is occupied by a vast attic (*gambara*) serving as a drying-room and store-room for all the agricultural products of the farm. This granary has no side wall, for the roof slopes steeply down on either side, and at the front and back it is enclosed by a fabric of rough axe-hewn boards or shingles known as *aizkola* and similar to our traditional weather-boarding, nailed to a framework of wooden beams. In Philippe Veyrin's view the modern Basque farm is derived from this primitive dwelling. In later years the use of stone was extended upwards, and the beams have largely disappeared everywhere save in

Labourd and Vizcaya, where they have been retained principally for their decorative rather than for their constructional value.

There is something to be said in favour of this theory. The Labourd farms are half-timbered, the ground-floor being always of stone and the upper story or stories of brick or plaster which may have replaced some more primitive material. In many parts of the country, such as the Bidassoa valley, where the whole house is of stone, there is a small granary immediately under the gable, the front of which is either open or roughly boarded up.

The plan of the ordinary Basque farm varies but little. Through an entrance so wide that a cart may pass through it one walks straight into the *eskaratza*, a vast hall with an earthen floor used for housing carts. The other ground-floor compartments are usually reached through the *eskaratza*. They consist of the *estaulia* or ox-byre, the *tresnategia* and *zelauria*, used for storing agricultural implements and cattle-fodder respectively, and the *sukaldia* (kitchen), which has a separate and smaller outside door. The *sukaldia* is the principal living-room of the farm, for the *sala* or parlour on the first floor, like its English counterpart, is used only on special occasions. The bedrooms are all on the first floor except when the *etcheko primu* marries and, continuing to live under the paternal roof, becomes the *jaunastia* or young master. In this event there are likely to be a kitchen and bedrooms on each floor, for the two families usually prefer to maintain separate establishments.

The kitchen, which in Navarre is usually on the first floor, is the most important room in the farm, for from time immemorial the activities of the house have centred round the life-giving fire which seems always to be burning in the vast open hearth (*supazter*) and from which the *sukaldia* (beside the fire) derives its name. In the oldest type of kitchen, rarely found nowadays and then only in Navarre and Vizcaya, the fire is in the centre of the floor. The smoke escapes through a high conical chimney of brick, which is carried through the attic and the roof. In olden times, no doubt, this outlet did not exist, and the smoke, finding its way through the rafters, helped to dry the corn-cobs in the attic. In most kitchens, however, the fireplace is in the wall. Above it hangs the pot-hook (*laratza*) from an iron chain. From the low rafters of the ceiling are suspended hams and strings of onions or scarlet peppers. A *zizailu* or *txitxilu* is drawn up close to the fire. This most ingenious piece of furniture, which is

peculiar to the Basques, consists of a wooden bench with a back the middle part of which can be let down forwards into a horizontal position to form a small table between the two persons occupying the ends of the bench. Set out on a vast walnut dresser (*mankalkasia*) with its back to the whitewashed wall are rows of glistening crockery. Shelves built into recesses in the wall contain the pots and pans. Among these are two peculiar kinds of water-jar, the *pegarra* and the *phereta*, the first a tubby jar of earthenware, as broad as it is high, which the women still balance on their heads in some parts of the country, and the second a wooden bucket, narrowing towards the top and banded round with strips of polished brass. Among the smaller jugs one is often surprised to see pieces of old

P

English lustre, brought back from Newfoundland by Basque fishermen. Another utensil found in every  Basque kitchen is the *kaiku*, a wooden container used for milk, carved diagonally from a single tree-trunk so that its sides, though parallel, rise at an oblique angle to the base, giving it a curiously unsymmetrical appearance. A rough but solid table, a few rush-bottomed chairs and a clock complete the equipment of the *sukaldia*.

The bedrooms too are soberly furnished. Their immaculately whitewashed walls are broken only by a holy water vessel and one or two sacred pictures. The bed and cupboards of sombre walnut seem to grow out of the dark beeswaxed boards of the floor. In the corner stands the big umbrella without which the Basque seldom ventures abroad even in the finest weather.

Although the internal disposition of the house is approximately the same in the seven provinces, the exterior varies considerably from one province to another. But in the words of O'Shea, " these are but dialects of the same architectural tongue."

In France there are three distinct types of house corresponding more or less with the three provinces. The Souletin house with its steep roof, originally of shingles but now usually of grey slate, is hardly distinguishable from its Béarnais neighbour, from which it is certainly derived. The two remaining types correspond only roughly with the provinces from which they are named. It is not rare, for instance, to find Bas-Navarrais houses in Labourd, and conversely the Labourd type is frequently found in the northerly districts of Basse-Navarre. The truth is that each of these styles arises out of the materials most easily available in the district in which it appears. The Basse-Navarre house, built entirely of stone, seems to grow naturally out of the rocks of Arradoy and the Pic d'Iparla, while the half-timbered Labourd farm belongs more to the rolling wooded country away from the mountains, where stone, if not unobtainable, is more difficult of access.

The Labourd type falls into two sub-divisions : the village house and the outlying farm. The former stands in a cramped space where the houses, though usually detached from one another, are huddled close together and must be built on a small foundation with a narrow frontage for which they make up in height. The latter is low and spreading, with a frontage of perhaps thirty yards, which is often exceeded by its depth. In both types of Labourd house each story usually projects some eight inches or a foot beyond the one below. The weight of the upper stories is carried by strong horizontal beams often beautifully carved. The main cross-walls are brought out to coincide with the advanced wall-face and are carried on enriched brackets or corbels. The side-walls sometimes project as much as a yard in front of the wall-face to shelter it from the wind and to support the spreading eaves. This feature reappears on the Spanish side, where the projecting side-walls are called *fraileak* (monks). Here also the ground space outside the house yet sheltered by the eaves, known as the *itchasura*, is regarded as semi-sacred. A laurel is often planted within it, and any children of the house who die without baptism are buried there.

Where the ends of the structural walls emerge on to the face of the building they usually divide it into either two or three parts. Where there are three parts the two slopes of the roof are likely to be symmetrical, and in general it is only when there are but two such parts that one finds long roof-slopes stretching down on the windward side to within six or eight feet of the ground. An outside stairway, though by no means rare, is the exception rather than the rule. The balcony, seldom found on the Labourd house except near Sare, is a small and ramshackle affair, set in the angle of the roof immediately outside the store-room, the drying of the contents of which is practically its only function.

Another feature of the farms round Sare is the *lorio azpia* or *loriua*, a sort of rectangular portico on the ground-floor which occupies one section of the wall-face, the middle one if there are three. It constitutes a covered space open to the air, where threshing and other agricultural work may be done in shelter. The oven of whitewashed brick is often built into the corner of the *loriua*, and a door on which a number of crosses are chalked up leads from it into the *eskaratza*.

Porticoes akin to the *loriua*, but with a low arched entrance, are found in Vizcaya and Spanish Navarre, but they are rarely met with in Basse-Navarre. The houses of this province are distinguished principally by the decorative use of finely-cut and squared blocks of stone, grey or mauve in colour, placed irregularly round the windows and in a semi-circle over the arched doorway. On the corners they are set alternately in either wall with a pleasing zigzag effect. The Basques have always been famous as stone-cutters and were so employed by Philip II in the construction of the Escorial. On one occasion when they struck for better pay the King was forced to grant their demands, for both he and they knew that nowhere else could he find such skilled workmen.

The dark brown beams of the Labourd farms, the colour of which is derived from the bullock's blood with which they were, and occasionally still are, dyed, are seldom found in Basse-Navarre, but to compensate for their absence the balcony becomes a regular feature, especially near the Spanish frontier, and frequently extends the whole length of the façade. It is in Basse-Navarre that the largest number of lintel inscriptions are to be found commemorating the founding or reconstruction of a house and bearing the names of the first couple who inhabited it, e.g. :—

PIARRES ETCHEVERRI & JEANNE
INDART CONJOINTS MAITRES DE
IBARRONDO 1659

Sometimes these inscriptions are more detailed. The following figures on a house at Ainhoa : *Cette maison appelée Gorritia a esté rachetée par Marie de Gorriti, mère du feu Jean Dolhagaray des sommes par lui envoyées des Indes, laquelle maison ne se pourra vandre ny engaiger : Fait en l'an 1662.* A previous chapter contains a reference to the grave and austere character of some of these inscriptions. Others, none the less, are humorous or satiric : *Ici on donne à boire et à manger et bon caffé aujourd-'hui en payant et demain pour rien* (on an inn at Iholdy) : *Crédit est mort* (at Sainte-Engrâce) : *Rien n'est plus à charge à des gens occupées que la visite de ceux qui ne le sont pas* (Urçuray). Sometimes they testify to the pride of the owner :

> *Infançon sorthu nis*
> *Infançon hilen nis.*

(A nobleman I was born, a nobleman I shall die) : or they record unusual happenings : *La conque de fromant se vendoit à 15 et le millocq à 14* (Harambels).

In Spanish Navarre the houses closely resemble the Basse-Navarre type, although they are on the whole larger. The gable-roof tends to be replaced by the pyramidal as one moves eastwards towards the regions of heavier snow. The other three Spanish provinces are characterised by a greater variety of style than the French side. There is, properly speaking, no Guipuzcoan or Biscayan house. In Guipuzcoa, although both the Labourd and Basse-Navarre types, and sometimes even a combination of both, can be found, the front is usually undistinguished and lacking in both the half-timbering of the former and the decorative stone-work of the latter.

In Vizcaya the use of whitewash, which is less general in the Spanish than in the French provinces, grows decidedly sparser. The portico reappears (under the name of *karrajua*) usually in the form of a low arch, although sometimes it is rectangular, as in Labourd. When the houses are stone-built the individual stones are left to show through a thin covering of plaster or outlined in white cement, giving the walls a curiously dappled effect.   When they are half-timbered the structure comprises diagonal as well as horizontal and vertical unpainted beams which show through the upper part of the wall-face, and over which is pinned, in the Durango district, a facing of red tiles to protect them from the elements. The intervening material is composed of equal courses of red brick and mortar.

In Álava two fresh types of farmhouse make their appearance.   In one of these the second floor projects outwards, the middle part of this floor being higher than the sides to allow for the greater height of the *sala* which occupies the centre of the first floor.   In the other the ridge of the roof is parallel to the front of the house, along the whole length of which runs a portico of the *loriua* type supported on pillars.

Much has been written concerning the orientation of the Basque house.   The fact that the majority of the farms face East or South-east has been considered by some writers to be of profound and ancient significance, while others, less imaginative, attribute it to the owners' desire to turn their backs on the prevailing winds from the North and West.   It must be admitted that many houses, protected from the wind by natural features of the landscape, do not have a south-easterly aspect.   A possible explanation which would satisfy those who are not content with so dull a solution of the problem is put forward in the following chapter.

CHAPTER XII

DECORATION

BASQUE decorative art consists almost exclusively of wood carving and of engraving on stone.   Outside Vizcaya and Guipuzcoa, where the *kirruak* (bedspreads) and *zamauak* (offering cloths) are curiously worked in blue, there is no embroidery.   The wrought iron is copied directly from Spanish models.

Strangely enough, it is not until comparatively modern times that the Basques appear to have learnt the art of engraving on stone, for very few prehistoric or classical inscriptions have been found in their country.   According to Camille Jullian stone dolmens and menhirs found in the Lower Pyrenees bear rough representations of shepherds' crooks and woodmen's axes.   It may have

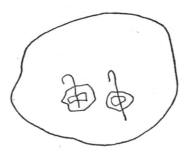

been some such stone that I found one day at the side of the weary stretch of road between Saint-Jean-Pied-de-

Port and Saint-Jean-le-Vieux. The stone was river-worn and bore a curious design which may well be a combination of crook and axe, a prehistoric counterpart, perhaps, of the sickle and hammer. Ever since the Stone Age, and especially in the Minoan civilisation, the axe has had a symbolical meaning connected usually with the Sun-God. The fact that in some parts of Europe (including Gaul) the Sun-God and the Thunder-God were looked upon as identical explains both the Ancient Greek belief that stone axes had the character of thunderbolts, and the modern Basque belief that the former have protective virtue against the latter.

Camille Jullian adds that the Basques, slow as ever to accept innovations, did not adopt the practice of inscribing stone until an epoch when the rest of Europe, seduced by the new discovery of printing, was almost ready to abandon it. Nor is this practice in true accordance with their nature and habits. " The Basque," he writes, " is a man for speech, for singing, for exclaiming and for improvisation : he is not one for putting his thoughts into form, for moulding them or setting them down for posterity."

Generally speaking the Basque applies decoration to only a limited number of objects. Of principal importance among these are his door-lintel and tombstone. There is an intimate connection between these two objects, for both are in a sense thresholds, the one of the home and the other of the grave. Both testify to the respect of the Basque for his ancestors and to his sense of the continuity of the family. While the lintel inscription commemorates the founders of the house and therefore of the family, the inscriptions on the older tombs indicate that these are the resting-places, not of an individual, but of countless successive generations. " This," they run, " is the death-stone (*hil-harria*) of such-and-such a house." House and tomb are so inseparable that when the house is sold the *etcheko hil harria* is usually included in the property.

" On one of my recent excursions," writes the late

Louis Colas, whose masterly work " La Tombe Basque "
is the last word on the subject, " I examined the little
cemetery of the hamlet of Biscaye (Basse-Navarre) where
I found some interesting tombstones. My attention
was particularly drawn to two of these. Magnificently
sculptured, they bore the following inscriptions :—

ICY GIST GRATIANE

MAISTRAISE DE MENDIBURE

1684

ICY GIST IONNES IRIGOIN

MAISTRE DE MENDIBURU

1684

Side by side lay the *etcheko jauna* and the *etcheko andrea*.
As we contemplated the mound of earth crowned by
these two monuments the Abbé Recalde told me that
for three hundred years this had been the tomb of the
Mendiburu family, who still live in the house of that
name."

No one who has wandered round a Basque cemetery,
more especially on the French side, can have failed to
notice that the oldest tombstones, worn and lichen-
covered, tucked away in a corner of the churchyard or
deep-sunken into the earth are of a shape rarely seen elsewhere. They consist of a thick stone disc growing out
of a wedge-shaped base and are often profusely decorated
on both sides. Although these discoidal tombstones are
not peculiar to the Basque Country, since they are found
the whole length of the Pyrenees, in Spain and Portugal
and even in England (their resemblance to the Celtic
" wheel-cross " is obvious), the Basques have adopted
them and made them their own. There is no doubt
that the type is an ancient one. Tombstones of this
shape, covered with inscriptions in the mysterious Iberian
characters, have been found in different parts of Spain,

and this fact has been eagerly seized upon by those who hold that the Basques are a remnant of the Iberians. Colas for instance shows that their present area of distribution corresponds with the regions known to have been inhabited by the Celtiberians.

Unfortunately there is a break in the tradition, a break of at least fifteen hundred years between the Ibero–Roman discoidals and the oldest examples found in the Basque Country. Nevertheless Colas thinks that the discoidal tombs are of ancient origin and were anthropomorphic in their beginnings. When the primitive ancestors of the Basques buried their dead, he argues, they set up stones to mark the place of their burial. They could think of no surer way of perpetuating the memory of the deceased than by giving to these stones the rough outline of a human head and trunk, and the stone, set upright in the earth, represented the dead man, not in the stillness of death, but in the activity of life. The turban-crowned tombstones of Turkey were doubtless similar in their original intention. It is significant that even to-day the discoidal stones are called *gizonak* (men) in parts of Labourd and *kurutzeburubeltzak* (black-headed crosses) in Basse-Navarre. A stone found by Colas at Sorhapuru would certainly seem to lend colour to his theory. Uninscribed and unadorned, evidently of great age, it has two excrescences where the " body " merges into the head, which can only be intended to represent

arms. Another has what are apparently intended to
represent a pair of ears.

It is difficult to estimate the age of the oldest surviving
discoidal stones, for those which are of most ancient
appearance bear neither date nor inscription. The
oldest authenticated stone (found in the churchyard at
Izturitz) is dated 1501. Colas, however, believes that
some of those which he has seen are as much as six or
seven hundred years old, and there seems to be no reason
to doubt his opinion.

Although the peasant craftsmen of the sixteenth and
seventeenth centuries put their most patient work and
their most ingenious variety of design into these tombstones, wood-carving also affords a fruitful field for the
study of Basque decoration. Among the objects which
are thus carved are the wooden galleries running round
the interior of the churches, the principal beams on the
face of the houses and the purlins
which support the projecting roof.
The main street of Fuenterrabía is
full of splendid examples of these
last. Inside the house dressers,
cupboards and chests (*kutchak*) are
frequently carved with great rich-
ness and variety of design. So
also are many humble objects of
everyday use; shepherds' crooks,
spinning-gear, ox-yokes, cheese-
moulds, *phereta* and *kaiku*. The
sound-holes of the *ttun-ttun* are
nearly always fretted in an elaborate
pattern, and some of the most
interesting designs are to be found
on the *argizaiolak* of Guipuzcoa.
These last are little wooden
tablets wound around with a long

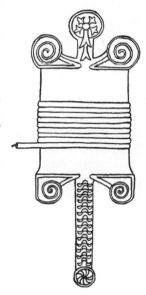

wax taper which is burned in church for the souls of
those who have died within the year. Their peculiar

shape, coupled with the fact that they are only found in those parts of Guipuzcoa where the discoidal tombstone does not appear, has given rise to the theory that like the latter they are anthropomorphic in origin. In shape, moreover, they are not unlike the paleolithic representations of man painted on pebbles of the Mas d'Azil type found in North-west Spain.

In the Basque country there are no essential differences of technique or design between stone-engraving and wood-carving, and it will be convenient to class them together for general consideration.

Practically all Basque decoration is in *champlevé*; that is to say that the ground is cut away and the design is left outlined in the original surface of the wood or stone. This surface is sometimes further decorated with simple incised lines or shading. Sculpture in the round or in bas-relief is rare, and the few examples known are primitive and clumsy, these processes being clearly beyond the powers of the peasant craftsman. For wood-carving and for a number of discoidal tombs the technique of chip-carving is used, the design being composed of inclined planes or facets and of the ridges and hollows formed by their intersection.

Although " Basque Art " has been so much discussed of late that the expression has become a *cliché*, serious writers on the subject such as Colas and Philippe Veyrin have raised the question whether such a thing as Basque art can be truly said to exist. " Should we not rather say that there is a Basque style, a Basque manner ? " asks Colas. " The word art presupposes inspiration, implies invention and creation, conjures up the idea of great originality. Style and manner are determined by secondary causes, by various and divergent influences which can be traced and defined."

Colas is right. The originality of Basque decoration lies not in the creation of new forms or in the invention of new motives, but in the individual treatment of borrowed designs. Ignoring the natural models which abound

ENGLISH CHEST OF THE EARLY THIRTEENTH CENTURY SHOWING
TYPICALLY BASQUE DECORATION.

(Reproduced by kind permission of the Director, Victoria and Albert Museum.)

DOORWAY OF A DORREA AT OYARZUN (GUIPUZCOA).

around him, the Basque carver nonetheless succeeds in investing his work with a distinctive quality derived not so much from his own æsthetic sense as from some unifying principle which welds into a homogeneous whole the diverse elements on which he has drawn.

There are two outstanding traits of the Basque manner which can be defined forthwith ; the rare use of natural subjects which, when they appear, are treated with Gothic *naïveté* or conventionalised to a very high degree ; and a marked preference for geometrical patterns such as do not necessitate freehand drawing and can be designed with compass and ruler. In the ingenious variation and disposition of these the Basque excels. To what extent these characteristics express a racial preference or how far they are dictated by limitations of technique it is difficult to say. Probably both factors play their part.

The Golden Age of Basque decoration was in the sixteenth and seventeenth centuries. In the eighteenth century the tradition waned and in the nineteenth it died. The sources from which the Basque craftsman drew his inspiration ranged from the most ancient designs to those of the Renaissance which were contemporary with his best work.

One pattern, in particular, is of interest, if only for the importance which has been attributed to it in connection with the problem of Basque origins. This is the swastika, familiar to orientalists as the Hindu symbol of blessing and blessedness. The name, which is composed from the Sanscrit roots *svasti* (well-being) and *tika* (sign or token), was applied as early as the first century B.C. to a symbol which is undoubtedly far older, for excavators have found it in the second city of Troy and, in Greece, on objects dating from the Bronze Age. In the third century A.D. it was widely used as a Christian symbol like the Fish and the Anchor. It is also found on ancient Iberian pottery.

The way in which this sign is geometrically constructed is both curious and interesting. Describe a circle, draw a diameter and then, on each radius, describe a semi-circle, the two being on different sides of the original diameter. When the latter is erased the figure thus formed constitutes the only possible way (other than a diameter) of dividing the circle into two equal, complementary and congruent parts (Fig. A). In the minds of the primitive men who first constructed this figure the two halves of the circle symbolised the opposing principles of life; male and female, light and darkness, good and evil.

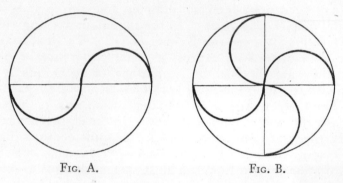

FIG. A.   FIG. B.

Now let the process be repeated on a diameter drawn at right-angles to the first, and a figure is constructed which consists of four arcs of a circle radiating from a point (Fig. B). This is the most primitive form of the swastika.

Those races which, lacking the notion of compass drawing, were yet unable to reproduce the swastika freehand, conventionalised it by turning each arc into a line bent at its centre in a right-angle, and it is in this form that the swastika is most widely found outside the Basque Country (Fig. C). In Germany, for instance, it is called *Hakenkreuz* and used as an anti-Semitic symbol. In other countries it is regarded as a talisman; for good if the lines bend clockwise, for evil if they go widdershins.

This form is very rarely found in the Basque Country and is not indigenous. The usual form in which the

swastika appears is that known as the Oviphile Sign.
This can be constructed by extending the process
described above. Let each radius in Fig. B be treated
as a diameter and divided in turn into two radii. If
smaller semi-circles be then described as before, a figure
is obtained which can be described roughly as four
commas springing from a common point (Fig. D). The

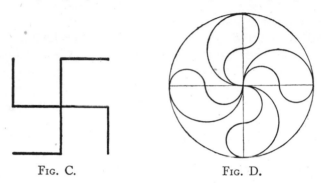

FIG. C.   FIG. D.

Oviphile Sign is used in many countries as a fertility
symbol. In the Basque Country it appears on both
tombs and lintel-stones, and, according to Colas, more
especially on sheepfolds and on the houses and tombs of
shepherds and priests, the latter, perhaps, being regarded
as spiritual pastors. A seventeenth-century treatise on
medicine and magic by Paracelsus gives the following
specific against sheep diseases: "Having taken earth
and sand from the nearest stream at which the sheep
drink, and that at the time of the waning moon, with this
same earth and mud you must paint on the folds this
incantation." [1] And there follows a complicated jumble
of Latin and Greek words among which appear three
clearly drawn oviphile signs.

The appearance of this sign in Basque decoration is
one of the unexplained mysteries of the race. Its solution
might well contribute to that of the problem of origins.
" It is certain," writes Camille Jullian, " that this was a

[1] " Paracelsi Opera Omnia," Vol. 1, Geneva, 1658.

favourite symbol of the Iberians, by whom I mean the natives of Spain immediately before the Christian era. Gaul knew it but soon forgot it. The Pyrenees clung to it tenaciously : in Roman times as soon as one approaches the Basque Country, the swastika makes its appearance." Jullian saw a swastika being graven on a tombstone as late as 1900, but he does not attempt to explain the puzzling fact that the sign appears on no tomb or doorway earlier than the end of the sixteenth century. If it be indeed an Iberian inheritance it must, like the discoidal tombstone, have gone underground for some fifteen hundred years. He is probably nearer the mark when he adds, seemingly as an afterthought : " And if it has taken root in the Basque Country the fact is perhaps due to primitive Christianity rather than to any pagan survival." A possible, though rather fanciful, explanation of its origin has been suggested to me by a sentence in George Birdwood's book " Sva " : " Any house facing the East is a *Svastika ;* and *svasthya* are the freehold lands held in their villages by the Brahmans." Could there possibly be a connection between the swastika and the eastern orientation of the Basque farmhouses, both phenomena being of similar origin and intended to signify the freedom of tenure which has always reigned in the Basque Country ?

The comma-like designs, four of which together constitute the Oviphile Sign, appear frequently by themselves, especially on the horizontal beams which support the galleries of churches and the overhung façades of houses. Indeed Philippe Veyrin regards them, not as the Oviphile Sign resolved into its component parts, but as an independent and elementary design from which the Oviphile Sign may even have been formed. He points out that in many cases one or more points of the five-pointed star, a favourite Basque design, are extended into

mas.[1] On the other hand, two discoidal
:he cemetery of Banca (Basse-Navarre),
decorated by the same hand, seem to lend
coɪ⏤   eory that the Basque engraver consciously
connects the comma, if not with the Oviphile Sign itself,
at least with the geometrical construction by which it is
formed. On both tombs the circular ground is quartered
by a cross, and in each of the corners there appears on one
stone a comma and on the other a reproduction of Fig. B
in which the circle is divided into comma-shaped halves.

On tombstones particularly there figure many other
signs and symbols borrowed from various sources. There
are, for instance, rough representations of the sun with
straight or curved rays, five- or eight-pointed stars, and
various phases of the moon. Signs like these figure on
Iberian tombs and inscribed stones, and recall the times
when the Basques, as yet unconverted to Christianity,
worshipped the Sun and the Moon.

Christian symbols, however, are met with more frequently. The Cross, simple on the older tombs, grows
more ornate with the years. The Maltese Cross appears.
The ends are often splayed out into something like a
fleur-de-lys, and one or two discoidal tombs reproduce
crosses adorned with bells, the use of which was strongly
condemned by de Lancre. For in those days bells were
associated with dancing, and dancing smelt of witchcraft.[2] " The close proximity of Spain and their relations with that country," wrote de Lancre, "have imbued
them with this evil custom to such an extent that throughout Labourd their crosses tinkle and their priests are in
the forefront at any village dancing."

[1] Philippe Veyrin : " L'Art Basque Ancien," p. 23. He also quotes
a pattern (found only in the neighbourhood of Iholdy) in which these
commas have been combined to form a conventionalised pot of flowers.
(See also drawing on page 159.)

[2] Bells are also thought to be a protection against the Evil Eye.
At the pilgrimage church of Urquiola (Vizcaya) cattle-bells are blessed
by the priests in order that the peasants may attribute to this any protective virtue with which they may credit them.

Q

The Christian monograms I H S, M A, M A R I A and I N R I are treated with great freedom and variety. The first is by far the most common and is sometimes accompanied by a combination of Alpha and Omega. The I is usually presented in the form of a cross and sometimes also in that of a fleur-de-lys. The H may lack a crossbar or the S be inverted if the exigencies of the design demand it. On one or two stones the monogram is so completely distorted that the engraver must clearly have lost sight of its original meaning and seen in it no more than a decorative pattern. Other symbols used are the Flaming Heart and the Dove. Some tombstones, those of priests, perhaps, bear curious reproductions of chalices, censers, candlesticks and other objects connected with Christian worship, which, to judge from their style, would appear to have first been used as models early in the seventeenth century, since when the engravers have been content to copy their predecessors.

Side by side with these Christian symbols the tombstones show mediæval caballistic signs such as Solomon's Seal (formed of two equilateral triangles interlaced), of which the Pentacle, more rarely found, is but a simplified form. Some artists, seeking new models, borrowed their themes from the coins of the period. There are discoidal tombs whose circular designs recall English coins of Edward I or French coins of Philippe le Bel, Saint Louis and Jean le Bon. A few engravers took heraldic models, and one finds designs improvised out of the Chains of Navarre or the Baztan chequers. The fleur-de-lys of which there are many ingenious variations, is the most widely and freely used of these heraldic devices. Incidentally the escutcheons in Navarre testify to the genius of the Basque engravers for varying a given design. In the village of Maya, where a Bell is usually quartered with the Chequers of the Baztan, the combination of these two devices is composed differently on every house with more fertility of imagination and decorative sense than respect for heraldic tradition.

Apart from purely ornamental decoration it was a very usual practice for a man's tomb to bear as an indication of his trade a representation of the implements which he used during his lifetime. Tools of every sort appear on the face of the discoidal tombs and, more rarely, over the doors of farms. One sees the hammer and anvil of the blacksmith, the farmer's scythe and plough, the woodman's axe and the shepherd's shears, the carter's oxen, a crossbow with quiver and arrows (on a stone dated 1503 which is thought to commemorate the death of Berterretche), a notary's seal with a scroll of parchment, a bottle and glass that may denote an inn-keeper . . . or a toper, the gear of the cheese-maker, the sandal-maker, the weaver, the rope-maker, the carpenter and, last but not least, the engraver upon stone. Sometimes as many as six or seven tools are portrayed together. These stones are interesting for the evidence which they furnish concerning primitive implements now obsolete or obsolescent; the *martimulua*, for instance, a form of roller used for levelling ploughed land before sowing it; and the *laya*, forerunner of the plough, a heavy two-pronged fork which the Basques used to use, one in each hand, for digging up the earth.

Nor are women's occupations disdained. One finds a spinning wheel with spindle, bobbin, shuttle and miniature mallet; a bunch of keys in memory of a careful housewife; or the needle, thimble and scissors of a dressmaker.

The tombs, too, have their unsolved mysteries. One discoidal stone bears a long inscription in an unknown alphabet, a practical joke perpetrated by some village *mystificateur* on an illiterate client or perhaps, more simply, on posterity. One or two others bear inexplicable patterns, quite unsymmetrical, which might just conceivably be interpreted as maps or plans.

For the rest the Basque engraver relied principally on compass and ruler, and on a few simple foliage and scroll patterns which he could execute freehand. It is in the former rather than in the latter, however, that the chief merit of his work is to be found. The circle, more even than the straight line, is the foundation of Basque decoration, and it appears in countless intricate and ingenious variations and combinations from the simple six-pointed star to certain strange octopod and spiral designs which recall the art of Knossos and Mycenæ.

Whorls and roundels absolutely identical with those which figure on Basque chests and tombstones are found on two or three early thirteenth-century church chests in Sussex and Hampshire. One of these is at the Victoria and Albert Museum (see Plate facing p. 220), another at Stoke d'Abernon. When they were carved England was in possession of Gascony, and Sussex and Hampshire were the two counties which had the closest relations with that region. It is impossible to believe that there was no interchange of artistic ideas, but the question is : in which direction did the current flow? On the one hand the Basques have never been original creative artists, and moreover none of their surviving carving can be said with certainty to date back further than the sixteenth century. On the other hand to the best of my knowledge this group of chests stands alone in English art which, at that period, was purely Gothic in feeling. Fred Roe (" Ancient Church Chests and Chairs ") considers that all the chests in question must have come from one workshop. It is by no means impossible that that workshop was Basque. But the original source of these designs may prove to be Coptic or Merovingian.

To-day the decorative tradition is dead, save on the coast, where it survives in an anæmic form to cater for the tourist industry. Throughout the country the severe and simple discoidal tombstone has been replaced by nauseatingly ornate crosses. The old dressers and chests of walnut are no longer made. It is less trouble to buy shoddy stuff from Bayonne or Bilbao.

But this is not the worst. It might have been hoped that, although the Basques have lost the inspiration and

patient craftsmanship which brought these beautiful
though unassuming objects into being, they would at
least appreciate the work of their ancestors and do all in
their power to save it from destruction.   The furniture,
of course, is prized for its market value.   But the lintel-
stones and discoidal tombstones are worth no more than
their weight in stone and only too often are broken up to
mend the roads or serve as building material.   A handful
of lovers of Basque art have done what they could through
church and schoolroom to instil into the peasants some
measure of respect for these relics of their past.   Their
efforts have been rewarded with no very great measure of
success.

CHAPTER XIII

PELOTE AND OTHER GAMES

Pilotak ohore du Eskual herrietan,
Zeren den ederrena joko guzietan.
Eskualdunak gaztetik, pilota plazetan,
Agertzen du baduen odolik zainetan.
ZALDUBY.

Pelote is the glory of the Basque provinces
For it is the finest of all games.
On the pelote courts the Basque, from his youth up,
Shows that he has red blood in his veins.

In every Basque village, however small, there are three
things that lend charm and character to the landscape.
The first is the church and the second the cemetery that
encircles it with weathered tombstones and dark cypresses.
The third, the pelote court, is never more than a stone's
throw away. It has been said that these three form a
triple symbol of the Basque race. The church stands for
faith, the cemetery for tradition and the pelote court for a
hard and vigorous outdoor life.

Apart from its symbolism and its practical utility the
pelote court has a strong decorative value. The rudely
whitewashed stone wall, shaped like an elongated Byzan-
tine triptych with arched centre, looks down a long open
space, paved at first with flag-stones and then degenerating
into rough grass or bare earth. Down either side there
usually runs a long double step of rough masonry which
serves to seat the onlookers. Different courts vary
greatly, however, and in Spain there is usually a long

side-wall on the left-hand side.   At the far end there may
be a smaller wall where the little boys learn to become
the *pilotaris* of the future.   Balconied houses overlook the
court from all sides, and immediately behind the wall
there rises often enough the tower of the village church.
Sometimes, indeed, the church itself furnishes the object
wall.   It can hardly offend the God of the Basques
(whose priests not only play in cassock and biretta but
have more than once been known to make pelote the text
of their sermons) to hear the stinging smack of a fairly
hit ball on the walls of His dwelling.   In many villages,
however, civilisation has brought more delicate ideas of
reverence, with the result that the church now bears the
inscription : *Debekatua da Pleka haritzea.   Il est défendu
de jouer au blaid.*

   Blaid is the name given to the least complicated form
of pelote, to that common denominator of all wall-and-ball
games which consists of hitting the
ball against the wall and returning
it on the first bounce.   In spite of
all the more complex forms of the
game which are played by pro-
fessionals and skilful amateurs the
game of *blaid* is the people's
favourite.   In the towns and larger
villages they may flock to watch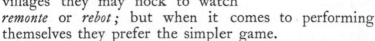
remonte or *rebot;* but when it comes to , performing
themselves they prefer the simpler game.

   You may see *blaid à main nue* played under ideal
conditions at the *Fête Patronale* of any of the smaller
villages.   A match, pompously advertised as a *grande
partie de défi,* has been arranged between a local pair and
two players from another village.   If the latter come from
the other side of the frontier so much the better, for the
match will then assume an international character.   In
addition to their white shirt and trousers the French
players wear a dark blue béret, a blue sash and blue strings
to their *espadrilles,* while the Basques from Spain are

distinguished by their red trappings. The peasants line the edge of the court and follow the game with expert eye. From behind one has an impression of stooping shoulders and wrinkled necks. On the other side the innumerable white specks of spotlessly clean, collarless shirts stand out against the sombre black of béret and *chamarra* (smock). The match proceeds in an atmosphere of informality. Wine is carried round, and everyone helps himself and in return contributes a small coin towards the expenses of the festivities. The onlookers shout encouragement to the players. They have usually betted freely on the result, and if the game is going against them their comments become more and more indignant or sarcastic until sometimes the players are constrained to interrupt the match in order to answer back.

The game is extremely simple. Each side has one player standing near the wall, who acts as server, while the other stays further back to take the deep shots. The server bounces the ball on the ground and hits it hard with clenched fist at the wall, on which is marked a line some three feet above the ground, below which no ball is good. The game proceeds along the lines of fives. Every point is counted in the score, and the server retains the service until he is put out. Game is usually up to 45 or 50, and the score is kept by an umpire, who chants it aloud at every point, and who in olden days was made to swear upon a crucifix that he would judge the game fairly. The ball normally weighs some three-and-a-half ounces. It is composed of a rubber core, wound round with wool and encased in leather, which is sewn while it is wet so that it shrinks and tightens when it dries. It is extremely hard, as I discovered one day to my cost at Guetaria (Guipuzcoa) when I rashly joined in a game. I went on my way half an hour later with my hand swollen black and blue. For three days I could neither clench my fist nor open my fingers properly. I have since avoided the *main nue* game and have noticed that the hands of regular

A MULETEER (NAVARRE).

A PELOTE MATCH AT IBARRON (LABOURD).

players are not only hardened but swollen to double their normal thickness.

Strangely enough, although *blaid à main nue* is the most rudimentary of the many modern forms of pelote, it is not that from which the game was originally derived. Although this much is certain the origins of the game are very obscure, for both written record and oral tradition have little to say on the subject before the end of the eighteenth century. There are not wanting Basques who claim for their race the honour of having invented the game, and Peña y Goñi, whose history of pelote was published in the 'nineties under the title of " La Pelota y los Pelotaris," has the complacency to announce that he will " pass over in silence the period from Adam to Perkain " (this last a famous player of the French Revolution period). Yet those intransigent Basques who would have it that pelote was played in the Earthly Paradise (with the original apple of transgression, perhaps, for the pun on *pomme* and *paume* is so tempting !) need hardly be so jealous of their national honour. The invention of the barest essentials of the game is of little account in comparison with the great skill and enthusiasm with which the Basques play it and the numerous elaborations of the game which their ingenuity has devised.

The lack of documentary evidence on the subject is quite astonishing. Yet, sparse as are the literary references to pelote, they indicate unmistakably that the game was popular in the Middle Ages. The Venetian historian Andrea Navagero, who travelled through the Basque Country in 1528, wrote as follows : " In front of their houses they have a square space enclosed on every side, where the animals may not enter, covered with a roof of branches, levelled so that there is no unevenness and sprinkled with sand in order to keep it dry ; everything done, in fact, with extreme care. Here the men remain all day (*sic*) playing at ball, bowls and other games which are usual here."

Henry VII of England is mentioned in an old chronicle

as having given £100 to a Biscayan who had played before him, thus showing that Edward VII, who followed the game with great interest, was not the first British Sovereign to be a confirmed *plaza gizona*.

Two discoidal tombstones found in the French provinces by Louis Colas throw a little light on the subject.  The first is that of Maistre Guilem Diriarte of Garris who died in 1629. The design portrays a nude figure about to strike a ball with the flat of the hand. The second, that of Manech Suhuruchahar (1784), shows a hand, a ball and a kind of wooden bat called *pala*. Manech may have been one of the players in a game at Bayonne, which is described in a letter dated 1755 from Monsieur de Lesseps to a friend in Paris :

> " Yesterday, a great game of pelote on the Place de Gramont between seven Basques among whom was Monsieur Hiriart the Doctor of Macaye, a brother of our late Mayor, dressed like the others in a peasant's béret and shirt. The match attracted many other Basques and people from the Spanish frontier. . . . The Doctor and his side had the misfortune to lose, but they are counting on getting their revenge in a match arranged for Thursday next."

This is all that is known of the game until we reach the time of Perkain at the very end of the eighteenth century. It is therefore all the more surprising that, from that moment, the mists dissolve completely, and both oral tradition and the written word furnish us with a detailed history of the game. There is no gap in the dynasty of Perkain. He is succeeded by Michico, Gaskoina, Mathieu Borotra, Chiquito d'Eibar, Paysandu and

Porteño (this last a Biscayan from South America, who seems to have been the Admirable Crichton of the game, for he was equally at home in every form of pelote). A host of other great players handed the tradition down to the " aces " of the present day, Mondragones, Irigoyen and Chiquito de Cambo. Hardly less famous than these champions of the game are certain matches of the past which have been commemorated in song. There is Perkain's great game at Les Aldudes, for instance, a match between Guipuzcoa and Navarre in 1820 at Irún, a game at Ernani in 1826 and, above all, the immortal *Irungo Partida*, the first international match, played at Irún in 1846.

Whatever measure of popularity the game may have enjoyed in those dark ages which are so recent there is no doubt as to the enthusiasm which it arouses nowadays. The Basques may no longer throng to see Chiquito de Cambo, once one of the great figures of the game, perform in exhibition matches for the benefit of foreigners, attended like a *prima ballerina* by his own *corps de ballet* of second-rate players carefully trained to let him win. But one has only to observe them at a game of *trinquet* or at some village match of *blaid* or *rebot* to realise the hold that the game has on them. Many stories illustrate their passionate devotion to the national game. Legend relates that fourteen Basques deserted from Napoleon's army in order to play in an important match at Baigorri. (One cannot help wondering how many a side this match was played!) The truants returned to the ranks just in time to fight at the battle of Austerlitz, where their gallant conduct earned them pardon. More recently a young priest was asked by his Bishop, a little maliciously perhaps, who he would rather have been, Bossuet the preacher or Perkain the *pilotari*. The answer came without a moment's hesitation: " Perkain ! "

There is every justification for this whole-hearted enthusiasm, for pelote is wonderful exercise and such excellent training for hand and eye that it is easy to understand why the Basque troops were the best bombers in the French army during the Great War. There is no game, moreover, which is so intrinsically beautiful to behold and which produces such graceful movement and such magnificent postures. The delicacy of the footwork is a joy to the eye. The gesture of the *main nue* player who flings himself at a low volley, the backhand follow-through with the long *chistera*, the overarm return of a high ball at *remonte :* the beauty of these and many other shots can be appreciated equally in the heat of the game and at leisure in the paintings of Ramiro Arrue and Cabanas Oteiza or the drawings of Garmendia.

To return to the origin of pelote, there seems little doubt that the game is derived directly from the mediæval *jeu de paume*, just as the latter in turn is descended from Greek and Roman ball-games. This is borne out by the name itself, which is clearly derived from the Greek *pilos via* the Latin *pila*, and by the lack of pure Basque words for the technical terms of the game. Texts and vase-paintings show that the Ancient Greeks played a game with a ball made of hair sewn into a case of coloured leather. This game was taken up by the Romans and was in all probability the ancestor of the modern Italian *pallone*, of the Belgian *tamis* and of the French *jeu de paume*, which is thought to have been imported from Italy at the end of the thirteenth century. The word *paume* first appears in French literature in 1316.

Longue paume, the original form of the game, was played up-and-down over an imaginary net in any open space. Towards the middle of the fourteenth century special spaces were enclosed and roofed in for the game, and the four walls gave rise to new rules, those of the game called *courte paume* [*courte* (short) is the origin of the English word "court" as used in tennis and other games]. This game became so popular that in the year 1570 Lippomano, the Venetian Ambassador, recorded the existence of eighteen hundred courts in Paris alone, and an Englishman, Sir Robert Dallington, exclaimed

that there were more courts in France than drunkards in
England. Many of these courts were formed from older
buildings such as stables and contained various accidental
features which added the element of the unexpected to
the game. Eventually one court (possibly the royal
one ?) imposed its own individual features on the game to
such an extent that they were universally copied and still
survive in the real tennis court and in the Basque *trinquet*
of to-day. A casual roof was the origin of the pent-
house, and the *dedans*, the *grille* and the *tambour* are
thought originally to have been a wired-off poultry-run, a
trap door for the passage of dishes and a chance irregu-
larity in the wall. The method of scoring 15, 30, 45
arose from a rule permitting the server, who started forty-
five *pieds du roi* from the net, to approach fifteen paces for
each point scored.

If *courte paume* displaced the *longue* in Paris the latter
probably held its own in the countryside, and it is from
the older game that Basque pelote is derived. At the
end of the eighteenth century, when the mists lift, we find
that the four existing forms of pelote are all played up and
down the court over a line (*paso*) drawn across it, with a
complex scoring system of points and chases. One of
these games, *bota luzea* or *largo* as it is called in Spain
(the name meaning " long " is a sufficient indication of
its origin), differs from *longue paume* only in one or two
insignificant details. The type of court used for this
game is an open space called *sorhopila*, situated usually
on a mountain plateau but occasionally in a village as at
Añiz (Navarre). There is no wall, and, were it not for
the *bota harri* (serving-stone), which is usually in the form
of a tripod supporting a sloping piece of wood on which
the ball is bounced before service, one might not realise
that it was intended to be a pelote court.

The obsolete Basse-Navarre game of *mahi-jokoa* is a
variant of *bote luzea*, in which a table is placed in the centre
of the court to serve as a hazard.

The games of *lachoa* and *rebot* do not differ greatly

from the two above mentioned. The principal innovation is that a wall at one end of the court is used in
service though in no other part of the game. *Lachoa*
was the favourite game of Perkain and his contemporaries,
but *rebot*, which it closely resembles, has replaced it
everywhere to-day, and it will therefore be convenient to
take the latter as an example of the complicated rules of
these old games.

The " serving-stone " is set on the *paso*, which is drawn
forty yards from the wall. Each side of five players
alternately attacks and defends, according to the fortunes
of the game. The spear-point of the attack is the server,
who bounces the ball on the *bota harri* and hits it against
the wall. The defending side, drawn up in **V** formation,
hold the space between the wall and the *paso*, their apex
being the *refileur*, usually their best player, who stands
close to the wall and returns the service off the wall,
hitting it down to the far end of the court. In the
ensuing rally the ball need no longer hit the wall. If the
attacking side miss the ball they lose the point outright ;
if, on the other hand, they can make the ball cross a line
drawn two yards from the wall into what is called the
barne they win it. Should the defending side miss the
ball without this happening or should they allow the ball
to cross the *paso* along the ground a chase (*chacha*) is
called. A green branch is placed opposite the point
where the ball was missed or stopped, and, until the point
is either definitely won or lost, the *paso* is regarded as
running through this spot. Scoring is as in tennis, the
match being thirteen games. Should a chase be scored
when the serving side stand at forty or should a second
chase be scored the sides change ends, and the two chases
are played off successively.

These, then, were the games played by Perkain and
his scarcely less famous contemporaries, Curutchet
Ezkerra the left-hander, Azantza and the latter's famous
sister Tita of Cambo, the only celebrated woman *pilotari*
in the annals of the game, of whom we are told that she

A Rebot Match at Saint-Jean-de-Luz.

Pelote Court at Narvarte (Navarre).

was feared even by Perkain, that her service was incomparable and that one day she threw out two national guards, emissaries of the Convention, who had come to arrest her brother.

A famous song tells of a game at Saint-Palais won by Perkain from Azantza after the latter had led by nineteen to seven (the match being presumably up to twenty). Another recounts a match at Tolosa which the authorities had prohibited owing to the enormous wagers which had been laid upon it. Perkain, however, arranged with his opponent Harosteguy to play the match under the pretence that it was only a friendly game. Again he was victorious.

His greatest exploit was the almost legendary game at Les Aldudes in 1793. It appears that he had got into trouble with the revolutionary authorities and, to escape the guillotine, had fled into Spain. Hearing, however, that his great rival Curutchet was to play at Les Aldudes, he risked his life to take part in the match. While he was playing the gendarmes arrived to arrest him, but he was protected alike by players and onlookers and crossed safely back into Spain. A none too reliable historian adds that he killed the Chief of Police with a more than usually vigorous stroke.

A number of not very exemplary stories are told of Perkain's domestic life. He appears to have suffered from a nagging wife. One night, when he returned home very late after having been away for eight days, his wife, instead of heaping abuse upon him, lay back in bed in perfect silence, gazing at him with baleful eye. But he was equal to this new form of protest. He went out again at once and fetched the village priest, telling him that his wife must be at the point of death, since she could no longer talk. The two returned together bringing with them the Holy Sacrament, which, as can readily be imagined, was received with anything but " extreme unction " by the lady, who was far from being at death's door.

In those days the *chistera* or long curved basket which is such a familiar feature of the Basque Country to-day had not been invented, and Perkain's contemporaries used either their bare hands or more often a sort of hollowed leather scoop fitted on the convex side with glove-fingers or loops like those of a batting-glove. With this leather surface a cut could be put on the ball which was sliced with a left-to-right movement. The longer the surface of the " glove " the more cut could be imparted, with the result that, instead of the ten-inch glove of Perkain, one about sixteen inches long was in use when Gaskoina rose to fame just before the middle of last century. Gaskoina (the Gascon) was the nickname bestowed on Jean Erratchun, who, though he was born in 1817 at Hasparren, spent his childhood at Labastide-Clairance, just outside the limits of the Basque Country. By profession a drover, he soon established a tremendous reputation as a pelote player. Like many famous *pilotaris* he was heavy and fat but wonderfully quick and light on his feet. He is still spoken of as one who never played sensational shots for the gallery but was a master of placing and especially of a service which, " yorking " the wall, was quite untakeable. He died of typhus in 1859 and may be classed among those great men whose last words, assuming for the moment that they are not apocryphal, were worthy of their lives. It seems that he was to have played in an important match at Mauléon on the very day that he died. " Is there any news of the game ? " he asked in a whisper on his death-bed. " None," they replied. " I should have liked to know how it went," he sighed, and breathed his last.

Gaskoina, greatest of all players, was the hero of the greatest of all games, the international match played at Irún on Sunday, August 9th, 1846. By dint of comparing various accounts in both verse and prose it is possible to follow the main outlines of the game. The French team, besides Gaskoina, included Gamio, a priest from the Baztan, who had been exiled from Spain for his

Carlist sympathies, Dominique Harriague of Hasparren the server, Dominique St. Jean or Ezkerra and Domingo of Espelette. Spain was represented by Melchior, Tripero, Molinero and two others whose names have been lost. This was the first time that a representative international match had been played, and it is easy to imagine the excitement that it caused and the crowds that it attracted. Twelve thousand persons are stated by an eye-witness to have been present.

Tradition has been busy with the wagers lost and won that day. They are said to have amounted in all to 140,000 francs, of which total one student from Bayonne was responsible for 40,000. A Guipuzcoan tinker staked not only all his money but his two mules and his entire stock-in-trade. With so much depending on the issue it was not likely that there would be any lack of dirty work. Just before the game began Gaskoina was offered eight thousand francs by a " rich hidalgo " if he would lose, to which handsome offer he promised a reply " within two hours." The fact that he won the game is always quoted as a proof of his integrity. And, indeed, it is doubtful that he would have deliberately lost. But if he had been fairly beaten one wonders whether the Spaniard might not have been asked to part with his money. Such a " heads-I-win-tails-you-lose " trick would appeal to the Basque sense of humour. A Spanish priest is said to have accepted eight hundred francs not to take part in the game, and the absence of another was regarded with suspicion, although it was stated that his Bishop had refused him permission to play. After all, the Bishop himself may have had something on the game.

As soon as the match began a crop of nails appeared on the court for the benefit of Gaskoina, who was playing bare-footed, and a group of Spaniards bribed one of his friends to give him frequent drinks from his own wine-skins in the hope of making him drunk. Neither of these tricks was successful, for Gaskoina's tough soles were

R

impervious to the nails, and as for the wineskins, the prudent drover had filled them with soup!

Nevertheless the game did not open auspiciously for the French. After the first few points Harriague played magnificently, but Gaskoina was uncertain and Gamio played so badly as to lay himself open to the gravest suspicions. The Spaniards established a winning lead. Then at last Gaskoina found his form and with a wonderful succession of shots drew level. Game succeeded game and there was seldom more than a point between the two sides. Finally with only two points to go the score was still level. The excitement was intense. A Frenchman offered Gaskoina a pair of oxen if he could pull off the match. Gaskoina made the next point, but in the rally that followed Gamio poached Gaskoina's ball and hit it down. Again the sides were level. Then amid tremendous enthusiasm Gaskoina made a chase and won the next rally to finish the match. He was escorted back to France in triumph by his friends, who, suspecting foul play, refused to let him accept a drink or a cigar on Spanish soil. In addition to the pair of oxen Gaskoina made four thousand francs on the day's work.

Thus far, apart from the longer glove, the game had not altered appreciably since Perkain's day. But profound changes were imminent. In the early 'fifties the miller of Mauléon introduced a very much longer glove at the end of which the ball could be held for a fraction of a second before being slung at the wall. The old sliced shot (*chirrichta*) was replaced by this more powerful and accurate shot, which was called *atchiki* from the Basque word meaning " to hold." The result, however, was a falling off in the popularity of the game, for the new type of glove was not only very heavy and difficult to wield, but extremely expensive. Consequently children and poor people began to look about for some sort of bat that was lighter and cheaper. In the late 'fifties several queer instruments became popular. In the valley of the Nive people took a big three-pronged wooden fork, cut off most of the handle, tied the prongs together with cord and filled in the intervening space with a rough string mesh. This instrument, called *matsardia*, must surely be the most primitive form of racquet on record.

Simultaneously other experiments were being made in the adjoining valley of the Nivelle. The frames of old sieves were cut into three pieces, each of which was made into a rough kind of curved bat called *zetabea*. This was tied to the wrist with a handkerchief, or holes were bored in it and it was fastened on with cord. Needless to say it was not much more serviceable than the *matsardia*.

One day in the early 'sixties a thirteen-year-old boy named Gantchiki Dithurbide of St. Pée was playing pelote with his friends. His father was the maker of a certain kind of elongated basket used for gathering beans or fruit, and for a joke Gantchiki played a stroke or two with one of these baskets. The result was so successful that he conceived the idea of using wicker for pelote gloves. His father set to work to make the new type of *chistera* (the name of the original fruit-basket), which rapidly supplanted the leather glove.

The *chistera* of those days was shorter and straighter than the modern kind. It was, in fact, an exact reproduction in wicker of the old leather glove. The stroke used was still the slice or the *atchiki*. But the greater force which could be imparted to the ball, coupled with the improvement recently effected in the latter by the introduction of a rubber core, resulted in a complete transformation of the game. Hitherto the ball, which had been composed of tow covered with leather, had been very dead, and it would have been impossible to knock it up against the wall. The introduction of a rubber core made all the difference, and in place of the old up-and-down games people began to play after the manner of fives. The innovation was strongly opposed by the traditionalists, and on many courts notices were put up forbidding *blaid* to be played. But the new game rapidly became popular and displaced the old to a considerable extent. There were several reasons for this. For one thing the ball now went so much further that many courts were too small for *rebot*. At Sare I have seen the *refileur* hit the first-floor windows of the houses at the far end of the court over a hundred yards away. *Blaid* was less expensive than *rebot*, less difficult and less complicated. Moreover, it could be played one- or two-a-side, while ten people were required for the older game. About this time, therefore, most of the walls of the village courts, which hitherto had been quite small, were enlarged to enable *blaid* to be played, and the old masonry can still be distinctly seen framed within the new.

The disadvantages of the game as played with the old short *chistera* were that it tended to damage the arm-muscles and that the back-hand, being extremely difficult, could only be used as a defensive stroke. In 1888 Melchior Curuchague, playing at Buenos Aires, broke his wrist. In order to be able to play again when it had healed he manufactured a very long and curved *chistera* with which he played back-handed, using his left hand to support his weak wrist. The new instrument and the new style found favour, especially among foreigners, and a new game, almost exclusively professional, came into being under the name of *a punta* in Spanish and *atchiki handi* in Basque. This is the game loosely called *pelote à chistera* of which Chiquito de Cambo is the principal exponent.

Professionalism developed greatly towards the end of the nineteenth century, especially in Spain, where enormous closed courts were built for the games of *remonte* and *pala*.

Nobody with an afternoon to spare in San Sebastian should miss seeing one of the daily games of *remonte* played at the Fronton Jai Alai by four of the big aces of the game. The court is some sixty or seventy yards long by eleven wide. There is an object-wall, a long side-wall and a back-wall. The right-hand side is filled with

tiers of seats for the spectators.   For a few minutes the
newcomer, deafened by the din which assails his ears,
will scarcely be able to follow the game, for in front of the
spectators there stand a row of bookmakers, their backs
turned to the game, who never stop shouting the odds
which vary with every point scored.   Wagers are all
between one spectator and another.   The management
takes a percentage on winning bets, and the bookmakers,
their employees, act only as go-betweens.   The *habitués*
signal to them the odds which they are prepared to give,
and they shout them out in *duros* (five-peseta pieces).
" *Treinta a cuarenta azules* " (thirty to forty on blues),
one hears them cry : or " *quince colora'os* " (fifteen on
reds, evens).   Other spectators take up these wagers
and signal their acceptance to the bookmaker, who
registers them on a bi-coloured betting-slip which he
tears in half.   He places each half in a little wooden ball
which he throws to each punter, who takes his slip and
returns the ball.   Fortunately the bookmakers are
usually old *pilotaris* with a good eye, and there is very
little risk of suddenly getting a ball in one's face.   The
danger from behind, however, is appreciably greater.
Bets are settled in cash at the end of the game, and I have
never heard of any welshing.   The great thing is to
profit by the ups and downs of the game so as to lay
favourable odds on both sides and thus make a profit
whichever wins.   I have often heard it alleged that the
course of the game, if not its final result, is arranged
beforehand, but I have no idea whether there is any truth
in this, although the introduction of professionalism into a
game naturally tends to lead to this sort of abuse.
     Personally I find that I can enjoy the game far better
as a spectacle if I have no pecuniary interest in its result.
Remonte is played with a very hard, lively ball, and is
extraordinarily fast.   The player seems to fling himself
at the ball, and practically the whole force of the body is
put into every shot.   Although the ball in reality hits the
glove-basket near the wrist and travels down it and out

at the far end the whole thing happens so quickly that to the eye the stroke is as instantaneous as a straightforward rebound.   It is only the bound of the ball that enables one to see that it has been heavily sliced.   So great is the spin imparted that a ball hit from near the side-wall to the middle of the end-wall can be made to return along the same path instead of glancing off at the corresponding angle.   As a ball travelling along the side-wall can only be played back-handed, and even then the player is hampered by the wall, it is deliberately placed there whenever possible.

Each side consists of a forward and a back.   Service is from a point near the back-wall, and the serve must pitch between two lines drawn, the one about a quarter and the other about half-way down the court.   The simplest stroke is extraordinarily difficult if one has not learnt the knack.   When I first tried the easier *atchiki* shot with the long *chistera* I slung the ball over my head far away behind me.   But before long by dint of keeping my wrist bent back as far as possible I was able to return the ball against the wall.   I have never tried the *chirrichta* shot, but my friend Vega, one of the stars of *remonte*, tells me that even if I were to stand only a yard or two from the wall and try to return the gentlest lobs I should probably fail to get a single one back.   Actually the most difficult stroke is a back-hand off the back-wall, which it is almost impossible to take without falling over.

The *remonte* court is often used for a game played according to the same rules but with a *pala* or long and narrow wooden bat tapering towards the handle.   This bat is probably a descendant of the *battoir* which was once used in the *jeu de paume*.   The game is, if anything, faster than *remonte* and the ball is extremely lively.   In the Argentine an instrument called a *palette*, resembling a large ping-pong bat, is used with a heavy rubber ball especially manufactured in England.

All the games thus far described owe their origin to *longue paume*, but *courte paume* was not without its influence on pelote.   It was almost certainly played in many of the towns and larger villages of the Basque Country, for there are numerous trinquets on both the French and the Spanish side.   Some are of the type known as the *jeu carré*, but the majority are *jeux de dedans*.   It is probable that they were used for *courte paume* until the end of the eighteenth century, when the popularity of the game waned considerably.   The Basques then proceeded to make use of the empty courts for pelote, taking over, not only the net and the peculiarities of the court, but also a simplified form of the rules.   At the beginning of the nineteenth century the game in vogue was the now almost obsolete *pasaka*.   This was played either with the bare hand or with the short leather glove.   The ball was a very heavy one, weighing anything up to two pounds.   Unfortunately the popularity of *pasaka*, like that of *rebot*, was undermined by the general adoption of the rubber-cored ball, and the old game was supplanted by *blaid*.   The net disappeared, the third side of the pent-house was removed in order to furnish an object wall and the tambour was moved to the angle formed by the end- and right-hand-side-walls.   The pent-house on the remaining two sides, the dedans and the grille (*zilo* in Basque) were all retained and help to make *blaid à main nue au trinquet* a very diverting form of fives, in which, by the way, the scoring, as in all other forms of *blaid*, is no longer by games but by single points.

At the beginning of this century the tremendous popularity of pelote as a spectacle and as a pretext for gambling, with the attendant increase in professionalism, affected the game adversely, and, threatened by the spread of football, it lost ground as the national game of the Basques.   Of late years, however, excellent work has been done by the *Fédération Française de Pelote Basque* in reviving the older forms of the game, standardising the rules and generally placing pelote on a sound and permanent footing.   Although one can have nothing but praise for what the Federation have done and the way in

which they have done it, it is difficult not to regret the
palmy days when the game needed no artificial prop
and when the lack of any centralised governing body did
not result in the confusion and abuses which grew up
in the early years of this century.

The games of ninepins and skittles which are played in
the Basque Country are quite undistinctive. But a form
of field event, extensively practised in the Spanish
provinces, presents some interesting features. This is
called *palanka* or *barra* and is first mentioned in the
literature of the eighteenth century. The *palanka* is
something between the javelin and the discus of the
Ancients, for while it retains the form of the javelin it
weighs anything from ten to twenty-five pounds. There
are four traditional ways of throwing the *palanka*. The
first, known as *bularrez*, is the same as the ordinary javelin
throw. The second, *biraka*, is preceded by a half-turn,
as in the first movement of the discus throw. Then come
the curious and difficult *isterpe* or *anka-pe*, in which the
palanka is thrown from between the legs, and finally
a Guipuzcoan speciality called *zazpi bira* (seven turns),
resembling the three turns of the discus thrower.

Gabino Lizarra of Berastegui is credited with the
following record performances, all made in 1913 with the
amarreko or ten-pound *palanka* :

Bularrez : 118 feet (equalled by Andres de Uriguen).
Biraki : 186 feet.
Isterpe : 100 feet.

The Spanish provinces are also the scene of various
contests, half sporting and half professional in character,
which arouse great interest. The *aizkolaris*, for instance,
have to hack through a given number of beech logs in
the shortest possible time. The *jasotzales* are weight-
lifters, and the *arri-zulatzales* are stone-borers from the
quarries at Motrico and Deva. Paolino Uzcudun, the
famous boxer, first distinguished himself as an *aizkolari*.

With a certain degree of reluctance I must also mention
the *Antzar-joko* (Goose-game) and the *Oilachko-joko* (Hen-

game), neither of which have I ever seen, nor frankly would care to see. For the former, therefore, the following description, taken from Fabre's " Antonio le Navarrais," must suffice :—

" At one end of the square was a cord stretched between two posts on which an unfortunate goose was hung by its legs, with its beak transfixed by one of its own torn-out feathers. . . . The young men who were to compete were drawn up in a row on horseback. . . . The signal is given. . . . A horseman dashes forward, swift as an arrow, and as he passes the wretched bird he tries to sever the head from the body with his bare hand, a barbaric sport which could be compared to bull-fighting, did it not lack the danger of the latter."

The Hen-game would have nothing more to recommend it were it not for the ceremonial which attends it. For the following details I am indebted to Philippe Veyrin, who saw it revived (for the first time in fifteen years) at Amotz near St. Pée. At the appointed spot a rough platform is erected, on which a throne is improvised from a couple of chairs covered with a piece of red velvet. Close by, a hen is imprisoned in a wooden box with a narrow hole in it through which the bird's neck is passed as though it were in the stocks. The actors in the game then approach in procession. First come the King and Queen preceded by two musicians (clarinet and cornet !), the former in a red béret, white breeches and a scarlet coat with green ribbons and brass buttons, armed with a big sword and a bouquet for a sceptre ; the latter in a white dress with flowing train and a diadem of artificial pearls. Their immediate retainers are followed by a score of young men and girls walking hand in hand in couples, clad in white with the red trappings of dancers. One young man has no partner. When the King and Queen have seated themselves on the throne, this young man takes up his position near the hen with a sword in his hand and a clean napkin folded over his left arm. The music begins to play, and the row of couples dance up to the

King. Then they stop. The sword-bearer hands his
sword to the first of the maidens, who takes it, kneels
down on a cushion and, with the gesture of a pagan priest
offering sacrifice, brings it down on the neck of the hen.
Were the sword sharp all would be well.   But it is not,
and the whole ceremony must be repeated ten or twenty
times before the head is finally severed from the body.
In bygone days the hen was buried up to its neck in the
ground, and the maiden executioners were blindfolded.
One cannot help wondering from what grim pagan rite
this bloodthirsty custom may have sprung.

CHAPTER XIV

SUPERSTITION AND WITCHCRAFT

In the character of the Basques there is a strong vein
of superstition, the common heritage of all simple and
primitive peoples, which at first sight seems strangely out
of harmony with their sincere and sober religious feeling.
When, however, one comes to look more closely into their
spiritual composition one sees that there is an element
underlying their piety and their superstition which
explains both and makes it possible for both to exist side
by side in the same individual. That element is fear.
The Basques fear their God more than they love him,
and, although little or no superstition enters into their
religious beliefs and practices, they have also conserved
the fear of primitive man for the forces of nature and the
powers of evil.

Many of their superstitions concerning good or evil
omens are shared with other races. Others are peculiar
to themselves. They consider it unlucky, for instance,
to see a woman beneath a window, to kill a cat, to pass in
front of a sleeping dog, to see a cat jump through a
window or to hear an owl hoot. There are just as many
favourable omens. A black hen is as lucky to the Basques
as a black cat is to the English. A goat in a stable is a

preservative against evil spirits.   A swallow's nest brings milk and honey to a house.   A man who has money in his pocket the first time he hears the cuckoo sing will never lack it for the rest of the year.

As in many other countries, Christmas Eve, New Year's Eve and Midsummer Eve are associated with various superstitious beliefs and practices.   Garlic sown on Christmas Eve is regarded as a cure for madness, as is also *ogisalutadore* (Saviour bread), the crust of the bread eaten on Christmas Eve, over which the sign of the cross has been made.   *Ogisalutadore* also serves to calm a rough sea, to make floods go down and to abate rainstorms.

Needless to say there are countless superstitions connected with death.   It is a sign that Death is hovering near should a dog howl in the night, a bell-peal resound an unnaturally long time, or the bell ringing for the elevation of the Host coincide with the striking of the hour.   If the fire goes out on Christmas Eve it is a sign that someone in the house will die before the year is out.   Curiously enough it is an equally sure presage of death to find, on going to pay a bill, that one has exactly the right sum in one's pocket.   When death does indeed visit a house a tile is taken from the roof to release the soul of the deceased, and, after the funeral, the *lastaira* (stuffing) of the dead man's mattress is burnt at the nearest crossroads.

In some Spanish Basque villages it is the custom to place on the bee-hives a piece of black cloth cut in the shape of a cross, as a sign of mourning.   In any case, the bees must always be told of the death of their master, although the reason offered for this custom varies in different parts of the country.   In some districts it is explained by the fear that they will desert their hives; in others they are adjured to make wax for candles to be burnt for the peace of the departed soul, and a special formula is used for breaking the news to them : *Jauna il dek ta eizue lan ari argi eiteko*—(The Master is dead, and

you must set to work to make light for him). The
cattle, too, will not be tranquil until they have been told
of their master's death.   It is said that when the *etcheko
jauna* of the house of Olha at Sare died away from
home, the first that his family knew of his death was that
the cattle filled the air with strange lowings and would not
be silent until the news came, and was imparted to them
according to custom.   Joseph Nogaret has told me of
villages where, if death visits the house, the cattle are
awakened and no longer allowed to remain lying down,
and where, most symbolical of all superstitions, the fire is
taken from the hearth and either buried or cast to the
four winds of heaven.

The belief in ghosts is not very widespread, although
it undoubtedly exists.   The Basques believe that the
spirits of those who have left some desire or vow unful-
filled return to earth clad in their burial clothes.   They
are visible only to those in a state of grace and are exor-
cised as soon as their desire is fulfilled.   The following
story was related to Manuel Lekuona of Oyarzun by his
mother : " The last phantom to appear was that of the
young wife of Emieta.   Some time after she had died she
began to appear to her sister-in-law Etcheberri of Carrika.
The phantom used to appear at night first in the form of a
vague mass at the foot of the trees, then hammering at
the window with ever greater strength.   Unable to stand
it the woman consulted a priest, who advised her to ask
the phantom if it were of good or of evil omen.   It
replied ' of good omen.'   She asked what it wanted.
The phantom replied that it had vowed two Masses and
that it was waiting for them to be celebrated.   The sister-
in-law states that she paid for the Masses to be celebrated
and that she went to the church and heard them herself.
On coming out someone sprayed her with holy water ;
she saw no one but says that it was the spirit of her sister-
in-law who thus besprinkled her."

In various parts of Guipuzcoa and Vizcaya the belief
exists that souls in Purgatory wander about the earth

from midday on All Saints' Day till the same hour on All Souls' Day. At Larrabezua the people believe that the souls of their ancestors return to their homes on Christmas Night and leave footprints in the ashes of the hearth.

The Basques share the fear of most Southern races for the evil eye, which they consider to be especially dangerous to small children. Some twenty or thirty years ago an English lady of my acquaintance had great difficulty in escaping unharmed from the inhabitants of a Spanish village who had made up their minds that she had the evil eye. They make use of special amulets against the *begizko*, as they call it. A *kutun* (amulet) will probably contain an assortment of substances such as jet, charcoal, ashes, laurel and other herbs, holy bread, and chicken dung. Amulets of jet have been found in Basque dolmens and tombs of the Bronze Age.

The Basques further believe in the possibility of casting death-spells on their enemies by means of incantations which are especially potent at certain hours of the day, or through such rites as twisting or burning a candle. Practices of this sort clearly owe their origin to the belief in witchcraft, and it is in this belief that the principal manifestation of Basque superstition is to be found.

The popular belief is that the *sorgiñak* or witches are persons of both sexes who have either deliberately sold themselves to the Devil in exchange for supernatural powers, or have fallen into the power of the Evil One through some slip made by their parents during the baptismal service. Their Sabbath is known as the *akhelarre* or field of the goat, a name derived from the enormous black billy-goat which is said to be a prominent feature at their meetings. Originally no doubt the word was applied only to the meeting-place, but it has been extended to cover the assembly and all that goes on there.[1] The meeting-place is usually on a mountain-top. Aizchuri

---

[1] In Vizcaya the Sabbath is called *Petralanda* or *Eperlanda*, meaning probably " Peter's Field."

(behind the village of Zugarramurdi) and La Rhune both enjoy a bad reputation, though the funicular must surely have scared the *sorgiñak* away from the latter mountain. Sometimes the witches meet under a bridge or in a ruined building such as the old castle of St. Pée.

The Basque beliefs relating to sorcery correspond closely to those held universally and shown in the standard treatises on the subject. If a child or an ox sickens there is usually someone on whom the peasants can lay the blame, some old woman whom they have offended, some beggar or gypsy to whom they have refused alms. Webster states roundly that "witchcraft among the Basques has not yet arrived at the legendary stage. The difference is felt at once in taking down their stories. In the legends they are reciting a text learnt by heart. . . . But they retell the stories that deal with witchcraft in their own words, just as they would narrate any incidents which they believed to have befallen themselves or their neighbours." The following story, taken down by Pierre Lhande, reflects the popular belief as to what occurs at the *akhelarre* :—

" When Bidabe was a young man he arranged to get married. His betrothed had the reputation of being a witch, but witch or *lamiña* he was determined to marry her, for he loved her dearly. One evening he went to visit his betrothed and her parents. As a present for Kattalin he took a pair of sabots nicely cut and ready to put together. He took with him the leather uppers, the straps, the little nails of yellow brass, a hammer and an awl. He stayed some time with the family and it grew late. As it was a dark night he arranged with the people of the house that he should sleep on a wooden chest and leave at dawn. So he lay down and fell into a peaceful slumber.

" Just about midnight he was awakened by a slight noise. He did not move, but opened his eyes ever so little and saw Kattalin approach the fireplace. The girl lifted one of the hearth-stones and took out a bowl full of something that looked like oil. With this ointment she anointed her body and forthwith disappeared up the chimney. ' Now I know the truth about Kattalin,' said Bidabe to himself. He took the same bowl and, as Kattalin had done, he greased his body and made off in the same way. Without knowing where he was going he flew through the air and came to rest in a beautiful plain, where was gathered together as fine an assembly as ever you could see.

" Quite a number of Bidabe's friends were there. He saw Kattalin dressed in red silk, and stayed hidden, petrified with fear. He learnt a great deal about the Witches' Sabbath and found out, for instance, what virtue there is in alder-bark, what one can do with a stick of holly-wood, and what illness can be cured with mole's blood. He learnt furthermore how a man can pass through a key-hole and how one can discover the greatest of all secrets. Who knows what things he did not so unexpectedly learn ? But Bidabe had to keep these horrible things to himself under pain of being flayed alive.

" The hour had now come for rendering special honours to the Chief of the Sabbath. This was a big man, black of face, with great ears like two big cabbage leaves, long teeth and a narrow forehead. All the witches of the Sabbath were obliged to kiss his hind-quarters. When Bidabe saw what manner of salute this was, he began to scratch his head. However, he did not dare hang back. So he swore an oath as big as a mountain : ' A thousand million carts full of devils can carry you off yelling before you receive this honour from me ! ' When it was his turn he took the awl from his pocket and . . . zist ! he plunged it into the King of the Sorcerers. The black brute gave a roar which would have shaken the desert. Of a sudden all the lights went out and the witches disappeared.

" Bidabe found himself in a thicket of prickly bushes, in the ravine of Kakueta, and it was eight days before he could get out. The people of the house did not worry, for they thought that he had gone to the inn to get drunk with one-eyed Gilgorri. For two months Bidabe was ill with fright. As soon as he was better he started to look for another wife. And I promise you that Marie, she whom he married, was no witch."

Many of the beliefs connected with witchcraft are very curious. It is thought that if a priest were to forget to shut the Missal after reciting the prayers which follow the Communion, all the sorcerers would remain rooted in their places so long as the book lay open. A sorcerer or a bewitched person cannot die until his familiar spirit (called *familiara* in Basque and *enemiguillo* in Spanish) has been either sold or given away. These familiars are said to be acquired from the Chapel of Saint-Esprit on La Rhune. If they are sold, it must be for at least one maravedi more than was given for them. Some say that they may be given to a person, to an animal or even to an inanimate object. Any person accepting them usually takes care to do so for a limited time, making use of some such formula as : " I will take it from you for as long as this handful of straw continues to burn." In certain Spanish Basque villages the peasants go round their fields on St. John's Eve bearing burning bundles of straw or laurel and singing incantations :—

> St. John, St. John,
> To-day, to-morrow, St. John.
> The day after to-morrow,
> The day after St. John's Day
> Let there be on our property
> Neither thieves nor witches.
> If any there be, let them be burnt.
> May the corn and the maize be protected,
> And the thieves and witches
> And all vermin be burnt.

There appears to have been an outbreak of witch-craft in Navarre during the fifteenth century : and in 1558 Diego de Guinea, Maria de Guesala and other

s

inhabitants of Ceberio were tried at Valladolid and
sentenced to the "*tormento de agua e cordel*" on the
evidence of Catalina de Guesala, a child

of eight. Little is known of these
spasmodic outbreaks, and in any case
they cannot be compared with the
astonishing epidemic which devastated
Labourd at the very height of its
prosperity over a century later. This
epidemic may quite possibly have been
due in part to the presence of the
gypsies expelled from Spain. The supernatural has always been part of the
Romany stock-in-trade, and in Labourd
it was against the Romany folk, and
especially against their women, that the
first accusations of sorcery were levelled.

In 1576 Boniface de Lasse was dele-
gated by the *Bailli* of Labourd to inquire
into allegations of sorcery which were
daily growing more frequent. De Lasse, who has been
described as a hard and inhuman man, proceeded at
once to arraign a large number of women, both gypsies
and Basques, on charges of sorcery, and to burn over
forty of them at the stake.

In spite of this salutary lesson, a number of apparently
supernatural phenomena reduced the countryside to a
state of panic some thirty years later. Animals sickened
and died or were smitten with sterility; children disappeared; graves were desecrated, and people were
awakened by strange noises and movements in the night.
Things came to such a pass that the *Bayle* applied to the
Parliament of Bordeaux for a commission to inquire into
the matter. The result of this application was the
despatch to the Basque provinces of Counsellors de
Cruzeau and de Tardeau and Procuror-General Desaignes,
who spent a month in the district, but left without having
done anything to restore order, confidence or calm.

Indeed, the situation grew rapidly worse, for men began to spread allegations of sorcery against their enemies with the object of paying off private scores. Eventually the *Bailli*, Jean Paul de Caupenne, felt constrained to address a report on the subject to Henri IV. The King, "having been advised that his land of Labourd was greatly afflicted with sorcerers," instructed the Parliament of Bordeaux to charge Counsellor de Lancre, whose name has already been mentioned in these pages, to "hunt out the crimes of sorcery in the land of Labourd and neighbouring places." It seems that the Bordeaux Parliament knew their man, for at their instance a certain Despagnet was attached to de Lancre with the object of exercising a moderating influence over him. Unfortunately, Despagnet, who, although he believed firmly in sorcery, was probably less fanatical than his companion, was recalled as soon as he had set foot in the Basque provinces. De Lancre was thus left with full powers to use what means he pleased to extirpate the sorcerers who infested the region "because, good monks having driven the devils out of India and Japan, these had settled in the Basque Country, where they had found persons well disposed to receive them."

Unfortunately for the Basques, de Lancre arrived in their country at the time of year when most of the men were away fishing on the Newfoundland banks or whaling in Arctic seas. The Counsellor established himself at Saint-Jean-de-Luz, and initiated a positive reign of terror. His method was to arraign all suspects, extort confessions and the names of alleged accomplices and then condemn them to the flames. At first the general public were on his side, for they believed sincerely in the evil doings of the sorcerers. Gradually, however, they began to see what abuses were being committed in the name of justice and to fear for their own lives. Then they turned against the Commissioner. But de Lancre had established himself securely, and they were not to be rid of him so easily. A regular panic ensued. Some fled into Spain, inventing pilgrimages to Santiago or Montserrat as an excuse for their hasty departure, and de Lancre found himself collaborating with the Inquisition for their extradition. Others denounced their neighbours with the object of diverting suspicion from themselves. No one was safe whatever his position, opinions or reputation. A woman was burnt on the sole evidence of a little girl of seven, who declared that she had seen her jump from the top of La Rhune to the beach at Hendaye seated astride a broomstick. It was discovered that the activities of the Basque witches were not restricted to their own country. They often went out to Newfoundland, perched on the mast of a fishing-boat, in order to poison the catch which the sailors spread out to dry. Jeannette d'Abadie of Ciboure admitted that she had been to Newfoundland in this manner, and that she had seen witches from nearly all the parishes of Labourd conjuring up storms and sending the sailors to their death.

The longer grew the list of his victims the greater zeal did de Lancre display. In his own account of the proceedings he admits that he thought it better to punish the innocent rather than to risk the escape of a single sorcerer. "To hang and to burn without picking and choosing," he writes, "that is the best way of ensuring the punishment of the guilty."

Meanwhile reports of what was passing had reached the Basque sailors at Newfoundland, who hastened back to protect their womenfolk. They could not influence the fanatical de Lancre, but their threats were sufficient to deter the executioners from carrying out his orders. De Lancre, baulked of his prey, turned his attention to the priests, of whom he expresses his strong disapproval: "No one reproaches them for haunting the cabarets, for dancing, for paying excessive attention to their dress, for playing ball-games in the streets, for walking about the villages pike in hand or attending the village feasts. They are in the habit of going on pilgrimages to Our Lady of Irún, and elsewhere in the neighbourhood, accompanied by three or four pretty girls.   This is the usual mode of life of the Navarrese priests beyond the frontier, and of our own, as I have often seen."

The Vicar of Ascain, an old man of seventy-five, was tried on the evidence of two women who testified to having seen him at the Sabbath.   No fewer than twenty-four witnesses declared that they had seen the Vicar and Curate of Ciboure celebrate the Black Mass in Ciboure Church. The Vicar of Ascain admitted his guilt, and the two Ciboure priests protested their complete innocence.   All three alike were defrocked and burnt at the stake. Eventually Monseigneur d'Echauz, Bishop of Bayonne, came to the help of his priests.   He wrote to the King and obtained the recall of de Lancre who, during the three months of his mission, had steeped the whole country in blood and left the prisons crowded with those whom he had had no time to judge.

It was some time before the country returned to a normal state.   Even after the departure of de Lancre accusations of witchcraft were not rare.   In one instance a man demanded eight sous from another who claimed that he owed him no more than five.   The matter was taken before the courts where the debtor declared that his creditor was a sorcerer and that the debt represented a fine imposed on him for not attending the Sabbath.   The crowd seized the creditor and, having extorted a confession from him by torture, put him to death.

The outbreak was not without its repercussions over the border, for in 1615 the Inquisitors of Navarre and Guipuzcoa issued an appeal to all those " who had strayed into the sect of wizards and sorcerers " to return to the fold of the Catholic Church.

In 1612 two Jesuit fathers were sent to purify and pacify Labourd.   Their report on their mission shows that, whether or not sorcery was practised in that province, there was at any rate a general desire to confess to every sort of diabolical practice.   " When they penetrated further into the Basque Country," runs the account,

" crowds came to them from all parts and, without having been interrogated or denounced by others, declared to them that they had given themselves over voluntarily to sorcery. . . . Monstrous things were told of the priests who professed these execrable practices. . . . In a cave filled with all sorts of impurities they went so far as to simulate the holy sacrifice of the Mass, and, in place of the Celestial Host, they offered the adoring communicants a piece of some substance black as pitch. . . . At these assemblies of sorcerers they concoct a poison which they boil in cauldrons in order to spread disease among crops, flocks and men.   Children aged from six to seventeen came to us in large numbers complaining that while still young and innocent of evil they had been carried off by the witches to their nocturnal mysteries and forced, with blows, to profess the infernal cult from which they had never since been able to free themselves either by force or by guile. . . . Besides these children there came to us to be cured many persons of advanced age, who had criminally served the Evil One for forty or fifty years. Among others there came to us a sorcerer who, to the detriment of many, had publicly professed sorcery in those parts, and who proved to us the sincerity of his abjuration by bringing to us his magical treatises to burn. . . ."

The sceptical mind of the twentieth century may find it difficult to understand how no more than three hundred years ago the belief in these things was general, not only among simple peasants, but even among the majority of educated persons.   Nevertheless, the Jesuits' account of their mission breathes a spirit of conviction which is more than credulity, which indeed is almost convincing. This epithet cannot be applied to de Lancre, whose work, nevertheless, is valuable in that it shows that witchcraft as practised or professed in the Basque Country differed in no important point from the contemporary beliefs throughout Western Europe.

It is impossible, therefore, to dismiss Basque witchcraft as the product of de Lancre's diseased and fanatical mind or to stigmatise it as a form of highly contagious hysteria. The belief must have had some foundation in solid fact. One is not bound to admit that throughout the Middle Ages human beings succeeded, like Faust, in conjuring up the Evil One and in selling their souls for the life-long enjoyment of supernatural powers, or that they actually rode through the air on broomsticks or devils' backs. But there are other possible explanations. In " The Witch Cult in Western Europe," Miss M. A. Murray puts forward a sane and objective interpretation of witchcraft, which, though by no means proven, does not directly conflict with the available evidence on the subject.

Briefly, Miss Murray's theory is that witchcraft constitutes a secret survival into Christian times of a pre-Christian religion or cult which had been, so to speak, driven underground by Christianity. For reasons which cannot be entered into here Miss Murray calls this religion the Dianic cult. An extract from the introduction to her book gives some idea of its nature :—

" The evidence proves that underlying the Christian religion was a cult practised by many classes of the community, chiefly, however, by the more ignorant or those in the less thickly inhabited parts of the country. It can be traced back to pre-Christian times, and appears to be the ancient religion of Western Europe. The god, anthropomorphic or theriomorphic, was worshipped in well-defined rites ; the organisation was highly developed ; and the ritual is analogous to many other ancient rituals. The dates of the chief festivals suggest that the religion belonged to a race which had not reached the agricultural stage ; and the evidence shows that various modifications were introduced, probably by invading peoples who brought in their own beliefs."

The existence of such a cult is not manifest at first sight in de Lancre's book or in the records of witchcraft trials throughout Western Europe in the fifteenth, sixteenth and seventeenth centuries, for in these the talk is all of Satan and the supernatural. Miss Murray explains this by the fact that " as every non-Christian god was in the eyes of the Christian the opponent of the Christian God, the witches were considered to worship the Enemy of Salvation, in other words the Devil." " Our sorcerers," notes de Lancre, " regard these devils as their gods." It is, moreover, most significant that, whereas according to de Lancre's book it was always Satan that his suspects admitted having served, in the folk-tales the Master of the Sabbath is usually called the *Jaun Gorri* or Red Lord. This tends to confirm Miss Murray's supposition that the word Satan or Devil which appears so frequently in the depositions in England, France and the Basque Country was not the word naturally used by the witnesses, but was put into their mouths by the judges or interpolated in the written records. Another point in favour of Miss Murray's theory, and one which can hardly be explained by any other means, is the astonishing readiness of many of the witches to admit their guilt, to glory in it and to go to the stake with the fanatical joy of the early Christian martyrs. " And there are sorcerers," writes de Lancre, " who are so attached to the Devil's service that no pain or torture astonishes (*sic*) them, and you would say that they went to true martyrdom and death for love of him as gaily as they would go to a feast of pleasure and public merry-making." This devotion seems to have survived even de Lancre's reign of terror, for when Francisque Michel wrote his book in the middle of the nineteenth century there lived at Saint-Jean-le-Vieux an old man of eighty, who prided himself on being the King of the Sorcerers and enjoyed a considerable reputation as a doctor and soothsayer. Wentworth Webster was even informed " on undoubted authority that, only a year or two back (*i.e.* in about 1875), a country priest was sorely puzzled by one of his parishioners, in his full senses, seriously and with contrition confessing to him that he frequented the Sabbath."

The devotees of the cult were organised in different congregations like any Christian sect. In England these congregations were known as " covens " (from the word " convene ") consisting each of thirteen initiates. There were two forms of assembly : the *esbat* (a name found only in France proper and not in the Basque Country) which was " only for the special and limited number who carried out the rites and practices of the cult," and the Sabbath, or general assembly of all its members. There is no reason to suppose that the central figure of the Sabbath, whether he were called Devil, Satan or Red Lord, was other than a human being, a high priest of the cult, in whom the god was personified, and who was usually masked or disguised with the help of skins as a bull, cat, dog, horse or, as was usually the case in the Basque Country, as a goat. Of this animal disguise Miss Murray writes that " from the analogy of other religions in which the custom occurs it would appear that it is a ritual for the promotion of fertility ; the animal represented being either the sacred animal of the tribe or the creature most used for food." The goat, be it noted, was the favourite sacrifice of the ancient Vascones. " The Devil," said one of de Lancre's witnesses, " was in the form of a goat, with a tail, and beneath it a black human face."[1] " When he receives someone to make a pact with him," adds de Lancre, " he always presents himself in human form." In England, though not in the Basque Country, there were a number of cases of witches recognising in the Grand Master of the Sabbath human acquaintances of their own. The minor dignitaries appear, in the Basque Country at any rate, usually to have been women, for de Lancre states that " in each village there was to be

[1] A two-faced God named Janus or Dianus was worshipped in Italy, and to-day the Fool who accompanies the dancers of Ochagavia wears a mask in front and behind. One of the earliest known mentions of witch-craft is a ninth-century decree attributed to a General Council of Ancyra, and quoted by Miss Murray (*op. cit.* p. 22) : " Certain wicked women, reverting to Satan, and seduced by the illusions and phantasms of demons, believe and profess that they ride at night with Diana. . . ."

found a Queen of the Sabbath, whom Satan held in delight like a privileged wife."

The ritual of the cult, which de Lancre describes in great detail, appears to have comprised initiation ceremonies including, of course, the renunciation of Christianity, and the renewal of vows, culminating in the ritual kiss which so horrified the hero of Pierre Lhande's story and in the branding of the devotee with a special mark. This was followed by the dances mentioned in a previous chapter, and a banquet. "After the dance," writes de Lancre, "they sometimes begin to jump." This is an indication that the dances were intended primarily to promote fertility, for, in Miss Murray's words, "the jumping dance seems to have had for its object the growth of the crops; the higher the performers jumped the higher the crops would grow." The climax of the *akhelarre* was the celebration of a Black Mass with black candles and a black host, degenerating finally into a sexual orgy which appears only slightly less monstrous when it is remembered that the religion was primarily a human and animal fertility cult.

Miss Murray shows that even the most apparently incredible features of witchcraft are capable of natural explanation. The transformation of the witches into animals, for instance, she regards as having been ritual rather than real: " that is to say that the witches did not attempt to change their actual form, but called themselves cats, hares or other animals." Marie d'Aspilcouette, who testified before de Lancre, seems to bear this out: " Those who thus transformed themselves said that they were not really transformed but only that they seemed so to be." Even the fantastic Ride to the Sabbath may have some foundation in fact, for Professor S. J. Clark contributes an Appendix to Miss Murray's book in which he shows that the flying ointment used by the witches, including such drugs as aconite, belladonna and hemlock, would produce " mental confusion, impaired movement, irregular action of the heart, dizziness and shortness of breath," and might actually produce the sensation of flying.

The fact that many of the Basque folk-dances apparently owe their origin to a fertility cult long since forgotten, might at first sight appear to be an obstacle to the acceptance of Miss Murray's theory.   On closer examination, however, there would seem to be no reason why the primitive religion should not have survived in two independent forms, the one a conscious tradition and the other an unconscious one.   " This heathenism," writes Miss Murray, " was practised only in certain places and among certain classes of the community.   In other places the ancient ritual was either adopted into or tolerated by the Church; and the Maypole dances and other rustic festivities remained as survivals of the rites of the early cult."   One must also not exclude the possibility that the continuity of the tradition from fertility cult to witchcraft on the one hand and to ritual dances on the other may not have been unbroken in the Basque Country itself, and that either of the two later manifestations may have been introduced from outside at a later date.

CHAPTER XV

FISHERMEN AND CORSAIRS

IT is not until he leaves his own country that the Basque appears to cast off the sloth and indolence which impede his progress at home, and to display his inherent energy and initiative. On the high seas the stimulus of exile brings out these latent qualities in an atmosphere free from the destructive influences of cosmopolitanism and of revolution and political intrigue, which tend to counteract the good influence exercised on the Basques by emigration to South America. The sea reveals their powers of courage and endurance in a finer light than any other field of activity, and this little handful of fishermen and mariners have as glorious a maritime history as any of the great seafaring nations.

It is uncertain whether the Basques were the inventors of whaling, or whether they learnt it from the Normans. They are known to have carried on this most hazardous occupation long before the English and other nations first copied them and then drove their whalers off the sea. But it will never be known exactly at what period Basque fishermen first ventured in their flimsy little craft to attack the whales (*Balena biscayensis*) which, fleeing from the colder waters of the North, used to pass within sight of their shores from the autumnal equinox till the end of winter. It has been suggested that the whaling industry flourished in the Bay of Biscay as early as the tenth century, but there is no evidence of its existence until the year 1199, when Jean Sans Terre gave to one Vital de Biel the tithe on two whales. In the thirteenth and fourteenth centuries whaling was still to all intents and purposes a Basque monopoly. All along the coast there were watch towers of which the memory survives to-day in the place-names of Guéthary and Guetaria. One such tower still exists at Saint-Jean-de-Luz, and there were others, which have now disappeared, at Bordegain and Sainte-Barbe. If any further evidence were necessary of the importance attached to whaling it could be found in the presence of a whale in the seals or arms of such towns as Biarritz, Motrico and Lequeitio.

In olden times, at the right season of the year, a watcher was posted on the tower day and night. As soon as he saw a whale blowing he set light to a pile of wet straw or branches at the top of the tower, and, to the sound of drums, the fishermen would put to sea, ten or twelve in a boat, and attack the monster. The industry, though highly dangerous, was extremely profitable, for there were few parts of the catch which could not be used. The fat, of course, was boiled down for oil, the meat was eaten (the tongue, a special delicacy, being sometimes reserved for the Bishop), the vertebræ were made into seats and the ribs were used for fences, or as beams in the construction of houses.

Andrea Navagero has left a very good description of the industry :—

"The whale-fishing is a marvellous thing. Each year they capture some here (at Bayonne) or at Saint-

Jean-de-Luz; but their capture is very arduous, for they have to fight them, and each year many die in these battles because of the resistance which the beast opposes. When they discover that a whale is heading for the land (which happens at a certain period of the year which they know and when they keep a look-out) well-manned boats put out in great number and cut off its retreat to the open sea, surrounding the whale as the latter comes nearer in to the shore. The whale, like other cetaceans, cannot stay long under water, but comes to the surface to breathe; at this moment those who are in the boats, as soon as they see it, fling certain small tridents fastened to cords. The monster, feeling the blow, makes a great to-do and disappears in the water, rushing towards the boats and striking them with its tail which it keeps in the air, so that it often causes many to perish; but the men make haste to fly, letting out the cord which is fastened to the trident, which last cannot come out as it is barbed. And when the beast comes to the surface to breathe, they strike it on every side with many of these harpoons described above, so that, many times wounded and finally exhausted and bound with an infinite number of ropes which leave it no freedom of movement, it cannot avoid being brought in; and thus, gradually driven towards the shore, it still has no means of struggling and ultimately finds itself in such shallow water that the men are bold enough to approach and finish it off. Then, overjoyed at having made so fine a prize, they drag it up on to the beach, on which, owing to its great weight, it makes so deep a track that one can see the mark for several days. They divide the booty into numerous parts; some of it is sold fresh, and they say that the meat is excellent; and some is salted. From the head they draw several barrels of oil, by reason of the natural grease of these beasts. They hold the tongue to be a very savoury dish; therefore they sell it. In fact they draw so much meat from the beast that the whole of France could eat from one whale: and those who catch one gain

no less than two hundred ducats profit thereby, sending
the oil and the salted flesh into all the towns of France.
It is said, however, that those they catch are not big ones
but only young ones, and that there is no way of taking
the big ones. They also recount as a marvel that a big
whale once came to the aid of its daughter which they
were playing; and that it was so furious and drowned
so many people that they were obliged to leave their prey
and to fly for their lives. That the whale must be a very
big fish I am persuaded by certain hooks displayed at
Bayonne, which are enormous, and of which they say that
the whale receives a great number in its head, in its body
and in its tail. Of those parts which are as of bone they
make little black rings."

These words were written early in the sixteenth century
when whales had already grown scarce in Basque waters.
A hundred years earlier they were still quite plentiful
to judge from an edict of Louis XII fixing the royal dues
to be paid on every capture. As they grew rarer the
Basques, deprived thus of so remunerative a means of
livelihood, set out to follow them, first to the coasts of
Spain and Cape Finistere and then to Scotland, Iceland
(1412) and Newfoundland, their claim to the discovery
of which in 1372 can hardly be disputed. Unfortunately, the same cannot be said for the suggestion that
they reached America a century before Columbus,
although there is a tradition that Columbus, while lying
at the Azores, was told of lands which lay beyond the
setting sun by the captain of a whaler from " Ande
Luz " (which might equally be Andalusia or Saint-
Jean-de-Luz). It is by no means impossible that Basque
fishermen discovered America before Columbus (just as
they in their turn may well have been forestalled by the
Vikings), for by this time their ships were no longer the
light craft which could not pursue the whale out of sight
of their own shores. Many were equal in size to
Columbus' two bigger ships and far larger than the third,
the " Nina," with her crew of eight. The Basque

whaling-ships were usually caravels, pinnaces and, in the seventeenth century, brigantines of from 40 to 100 tons. In the year 1621 no fewer than sixty vessels of this type were equipped at Pasajes.

From Newfoundland the Basques went to the mouth of the St. Lawrence, where they left their name in legend and in the *Île aux Basques*.

In 1610 Pierre de Lancre was told that the " Canadians trafficked with the French in no other language than that of the Basques." An old document states that " from the earliest times when the Basques fished for whale and cod in the Gulf of St. Lawrence they made friends with all the savages of that country . . . particularly with a nation called Esquimaux, which has always been and still is intractable with all other nations, and since their language was absolutely different they formed a sort of *lingua franca* composed of Basque and two other different languages of these savages, by means of which they all understood each other very well."

Although they reached Hudson Bay, Labrador and even Greenland (1512) it was only in Newfoundland that they established themselves, attracted not only by the whales which had drawn them thither, but also by the cod which they subsequently found there, and which caused them to give the name of *Île de Bacaillau* (cod) to the island. Every year large colonies of Basques spent several months in Newfoundland, drying and salting the fish, and as late as 1710 French maps still recorded a number of unmistakably Basque place-names such as Orrognoa (Urrugne), Biarritz, Uli Cillo (Fly Hole), Bariachuria, Buria-Andia, etc. To-day all these names have disappeared, and in " The Times Atlas " I have been able to find nothing beyond Port aux Basques and Port-au-Chois (originally Portuchoa . . . the little port).

The cod-fishers remained at the Newfoundland banks, but as the whales retired further and further into the icy North the intrepid Basque whalers followed them until, early in the seventeenth century, a vessel from Labourd, blown far out of her course, reached Spitzbergen, which had been discovered only a few years previously by the Dutch. Here whales were still plentiful. For a time the Basque three-deckers competed with the English and the Dutch in those grey Northern seas, and Spitzbergen still boasts a *Baie des Basques*.

Whaling in those days can have been no sinecure. Conditions on board the Basque ships were extremely primitive and insanitary, and even the Captain had no cabin but slept where he could. The provisions rotted, and the water became stagnant or gave out altogether if the ship were becalmed or met contrary winds. The foetid odour of putrescent whale fat was never absent until the day when Martin Sopite of Ciboure invented a process for melting down the blubber on board ship. In the early days when they landed on inhospitable shores the Basque sailors had to defend themselves against hostile Indians, and at sea they had always to be on the look-out for icebergs, the avoidance of which was usually more a matter of fortune than of skill. If they returned safely to Southern waters there was the ever-present danger of falling into the hands of corsairs or Barbary pirates and of losing, if not their lives, at least their ships, their liberty and the fruits of their expedition.

Yet it was not the perils and hardships of their life that led to a gradual decline in the fortunes of the Basque deep-sea fishermen. It was rather that the ever-growing pressure of foreign competition and above all the surrender of Newfoundland to England by the Treaty of Utrecht in 1713 eventually drove them off the high seas. Attracted by the profits to be derived from whaling, the English and the Dutch began, as early as in the fifteenth century, to copy the Basque example. At first their lack of experience prevented them from constituting very formidable rivals. Gradually, however, they made their competition felt, and there were many ways in which they were able to hamper Basque activities.

In 1636, during one of the numerous wars between

T

France and Spain, Saint-Jean-de-Luz and the neighbouring ports were totally destroyed. The fishermen,
attracted by offers of high pay, entered the service of their
Dutch and English rivals, to whom, to their own subsequent disadvantage, they taught all the secrets of their
trade, including the Sopite process. This was the beginning of the end. As early as 1613 the English succeeded
in forcing the " Grâce de Dieu," commanded by Michel
Harostéguy, and the " Quatre Fils d'Aymon," commanded by Michel d'Etchepare, to surrender half their
catch for the privilege of whaling in Bell Sound, Spitzbergen. The creation of the Dutch Company of the
North, which allocated to itself all whaling rights from
Nova Zemblya to Davis Strait, completed the exclusion
of the Basques from these waters.

    The Basques continued their whaling activities spas-
modically until the end of the eighteenth century, but
long before that time they had found another and equally
lucrative outlet for their maritime energies. Until the
end of the fifteenth century the sense of racial unity
had prevented French and Spanish Basques from attacking one another and from interfering with each other's
ships on their return from fishing or trading expeditions.
But the almost continuous state of war between France
and Spain throughout the sixteenth century put an end to
this happy state of affairs, and in defiance of the Treaties

of Good Correspondence the Basque sailors threw in their lot with one or other of the belligerent powers and waged bitter war on enemy shipping. The whalers first armed themselves in self-defence and then took to privateering on their own account.

The corsairs increased rapidly in number, and the range of their activities widened in proportion. In 1585, for instance, a privateer from Bayonne captured off the Guinea Coast three Spanish ships with a cargo valued at 350,000 ducats. Not even the Spanish colonies were exempt from these unwelcome visits, and the sixteenth century echoes with complaints addressed to the mother country by the Antilles, San Domingo, Venezuela and even Peru. Nor was it to be expected that in the intervals between hostilities the Basques would willingly give up so lucrative a pursuit and return to peaceful occupations. With or without letters of marque they continued their piratical exploits, and among the famous buccaneers who had their headquarters at San Domingo in the seventeenth century there were several Basque names including those of Michel le Basque, who planned and executed audacious attacks on Maracaibo in 1666 and 1667, and Junqua de Bayonne, who, in collaboration with the Duc de Gramont, successfully surprised and pillaged Vera Cruz.

The Kings of France and Spain were not long in seeing the advantages to be gained by harnessing the exuberant energies of the Basque seamen, whose expeditions they encouraged while striving to bring them as far as possible under their control. The first French letters of marque were issued in 1528, and in 1556 we find the French Sovereign granting Haristague, de Somian and d'Ansogarlo " pardon and remission of the penalties which they had incurred for having, without His Majesty's previous permission, carried off sundry enemy vessels and sundry merchandise in the region of the Indies."

Saint-Jean-de-Luz, which a Spanish author described in 1559 as being " treated always with consideration by the Kings of France because its inhabitants are very bellicose, especially at sea," appears to have been particularly famous for its corsairs, and the Spaniards sent expeditions to destroy the town in 1542, 1558 and 1636. Nevertheless in 1692 Saint-Jean-de-Luz captured 125 prizes, and such was the agglomeration of shipping in the harbour that the Governor of Labourd was able to inform Louis XIV that " one could walk from the house where Your Majesty stayed as far as Ciboure on a bridge of ships made fast to one another." It is probable that the famous corsair Duconte was responsible for many of these, for during the previous year he had taken eleven prizes single-handed. Other famous Basque captains of this period were Cépé, whom Louis XIV summoned to Versailles and congratulated in person, Harismendy, Saint-Martin and Dolabaratz, who on one trip took four magnificent prizes off Greenland.

It was at about this time that, in France at least, privateering was put on a sound and systematic footing by a series of strict regulations, the first of which provided that the " ship-owner wishing to privateer must first obtain a commission from the Admiral of France and deposit 15,000 francs as a caution for any irregularities which may be committed." The regulations specified further that no hands could be enlisted who were liable to be called up for military service. As soon as a prize was taken a scrivener must board her, make a full inventory and place everything under seal. On arrival in France the spoils were divided thus : one-tenth to the Admiral of France ; six-tenths to the ship-owner ; and three-tenths to the captain and crew in specified proportions.

The ships of the corsairs were usually frigates or Biscayan sloops chosen for their speed and their light draught. They were not heavily armed, but relied for their victories rather on boarding, a method which had the advantage of sparing the prize from serious damage. Discipline was extremely strict. A mutineer was first tarred and feathered and then marooned. A man who drew his knife was pinned to the mast by the hands, tightly bound and left to loose himself as best he might. A murderer was roped to the corpse of his victim and thrown into the sea. The relatively minor offence of smoking before sunset was punishable by three consecutive duckings.

Other customs were less barbaric but more curious. There was, for instance, a special ceremony of initiation for new hands. The newcomer was bound to the mast, and on his hind-quarters a big cauldron was fastened on which all the crew hammered in turn. This penance was continued until he had parted with all his loose cash. The corsairs were in the habit of swearing fidelity to one another on bread, wine and salt, and on these occasions a libation was poured into the sea. In 1582 this practice was prohibited by decree on the ground that it savoured of paganism, but although the severest penalties were imposed they had little or no effect.

The regulation and control of privateering do not seem to have affected it adversely. On the contrary, it is not until the eighteenth century that it can be said to have reached its apogee. The Basque corsairs were a sharp thorn in the side of England during the Seven Years' War. In 1757, in addition to their contributions to the regular navy, Bayonne and Saint-Jean-de-Luz were between them responsible for arming forty-five privateers, the crews of which amounted to upwards of seven thousand men under such famous captains as Larreguy, Haramboure, d'Etchegaray, Danglade and Duler. The last-named was entrusted at the age of twenty-two with the command of the "Victoire" and her crew of three hundred and fifty. At the end of the war when there was less scope for privateers, he devoted himself to exploration. One of his compatriots named d'Etcheverry succeeded at the risk of his life in obtaining from the Moluccas seeds of various spice-bearing plants of which the Dutch had hitherto jealously guarded the monopoly.

The wars of the Revolution and of the Napoleonic Period gave the Basque sailors new opportunities for plying their favourite trade, although they were no longer able to afford the magnificent vessels in which they had sailed fifty or a hundred years before. Nevertheless Dihiart, Dargaignaratz, Destibertcheto, Etchebaster, Hiriart and Pellot have left their names and their exploits to history. Within only a few weeks a thirty-ton lugger, the " Indépendant," succeeded in taking five English prizes. The last great corsair was Garat, who, with his ship the " Tilsit " and a crew of fifty-five, fought two English brigantines for two days and emerged victorious from the struggle. It was not, however, until the Treaty of Paris was signed in 1856 that letters of marque, which had long been out of use, were finally and officially suppressed.

Before bidding farewell to the corsairs I will outline the life of d'Albarade, one of the last and greatest of their number. Born at Biarritz in 1743 he went to sea at the age of sixteen in the " Outarde " and the following year embarked in a corsair, the " Labourt " of Saint-Jean-de-Luz, which took thirteen prizes during the cruise. In one of these encounters d'Albarade received his first wound. The following year saw him embark first in the " Minerve " and then in the " Triomphante," both of Bayonne. At the end of the Seven Years' War he enlisted in the regular navy, but in 1779 he was privateering again, in command of a Breton ship, the " Duchesse de Chartres " of Morlaix. Severely injured in an engagement with three English ships, he was taken prisoner and remained in captivity till 1780. He was then given command of the " Aigle " of St. Malo, in which he made a highly successful cruise, capturing seventeen ships, including the privateering lugger " Greyhound " (Captain James Nelson of Bristol), which had hitherto succeeded in outdistancing all pursuers. To d'Albarade's misfortune his triumphs aroused the envy of his less successful colleagues, and on their denunciation he was arrested on a charge, which may not have been ill-founded, of having enrolled deserters from the regular navy. In spite of his protests of innocence the " Aigle " was disarmed, much to the relief of the British merchant service, and d'Albarade's letters of marque were withdrawn. Nevertheless he was taken into the regular navy and decorated in 1787 with the Order of St. Louis. In 1792 he was given command of the " Astrée " and entrusted with the special mission of re-establishing discipline in the navy, which had become thoroughly demoralised as a result of the Revolution. In this task he was so successful that in 1793 he became Minister of Marine. His position was no sinecure. Not only was the navy thoroughly disorganised, but in Paris it was difficult to steer an even course between extremists and reactionaries. Nevertheless d'Albarade retained his portfolio for twenty-six months in spite of a denunciation which described him as a very dangerous traitor. When his term of office was over he was made a Rear-Admiral. In 1800, after having been first condemned for incompetence and then acquitted, he retired. In 1805 he asked to be re-engaged, but Napoleon evidently did not like the independent and truculent tone of his application and returned no reply. It was not until the Restoration that d'Albarade's services met with the recognition which they deserved. He was then pensioned and made an Officer of the Legion of Honour. Legend relates that shortly before his death, which occurred on the last day of 1819, he swallowed his Cross of St. Louis in order to make sure that it should accompany him to the tomb.

To-day the glory has departed, and the Basque sailors pursue no prey larger or more dangerous than the common sardine. It is probable that in the Bay of Biscay the sardine has been fished since time immemorial. So, at least, it would appear from a letter written in 1750, but in reality it was not until about that date that the French Basques, whose cod banks had been so sadly circumscribed by the Treaty of Utrecht, began to find the sardine industry more practical and equally paying.

Previously the sardine, which lay near the surface only in the summer months, had been pursued exclusively by the Spanish Basques, who were able to fish French waters with impunity, " even within sight of Saint-Jean-de-Luz," as an old writer says, while their French cousins were absent whaling, privateering or trawling the Newfoundland banks. As the Spaniards had no salt, however, they could only sell the sardines fresh, and consequently the industry was never carried on on a large scale. Moreover, they were very inexpert as regards both their methods and the construction of their boats and gear.

In 1750 a Fuenterrabía fisherman invented a new type of net and a new method of fishing which resulted in greatly increased catches. As this coincided with the tendency of the French Basques to seek employment at home, a new joint industry was created, in which the Spaniards supplied the fish, which were packed and salted in French ports. A year or two later Saint-Jean-de-Luz alone was exporting over twenty thousand barrels annually. This arrangement was especially convenient, since the sardine shoals appeared off the coast of Labourd only in summer when the heat made their preservation more difficult, while they were larger and more abundant off Vizcaya in October and November and off Galicia during the winter.

The new commerce soon attained appreciable proportions and aroused the jealousy of the Bretons, who had hitherto enjoyed a virtual monopoly of the sardine industry and now found serious rivals in the Basques, to whom they had in the past abandoned the cod fisheries. There was already in existence a decree dated 1748 prohibiting the importation of sardines from abroad, but it was consistently overlooked by the authorities and, needless to say, evaded by those born smugglers the Basques. The Bretons attempted to secure its application, but in so doing they defeated their own ends, for the French

Basques began more and more to fish for sardine themselves, and a decree issued in 1784 granted them the right
of bringing into French ports sardines which they themselves caught in Spanish waters.   Although a 20 per
cent. duty was later placed on sardines brought from
Spain the trade has never ceased to develop, especially
since it was discovered that the sardine was never absent
from Basque waters, but lay at a lesser or greater depth
according to the temperature of the water and could
therefore be fished all the year round.

The " Traité Général des Pesches et Histoire des
Poisons," by Duhamel du Monceau (1772), gives a
detailed account of the methods which were employed in
those days and which have survived till the present time.
The net was shaped like a purse, some 150 feet long by
22 feet deep, and weighted with lumps of lead weighing
six or seven ounces.   It could be closed by a cord passed
through horn rings which were attached to the edge of
the net at small intervals.   The opening was buoyed up
with pieces of cork.

The boats, manned by a dozen oarsmen, located the
sardine shoals by the presence of sea-birds or porpoises.
While the rowers did their best to encircle the shoal the
fishermen let their nets down on the port side.   Each
net was controlled by two ropes held, the one at the bow
and the other at the stern of the boat.   As soon as the
net was thought to be full these two ropes, drawn tight,
closed the mouth, and the catch was hauled on board.
Since 1910 the old type of tackle has been largely supplanted by a new form of net into which the shoals are
attracted by means of a special kind of bait.

CONCLUSION

It has been the aim of this book to paint a living picture of the Basques and of their civilisation and traditions, dispelling as far as possible the current idea that they have always been a race apart, living in savage isolation in a land of which the physical features have severed them from all contact with their fellow-men. In this connection I am reminded of an anecdote told me by an old Basque lady who happened one day to be talking her native language to a friend at the *Jardin des Plantes* in Paris. An inquisitive Parisian, puzzled by the strange tongue, asked her what language she was speaking. On hearing her reply he excitedly collected a group of companions and begged my friend to talk Basque for their benefit. "*Monsieur,*" she replied proudly, "*nous ne sommes pas des sauvages.*" And she turned her back on them.

The Basques are not "savages," and their geographical isolation is a myth invented to account for the preservation of their language and their survival as a distinct race. If the survival of a primitive Pyrenean tribe had been brought about solely by geographical conditions, it is surely in the central massif rather than in the gentle hills and valleys near the ocean that this would have occurred. Yet east of the Pic d'Anie everything is permeated with the all-conquering Latin influence. On the other hand, a closer acquaintance with the Basque Country reveals the fact that its wilder parts were not populated till quite recently, and that many of the most remote villages, Les Aldudes and Esterençuby, for instance, were founded no more than a century ago.

If the Basques have preserved a language and a stock which have survived nowhere else the explanation must be sought, not in their geographical environment, but in their character.   For two thousand years they have been in close and constant contact with the Romans and their successors.   Yet an intensely conservative instinct has enabled them to retain their language and their individuality.   They have retained little more, for, in Vinson's words, " one is forced to admit . . . that they have nothing original, nothing really their own save their language."   Their customs, their amusements, their arts and crafts, at first sight so distinctive, prove to be a fusion of elements borrowed from their neighbours, stamped with their own personality and then treasured up with a tenacity which preserves them long after the original models have disappeared.

Those who come to the Basque Country in the hope of finding a race which has always been unique will either be disappointed or hypnotise themselves into seeing something which does not exist.   Wherein then lies the fascination of the Basques ?   Perhaps Camille Jullian has provided the best answer to this question.   " Each vanished age," he writes, " seems to have bequeathed to Basque civilisation at least one ineradicable custom."   To those who approach them with an open mind the Basques are infinitely precious, not as some inexplicable exception among races, but as a living museum of human history where one may study all that is left of an older Europe, vanished elsewhere, but lingering yet awhile in this quiet corner of the Pyrenees.

London, April 1930.

BIBLIOGRAPHY OF WORKS QUOTED OR CONSULTED

ALFORD, VIOLET. "English Folk Dances." London. 1923.
—— "The Basque Mascarades." *Folk Lore*, April 1928.
—— "French Basques : Cascarots and Cavalcades." *Music and Letters*, April 1929.
ANONYMOUS. "Euzkel Abestijak." Bilbao. 1915–16–17.
—— "Gernikako Arbola." Bayonne.
—— "Eskualdun Kantuak." Bayonne. 1921.
ARANZADI, TELÉSFORO DE. "Reconstitución del Pueblo Escualdunac." Bilbao. 1902.
AZKUE, R. M. DE. "Música Popular Baskongada." Bilbao. 1901.
—— "Cancionero Popular Vasco." Edición Manual sin Acompañamiento. Barcelona.
—— "Cancionero Popular Vasco. Canciones Selectas Harmonizadas por el Autor." Barcelona.
—— "Diccionario Vasco-Espanol-Francés." Bilbao. 1905–6.
—— "Música Popular Vasca." Bilbao. 1919.
BAESCHLIN, ALFREDO. "La Arquitectura del Caserío Vasco." Barcelona. 1930.
BELL, AUBREY. "The Magic of Spain." London.
BIRDWOOD, WILLIAM. "Sva." London. 1915.
BLADÉ, CHARLES. "Études sur l'Origine des Basques." Paris. 1869.
BLAZY, E. "La Pelote Basque." Bayonne. 1929.
BORDES, CHARLES. "Douze Noéls Populaires Basques." Paris. 1894.
—— "Dix Cantiques Basques Anciens." Paris. 1898.
—— "Douze Chansons Amoureuses du Pays Basque Français." Paris. 1898.
—— "Cortèges et Danses du Pays Basque." Paris. 1914–15.
BORROW, GEORGE. "The Bible in Spain." London.
BROCA. "Sur le Caractère des Crânes Basques." Pau. 1863.
CERQUAND, LOUIS. "Contes Populaires Basques." Pau. 1874.
CHAHO, AUGUSTIN. "Voyage en Navarre pendant l'Insurrection des Basques de 1831–1836."
—— "Histoire des Basques." 1847.
"CHANSON DE SAINTE FOI D'AGEN." Poème provençal du xi siècle édité d'après le manuscrit de Leide avec facsimilé, traduction, notes et glossaire par Antoine Thomas. Paris. 1925.
"CHANSONS DES PÈLERINS, LES." Compostelle. 1718.
COLAS, LOUIS. "La Tombe Basque." Bayonne. 1924.

COLAS, LOUIS. " Marins Basques du Temps Passé." Biarritz. 1927.
DARANATZ, JEAN-BAPTISTE. " Curiosités du Pays Basque." Bayonne. 1927.
DETCHEPARE, BERNARD. " Linguæ Vascorum Primitiæ." Bordeaux. 1545.
—— " Poésies Basques de Bernard Dechepare d'Eyheralarre. Nouvelle édition. Absolument conforme à la première de 1545." Bayonne. 1874.
DIHARCE DE BIDASSOUET. " Histoire des Cantabres." Pau. 1825.
DONOSTIA, R. P. JOSÉ ANTONIO DE. " IX Eguberri Abestijak." Madrid. 1915.
—— " Deun Agaten Abestijak." Bilbao.
—— " 16 Seaska-Euzko-Abestijak." Madrid. 1917.
—— " De Música Popular Vasca." Madrid. 1917.
—— " Salaberi'k Bildutako Euzkel Eresiak." Pamplona.
—— " Como Canta el Vasco." San Sebastian. 1921.
—— " Zeruko Argia." Paris. 1924.
—— " XLI Eleiz-Abesti-Sorta." Paris. 1925.
DUVOISIN, LE CAPITAINE. " La Poésie Dramatique des Basques." 1841.
ECHEGARAY, CARMELO DE. " Compendio de las Instituciones Forales de Guipúzcoa." San Sebastian. 1924.
FABRE, M. H. L. " Antonio le Navarrais."
FISCHER, C. A. " Voyage en Espagne." Paris. 1801.
FRANKOWSKI, EUGÈNE. " Estelas Discoideas de la Península Ibérica." Madrid. 1920.
GALLOP, RODNEY A. " 25 Chansons Populaires d'Eskual-Herria." Bayonne. 1928.
—— " La Chanson Populaire Basque." Bayonne. 1929.
GARIBAY, ESTEBÁN DE. " Compendio Historial."
GASCUE, F. " Origen de la Música Popular Vascongada." San Sebastian. 1913.
GAVEL, HENRI. " La Chanson de Berteretch." Bayonne. 1925.
GOYETCHE, LÉONCE. " Saint-Jean-de-Luz Historique et Pittoresque." Paris. 1883.
GRAVES, A. P. " The Celtic Songbook." London. 1928.
HARISPE, PIERRE. " Le Pays Basque." Paris. 1929.
HARISTOY. " Les Paroisses du Pays Basque pendant la Période Révolutionnaire." Pau. 1895.
HÉRELLE, GEORGES. " Canico et Beltchitine, Farce Charivarique." Paris. 1908.
—— " La Représentation des Pastorales à Sujets Tragiques." Bayonne. 1923.
—— " Le Théâtre Comique." Bayonne. 1925.
—— " Les Pastorales à Sujets Tragiques Considérées Littérairement." Bayonne. 1927.
—— " Le Répertoire du Théâtre Tragique." Bayonne. 1927.
HIRIART, ABBÉ S. " Eskualdun Eliza-Kantuak." Bayonne. 1926.

HUMBOLDT, WILHELM. " Prüfung der Untersuchungen über die Urbe-wohner Hispaniens vermittelst der Vaskischen Sprache." Berlin. 1821.
—— " Diario del Viaje Vasco." San Sebastian. 1925.
—— " Los Vascos." San Sebastian. 1925.
IZTUETA. " Guipuzcoaco Dantza Condaira. San Sebastian." 1824–1826.
JAURGAIN, JEAN DE. " La Vasconie." Paris. 1881.
—— " Quelques Légendes Poétiques du Pays de Soule." 1897.
JOUAN, ABEL. " Recueil et Discours du Voyage du Roi Charles IX en Champagne, Gascogne, Bayonne et autres lieux."
JULLIAN, CAMILLE. " Histoire de la Gaule." Paris. 1910–12.
LAHETJUZAN, DOMINIQUE. " Essai de Quelques Notes sur la Langue Basque par un Vicaire de Campagne sauvage d'origine." Bayonne. 1808.
LAMAZOU, PASCAL. " 14 Airs Basques." Pau.
LANCRE, PIERRE DE. " Tableau de l'Inconstance des Mauvais Anges et Démons." Paris. 1613.
—— " L'Incrédulité et Mescréance du Sortilège." Paris. 1622.
LARRAMENDI, MANUEL DE. " El Imposible Vencido."
—— " Corografía o Descripción general de la muy noble y muy leal Provincia de Guipúzcoa." 1882.
LEIZARRAGA. " Jesus Christ gure jaunaren Testamentu berria." Rochel-lan Pierre Hautin. Imprimiçale. 1571.
LÉON, ALBERT. " Une Pastorale Basque : Hélène de Constantinople." 1909.
LE PLAY, F. " Organisation de la Famille." Paris. 1871.
LHANDE, PIERRE. " L'Emigration Basque." Paris. 1910.
—— " Autour d'un Foyer Basque." Paris. 1918.
—— " Le Pays Basque à Vol d'Oiseau." Paris. 1925.
—— " Dictionnaire Basque-Français et Français-Basque. A–Arrunt." Paris. 1926.
—— Ibid., " Arrunte–Desterri." Paris. 1928.
LUCHAIRE, ACHILLE. " Remarques sur les Noms de Lieu du Pays Basque." 1874.
—— " Du Mot Basque ' Iri ' et de son Emploi dans les Noms de Lieu de l'Espagne et de l'Aquitaine Antique." 1875.
MANTEROLA, JOSÉ. " Cancionero Vasco. Poesías en Lengua Euskera Recogidas." San Sebastian. 1877–80.
MICHEL, FRANCISQUE. " Le Pays Basque." Paris. 1857.
MURRAY, MARGARET ALICE. " The Witch Cult in Western Europe." Oxford. 1921.
MUXIKA, G. " Pernando Amezketara, Bere Ateraldi ta Gertaerak." San Sebastian. 1925.
NOGARET, JOSEPH. " Petite Histoire du Pays Basque Français." Bayonne. 1928.
—— " Saint-Jean-de-Luz des Origines à Nos Jours." Bayonne. 1925.

OIHÉNART, ARNAUD. " Notitia Utriusque Vasconiae." Paris. 1656.
—— *Ibid.* (In Spanish). San Sebastian. 1929.
—— " Proverbes Basques, rééditées par Francisque Michel." 1847.
—— " Supplément à ces Proverbes réédité par V. Stempf." 1894.
OLMEDA, FEDERICO. " Cancionero Burgalés."
OLPHE GAILLARD. " Le Paysan Basque de Labourd à travers les Ages."
    La Science Sociale. Paris. 1905.
ORMOND, PATRICK J. " The Basques and their Country." London. 1924.
O'SHEA, HENRY. " La Tombe Basque." Pau. 1889.
—— " La Maison Basque." Bayonne. 1898.
PARACELSUS. " Paracelsi Opera Omnia." Geneva. 1658.
PEÑA Y GOÑI. " La Pelota y los Pelotaris." 1892.
PEREIRA DE LIMA, J. M. " Iberos e Bascos." Lisboa. 1901.
PHILLIPS BARRY. " British Ballads from Maine."
RAMOS, M. G. " De Astronomástica Vasca." Tarragona. 1928.
RODRIGUEZ-FERRAR, MIGUEL DE. " Los Vascongados." Madrid. 1873.
ROE, FRED. " Ancient Church Chests and Chairs." London. 1929.
SALABERRY, J. D. J. " Chants Populaires du Pays Basque." Bayonne.
    1870.
SANDOVAL Y ROXAS, BERNARDO. " Nos los Inquisidores contra la Heretica
    pravedad y Apostasia." . . . Logroño. 1615.
SANESTEBAN. " Colección de Aires Vascongados." San Sebastian.
—— " Cantos y Bailes Tradicionales Vascos." San Sebastian.
SAROIHANDY, J. " La Pastorale de Roland." Bayonne. 1929.
SCHUCHARDT, H. " Baskische Studien. I. Ueber die Entstehung der
    Bezugsformen des Baskischen Zeitworts." Vienna. 1893.
SICILLE LE HÉRAUT. " Le Blason des Couleurs en Armes, Livrées et
    Devises." 1860.
SICULO, LUCIO MARINO. " De las Cosas Memorables de España."
    Alcalá. 1530.
SOUPRE, J. ET J. " Maisons du Pays Basque." Paris. 1928.
—— " Maisons du Pays Basque Espagnol." Paris. 1930.
" TRADITION AU PAYS BASQUE, LA." Articles by various authors. Paris.
    1897.
TREND, J. B. " The Performance of Music in Spain."
UHLENBECK, C. C. " Contribution à une Phonétique Comparative des
    Dialectes Basques." Traduit avec révision de l'auteur par Georges
    Lacombe. Paris. 1910.
URABAYEN, LEONCIO. " La Casa Navarra." Madrid. 1929.
URTELL, HERMANN. " Zum Iberischen in Süd-Frankreich." Berlin.
    1917.
—— " Zur Baskischen Onomatopoesis." Berlin. 1919.
VEYRIN, PHILIPPE. " L'Art Basque Ancien." Bayonne. 1927.
VINSON, JULIEN. " Bibliographie de la Langue Basque." Bayonne.
    1874.
—— " Les Basques et le Pays Basque." Paris. 1882.
—— " Folk-Lore du Pays Basque." Paris. 1883.

WEBSTER, WENTWORTH. "Basque Legends." London. 1878.
—— "Les Loisirs d'un Etranger au Pays Basque." Châlon-sur-Saône. 1901.
WHITE, BLANCO. "Letters from Spain." London. 1825.
WINCKLER, HEINRICH. "La Langue Basque et les Langues Ouralo-Altaiques." Halle. 1917.
YRIZAR, JOAQUÍN DE. "Ensayo sobre el Problema Arquitectónico Vasco." San Sebastian.
—— "Las Casas Vascas." San Sebastian. 1929.

PERIODICAL PUBLICATIONS

Anuario de la Societad de Eusko-Folklore. Vitoria. Published annually since 1921.

Bulletin de la Société des Sciences, Lettres, Arts et Études Régionales de Bayonne. Bayonne. Published quarterly.

Bulletin du Musée Basque de Bayonne. Published twice a year since 1923.

Bulletin Trimestriel de la Société Bayonnaise d'Études Régionales. Bayonne. Published quarterly from 1917 to 1921.

Euskalerriaren Alde. San Sebastian. Published monthly since 1911.

Eusko Folklore. Materiales y Cuestionarios. Vitoria. Published monthly since 1921.

Gure Herria. Bayonne. Published monthly from 1921 to 1926 and every two months since 1927.

Revista Internacional de los Estudios Vascos. San Sebastian. Published quarterly since 1907.

INDEX

U 2

PRINTED IN GREAT BRITAIN BY RICHARD CLAY & SONS, LIMITED
Bungay, Suffolk

1♥

B A Y O

B I S C A

Plencia

Bermeo

Las Arenas

Lequeitio

Ondarroa

Fuenter

San Sebastian

Pasages

Guernica

Zumaya

Guetaria

Renteria

Bilbao

Motrico

Marquina

Zarauz

Orio

Hernan

Andoain

R. Ur

VIZCAYA

Azcoitia

GUIPUZCO

Berrix

Eibar

Azpeitia

Cerberio

Loyola

Durango

Tolosa

Dima

Mañaria

Vergara

Zumarraga

Amezqueta

Ochandiano

Oñate

Zaldivia

Le

Ataun

Huici

Cegama

ALAVA

Alsasua

N

W E

S

Vitoria

Kilometres

10 5 0 10 20 30 40